Muslims in
the United States

Muslims in the United States

*Ilyas Ba-Yunus
and Kassim Kone*

GREENWOOD PRESS
Westport, Connecticut · London

Library of Congress Cataloging-in-Publication Data

Ba-Yunus, Ilyas.
   Muslims in the United States / Ilyas Ba-Yunus and Kassim Kone.
     p. cm.
   Includes bibliographical references and index.
   ISBN 0-313-32825-0 (alk. paper)
   1. Islam—United States. 2. Muslims—United States. I. Kone, Kassim. II. Title.
BP67.U6B32   2006
297.0973—dc22   2006014298

British Library Cataloguing in Publication Data is available.

Library of Congress Catalog Card Number: 2006014298
ISBN: 0-313-32825-0

First published in 2006

Greenwood Press, 88 Post Road West, Westport, CT 06881
An imprint of Greenwood Publishing Group, Inc.
www.greenwood.com

Printed in the United States of America

The paper used in this book complies with the
Permanent Paper Standard issued by the National
Information Standards Organization (Z39.48–1984).

10 9 8 7 6 5 4 3 2 1

$55.00

Contents

Introduction

He who has killed one innocent soul,
It is as if he killed all humanity.
And he who saved one soul,
It is as if he saved all humanity.
(Qur'an, 5:32)

It was a beautiful late summer day in the Northeast—scarcely a cloud appeared in the sky from Washington, DC, to Manchester, New Hampshire. As the sun rose over the Atlantic and the shadows of skyscrapers fell on the Hudson River, crowds gathered outside the ABC, NBC, and CBS studios, as they do every weekday morning. Girlfriends, mothers, children, teachers from Omaha, Minneapolis, and Tampa, and foreign tourists all waited, hoping for a chance to be on camera, to say hello to Grandma, or even to chat with the weatherman.

As the eight o'clock hour was coming to a close, the staff and crew at *Good Morning America* were hoping to pack up for the day. But during a commercial break, the news broke that the North Tower of the World Trade Center was on fire. Local channels were broadcasting images of smoke billowing out of the building. Soon the North Tower was on millions of televisions across the nation. And as we all watched the North Tower burning, an outline of a jet appeared and then crashed into the South Tower. The second tower burst into flames in front of our eyes.

More breaking news came about thirty minutes later: The Pentagon was on fire. Then came reports of a struggle in a jetliner over southwest Pennsylvania; the plane eventually plunged to the ground on a farm near Pittsburgh.

Three catastrophic events in a little more than an hour. All told, 2,976 innocent lives were taken (Wikipedia, September 11, 2001 attacks).

"WE ARE ALL AMERICANS"

On September 12, 2001, the front page of Paris' *Le Monde* newspaper
declared: "We Are All Americans" (*Nous Sommes Tous Am?ricains*). Indeed,
the outpouring of international support and sympathy for the stunned United
States seemed universal. In the months following the attacks, countries around
the world offered military and political support for the United States in its
attempts to find and hold accountable those responsible for the attacks. The
United Kingdom, Canada, Australia, France, New Zealand, Italy, Germany,
and the Northern Alliance all joined the coalition that destroyed the Taliban
infrastructure and Al-Qaeda strongholds in Afghanistan. Still more countries—
Indonesia, China, Russia, Pakistan, Jordan, Mauritius, Uganda, and Zimbabwe
among them—introduced antiterrorism legislation and froze bank accounts of
suspected Al-Qaeda supporters (Wikipedia, September 11, 2001 attacks).

Immediate reactions from the Muslim world were mixed—from reported
cheering in the streets in some major cities to outright condemnation by heads
of states, clerics, and scholars. Within the United States and Canada in particular, imams of large and small mosques denounced the attacks, saying they
should not have been carried out in the name of Islam: The Qur'an prohibits
the taking of innocent life in no uncertain terms.

For Muslims living in the United States—students, permanent residents, visitors, and U.S. citizens—the French proclamation was certainly more than apt.
But it would take on a different meaning in the months and years to come, as
the attacks and the U.S.-led war on terrorism changed perceptions of Islam
throughout the country.

BEFORE SEPTEMBER 11

Prior to September 11, Islam in the United States had, for the most part,
been a story of success, expansion, and hope. Muslims residing in the United
States entertained a degree of pride in being Americans. They perceived the
United States as a nation of immigrants, and a great majority of them entered
the United States legally, sponsored by family members, on work or student
visas, or as refugees seeking to escape persecution. Many who overstayed their
visas were eventually accommodated by the system.

With the establishment of mosques and various regional and national organizations, the Muslim population and Islam as a religion began to leave its mark
on U.S. society and culture. Large mosques appeared in New York, Chicago,
Los Angeles, Houston, Dallas, St. Louis, Atlanta, Washington, DC, southern
Florida, and eastern Michigan. Organizations were formed to help facilitate
dawah, or invitation to Islam, through conventions, conferences, publications,
marriage, and other interpersonal relationships. Islam was quickly becoming

the fastest growing religion in the United States. Far from being a hindrance to progress, Islam was shaping twenty-first-century America. Muslims were not giving up their fundamental identity, but a new and postmodern Islamic jurisprudence was in the making. The works of Jamal Badawi, Taha Jabir Alwani, and many others helped bring about this transition by examining the nature of Islamic law (the *Sharia*) and redefining a number of traditional practices, including those associated with the role and status of women.

The American Muslim population also began to become a political force. By the 2000 election, the political strength of this group was undeniable. According to a *Christian Science Monitor* report, 700 Muslims, indigenous as well as immigrant, were candidates for various offices in the 2000 election, and 153 of them were elected (Miller, 2003). Not only were American Muslims becoming active as candidates, but they were also demonstrating a tendency to be block voters. Following the recommendation of major Muslim organizations, more than 70 percent of Muslims voted for George W. Bush for president.

And American society began to recognize this growing Islamic presence. The media began to report on major Islamic holidays. Public television and CNN presented documentaries on the life of the Prophet Muhammad. During conventions of major Muslim organizations, restaurants around convention halls served *halal* (properly slaughtered) meat prepared in pure vegetable oil. In short, before September 11, Islamic roots were beginning to take hold in American society.

AFTER SEPTEMBER 11

September 11 began a new page in American Islamic history. This watershed event affected Muslim Americans of all walks of life: citizens, immigrants, visitors, students, overseas professionals, visiting scholars, tourists, and illegal residents. Feelings of confidence, faith, and pride in the United States were replaced with fear, apprehension, and uncertainty, especially among the immigrant Muslim population.

In the immediate aftermath of the attacks, President Bush's much publicized visits to Washington, DC-area mosques and his public declaration of Islam as a religion of peace and justice helped to reassure the Muslim community. In addition, the selection of the president of the Islamic Society of North America (ISNA), the largest Muslim organization in the United States, to lead the eulogy ceremony at the site of the destroyed World Trade Center amounted to a public display of support and confidence in the Muslim community.

On September 17, 2001, at a speech at the Islamic Center in Washington, DC, President Bush proclaimed, "The face of terror is not the true faith of Islam," and he further acknowledged that the attacks of September 11 "violate[d] the fundamental tenets of Islam" (Bush, 2001). Despite these repeated remarks and public shows of support for the Islamic community, it was an inevitable that some backlash would occur. Out of ignorance or malice or both, Islam became associated with terrorism. Conflicting and somewhat distorted images of Islam began to appear in the media, the implementation of new government policies seemed to single out Muslims, and rogue ordinary citizens took the law into their own hands.

The U.S. government response to the attacks, which culminated in the passage of the USA PATRIOT Act, had unintended consequences for Muslim Americans. In the eyes of many, including law enforcement agents, because all of the hijackers were Muslims, all Muslims became suspect. The number of American visas from Muslim countries was curtailed, Muslims who overstayed their visas in the United States were detained and required to attend deportation hearings, and many were interrogated at airports, among them a White House Secret Service agent and a highly respected Canadian Muslim minister.

As part of the effort to prevent future terrorist attacks, law enforcement agents and government officials called on ordinary citizens to be more vigilant and to report suspicious behavior. This request in part led to citizens taking the law into their own hands. Incidents of harassment and hate crimes, particularly against Middle Easterners, were reported. At least eight people were killed, including Balbir Singh Sodhi, who was shot and killed at his gas station in Phoenix, Arizona, on September 15, 2001. Singh Sodhi was a Sikh, and because of his beard and turban, was thought to be Muslim (Wikipedia, Balbir Singh Sodhi).

Cases of what appear to be prejudicial action on the part of officers of the law, some religious leaders, and individual citizens number in the thousands. Some Muslim organizations established hotlines for people to report such cases and seek help. The enormity of the situation made the inspector general at the U.S. Department of Justice complain about Muslims being denied their civil rights. In addition, Tom Plate, a professor at UCLA, stated, "If I were an American Muslim, I might be getting a little angry" (2004).

The cumulative impact on Muslim Americans has been disastrous. Thousands of Muslim businesses have been ruined. Many careers have been destroyed. And perhaps most destructive to the country as a whole, a widespread feeling of insecurity now prevails in the Muslim community.

UNCOVERING THE MUSLIM AMERICAN EXPERIENCE

In the wake of September 11, a spate of writings on Islam has appeared. However, very little research has focused specifically on Muslim Americans. In this book, we hope to remedy this lack of research and present the Muslim American point of view. As both of us are social scientists—a sociologist and an anthropologist—social science methods were applied whenever possible. Much of the information in this book is based on research sponsored by the Islamic Studies Institute of East-West University and through a partial grant from Project MAPPS of Georgetown University as funded by the PEW Foundation.

In the seven chapters of this book, we explore the Muslim American perspective on their religion and their major concerns in the United States. We also explore the dimensions of their population, the status of women, their organizations, and their communities. Because there is so much conflicting information about Islam in the United States today, we thought it prudent to start with a discourse on the fundamentals of Islam. Thus, in chapter one, we attempt to answer this question: What is Islam as it is perceived and practiced by its followers? Although the chapter centers on the Five Pillars, we also include a brief discussion on what we call the "macro dimensions of Islam:" economy, family, and polity. We hope this chapter answers many questions about the nature of Islam, the life and character of the Prophet Muhammad, and the major dimensions of Muslim worship.

In chapter two, we address the history and expansion of the Muslim population in the United States. We begin by examining slavery in the United States, when sixteenth and seventeenth century slave traders captured a number of Muslims in West Africa and brought them to this country. This makes Islam one of the oldest religions in the United States. In this chapter, we also show how to apply demographic techniques to estimate a population not covered by the census. In our research, we approached many registered and unregistered Muslim communities, examined the lists of families in those communities, calculated the average number of people in these families, and estimated the future growth of the communities.

In chapter three, we examine the history and nature of major national Muslim organizations. These national organizations show a tendency toward ethnic divisions—Arab, African American, and South Asian—in their membership, their organizational structures, and their major concerns. The two largest Muslim American organizations are also the only two of multiethnic composition, the Muslim Students Association of the United States and Canada (MSA) and ISNA. They hold their annual conventions together, and the president of MSA has a permanent seat in the Shura council, the highest decision-making body of ISNA. At the 2004 annual convention in Chicago, ISNA attracted 40,000 to 50,000 participants.

Chapter four takes a close look at the Muslim community in the United States. This is the home of the Muslim family, where Islam is shaped and reshaped and transmitted to the next generation. This is also where grass roots Muslim politics is beginning to blossom.

In order to examine a cross-section of the Muslim American community, we studied thirteen communities in five different locations. On average, we spent about three months studying communities in Brooklyn, New York; Syracuse, New York; Chicago and its suburb Villa Park, Illinois; Richardson, Texas; and the Finger Lakes region of New York State. These communities presented a range of ethnic diversity, from the small community of indigenous African American Muslims in Brooklyn to the Villa Park community of primarily Pakistani Muslims to the highly diverse population in Syracuse, which included African Americans, Arabs, South Asians, Turks, Iranians, Bosnians, and many others.

Perhaps the most unusual community we studied was a group of inmates at Auburn State facility in upstate New York. Almost totally African American, this community is relatively small when compared with Muslim communities outside the prison system, but it is one of the largest inmate Muslim communities in the nation. The growth in this community is due primarily to conversion to Islam of current inmates.

Except for the Auburn facility, information on these communities was collected through participant observation and interviews. For each community, we selected and consulted an informant with intimate knowledge of and involvement in that community.

Chapter five contains further analysis of the demographic information presented in chapter two. However, in this chapter, we focus on the changing status and role of Muslim women in the United States. Our research indicates a negative relationship between age and education of adult Muslim women: Younger women tend to be more educated than older women, and they also tend to be more career oriented. Because most Muslim American families are directly or indirectly associated with a mosque or Islamic center, most Muslim American women seem to cultivate primary group relations through mosque activities. Women are still rarely found in higher management positions in mosques, but mosques do play a more important role in the lives of Muslim American women than is true in the rest of the Muslim world.

In chapter six, we analyze the American reaction to the attacks of September 11 and its effect on Muslim Americans. This reaction falls in four major categories. First is the government reaction, in particular the USA PATRIOT Act. We then examine the reaction of Christian fundamentalists and following that, the reaction of Zionists. Finally, we explore the reactions of ordinary U.S. citizens.

In chapter seven, we turn inward and examine the major issues facing Muslim Americans today. In particular, we tackle the impact of Saudi Arabia on Muslim American communities and specific internal controversies that divide the Muslim American community.

What are the long-term prospects for Muslims in the United States? How long will this backlash against Islam last? These are crucial but difficult question to answer. Our educated guess is that September 11 and its aftermath represents a temporary dip in the otherwise upward trend Islam was experiencing. Perhaps discrimination against Muslims or, for that matter, any religious group will never disappear entirely from the United States. But we believe that with time and decreased publicity and political attention on September 11 and the war on terrorism, American perspectives on Muslims living in the United States, and next door, can change for the better.

REFERENCES

Bush, G. W. 2001. "Islam Is Peace." Remarks by the President at the Islamic Center of Washington, DC.

Hasan, A. G. 2000. *American Muslims: The New Generation*. New York: Continuum.

Miller, S. B. 2003. In war on terror, an expanding citizen's brigade. *The Christian Science Monitor* (August 13:1).

Plate, T. 2004. The near-saintly restraint of American Muslims. *Asia Media*.

Wikipedia: The Free Encyclopedia. "Balbir Singh Sodhi." http://en.wikipedia.org/wiki/Balbir_Singh_Sodhi.

Wikipedia: The Free Encyclopedia. "September 11, 2001 attacks." http://en.wikipedia.org/wiki/September_11,_2001_attacks#Fatalities.

1

Islam as a Creed and a World Religion

As we shall see in the following pages, American Muslims are a diverse population in race, ethnicity, and cultural background. They represent a microcosm of the multinational global community of Islam. Most people in the United States equate Islam and Muslims with the Arabs and the Middle East. In reality, not all Arabs are Muslims and not all Muslims are Arabs. Almost 12 percent of all Arabs are Christians of different denominations and only 20 percent of the Muslims in the world may be classified as Arabs. Although Islam originated in Arabia fourteen hundred years ago, what may be called the Muslim world today extends in an almost unbroken chain of countries from Morocco on the Atlantic to New Guinea in the Pacific, and from the central Asian steppes in the north to subtropical Africa in the south.

Evidently, Islam covers a vast territory, which spans ten time zones. When the faithful gets up in Marakesh at 5 A.M. for the early morning (*fajr*) prayers, it is almost 10 A.M. on a hot morning in Mecca, Saudi Arabia while at the same time, those in Dacca, Bangladesh, are finishing their lunch and getting ready for the early afternoon (*zohr*) prayers at 1 P.M., and those in Mindanao in the Philippines are finishing their late afternoon (*asr*) prayers at 4 P.M.

Were it a single political entity, the dream of the Muslim activist, the Muslim world would be described as the most pluralistic nation state. No doubt, Muslims are a portrait in diversity. Divided into more than fifty states, they belong to different histories and cultures. They speak hundreds of diverse languages from Swahili, Arabic, Turkish, Russian, Persian, Urdu, Hindi, Bangladeshi, Sinhalese, and Bhasha Indonesia to scores of local southeast Asian, central Asian, and Caucasian dialects. Lately, as they are settling down in large numbers in Europe and North America, Muslims and their children are becoming native speakers of the European languages.

Also, Muslims come in all colors and races, from dark-skinned Africans to brown-colored Arabs and light-skinned Turks and Persians to red-haired and blue-eyed Tartars, and the Malays of the Mongolian stock. These individual pieces of the mosaic, in its ethnic, historical, cultural, racial, and linguistic diversity, are stitched together only by the thread of Islam, which alone provides a great majority of these populations, their fundamental and most common self-concept or identity. Because Muslims, residing in the United States as citizens, immigrants, students, businessmen, or visitors, have come from all over the world, Muslims in the United States reflect this diversity. Indeed, it is not incorrect to say that the Muslim population in the United States reflects the extent to which Islam spread in the world during the past fourteen hundred years.

From the beginning of the eighteenth century until the end of the nineteenth century, Christianity was the fastest growing religion in the world, thanks mostly to the European colonialism and the Christian missionaries, who followed on its heels.

One hundred years hence, Islam is the fastest growing religion in the world, albeit without the benefit of any powerful states supporting it. In a number of countries where Islam is not the religion of the majority, the number of Muslims is staggering—almost 150 million in India, close to 80 million in China, and more than 20 million in the Philippines. Recently, Islam has been making deep inroads in Europe and North America mainly through migration, but also due to reproduction as well as conversion. In 1966 Rahman estimated that the total Muslim population in the world was around 500 million. By the year 2000, the Muslim population was estimated to have exceeded the one billion mark, meaning that one out of every five citizens of the world was a Muslim at the dawn of the twenty-first century. It is true that Christianity, including such diverse groups as the Mormons, the Jehovah's Witnesses, Eastern orthodox and the dominant Protestant and the Roman Catholic churches, is still the largest religion in the world with an estimated following of 1.2 billion. However, as the only religion with a continued growth in its demographic strength, Islam may become the largest religion in the world before long.

Extending over such a vast expanse of territory, Islam stands astride some of the most strategic and politically sensitive locations. The Muslims command the choke points of Gibraltar, the Dardanelles, Bosporus, Suez, Aden, Hermuz, and the Sunda and Malacca straits. Arabia and the Middle East, the birthplace and the cradle of Islam, lie at the juncture of three continents—Asia, Africa, and Europe. Although known mostly for oil and natural gas, Muslim lands also contain vast reserves of uranium and manganese under the sand dunes of the Sahara; sulfur and phosphorus in central Asia; and huge tropical forests along the equator in Southeast Asia.

In another vein, the Qur'an, the holy Book of Islam, has certain features that may be especially revealing to people of Christian persuasions. It may surprise many that the Qur'an is the only non-Christian book that recognizes and reserves the utmost reverence for Jesus Christ (and for all the prophets mentioned in the Bible). One whole chapter in the Qur'an is devoted to the virgin birth and the mission and the miracles of Jesus, who is referred to in the Qur'an more frequently than the Prophet Muhammad. Consequently, the Muslims are the only non-Christians who have the same respect for Jesus as for their own Prophet. Indeed, a Muslim who denies the divine ministry of Jesus defies the Qur'an itself. Thus, the Qur'an is responsible for extending the name, the history, and the mission of Jesus far beyond Christendom itself. No wonder Jesus (*Eisa*) has been one of the most popular names among Muslims.

Because of this conjunction of Islam and Christianity, Jesus may be the most referred-to name in the world. However, the Qur'an is by far the most frequently recited book in history. This is so because millions of Muslims engage in formal prayers five times a day. In these prayers they are supposed to recite portions of the Qur'an, without which their prayers cannot be performed. Furthermore, the Qur'an is perhaps the only book which has been, as a matter of routine, memorized from cover to cover by millions in each generation for the last fourteen hundred years. Among others, this memorization and frequent recitation is what kept the book intact in its original form and language through the centuries.

It is also thanks to the Qur'an that such a diverse Muslim population, divided by long distances, diverse languages, and varied cultures, owes its common ethos. After all, the same book recited so frequently and memorized by millions of people across many cultures and many nations must have some impact upon its practitioners. Thus, although the Muslim world is hopelessly fragmented today, its potential to become a powerful platform in world affairs is not lost on many.

During the past fourteen centuries, Muslims, the followers of Islam, have seen several fluctuations in their fortunes. Islam provided the basis of a great civilization, which for one thousand years after its inception, was creative and looked invincible. During its rapid spread, Islam cut across several cultures from Africa, Western and Eastern Europe to Persia, India, and China. Islam gave these cultures its monotheism, civil code, and justice system. From these cultures it also received art forms, philosophy, architecture, and medicine. This new blend of civilization gave to the world the Arabic numerals, decimal calculations, algebra, and logarithms that we use today in complex mathematical calculations. Further, in their heyday, the Muslims excelled in experimental chemistry, astronomy, architecture, irrigation, and agriculture.

Islam was not merely a city-based civilization. It was a city-making civilization. Before Islam, there was not a single city in the world larger than a few thousand inhabitants. The Muslims gave rise to, among others, cities like Rabat, Tripoli, Cairo, Beirut, Damascus, Istanbul, Baghdad, Basra, Tehran, and Delhi, which became centers of excellence in education, politics, and commerce with the passage of time.

However, like other civilizations, Islamic civilization also ran its course. With the help of technology and industrialization, Europe left the Muslim world far behind in economic development and the military power. Indeed, starting in the 1600s, Europeans embarked on the "age of discovery," which ushered the era of colonialism, from which Muslim people, along with the rest of the Third World, are just beginning to emerge with tattered economies, demoralized populations, and corrupt political elites.

THE ORIGIN

Of all the major world religions, Islam is the only one that grew in the full glare of history. The life of its founder, its development into a civilization, and its subsequent decline as a world power, have been and still are being debated and disputed by the academics with a fine comb.

As widespread as it is, Islam had a very humble beginning. It dates back to the Prophet Muhammad, who was born in or around A.D. 570 in Mecca, about forty kilometers inland from the Red Sea coast of the Arabian Peninsula. With an ancient center of worship called *Ka'bah*, or the Cube, at its center along with a freshwater spring, *Zam Zam*, nearby, Mecca is located at a point about half-way on the north-south stretch of Tihama, the Red Sea coastal strip of the peninsula. The caravans carrying goods of trade from Yemen and Ethiopia in the south and Palestine and Syria to the north, stopped in Mecca to rest and refresh, thus making Mecca an important trading post since ancient times.

When Muhammad was born, Mecca had already grown into an international commercial center as well as a focus of a lavish annual pilgrimage (*hajj*) to the *Ka'bah*, which attracted thousands from the desert tribes regularly every year. Most Meccans derived their livelihood, directly or indirectly, from these two sources. Many Meccans became prosperous by investing in the caravan trade, which provided employment to many. Muhammad was born to *Banu Hashim*, a clan of the *Qureish*, a Meccan tribe, which was responsible for looking after the pilgrims, and was thus the sole beneficiary of the monetary and other benefits acquired during the annual pilgrimage.

But the *Banu Hashim* were the poorest of the *Qureish*, and Muhammad was born an orphan. His father died a few months before he was born. His mother also passed away early in his childhood. His grandfather adopted him, but he also did not live very long. Finally, when not yet a teenager, Muhammad was adopted by one of his uncles in whose family he grew up.

Many historians mention Muhammad's childhood not just merely in passing. His being orphaned at an impressionable age and his transfer from one adopting home to another did not offer much chance for formal or informal education like that received by the other more fortunate youngsters of his age. Consequently, Muhammad did not learn how to read and write. He remained an unlettered person all his life (an *ummi*). He also learned, from the very outset of his life, the meaning of being an orphan, of being deprived of ordinary pleasures of childhood and of being dependent on others.

However, by all accounts he grew up to become an upright, serious, and honest person. People called him trustworthy (*al-Ameen*), a rare treat in a highly materialistic Meccan culture. In his critical review of the Prophet, Ruthven (1984:57) writes:

> Despite the hagiographical tendencies of Muhammad's biographers, a convincing personality emerges from the earliest sources. He was evidently well favored and mentally astute. ... He conveyed the impression of great energy, but his contemporaries found him unusually taciturn and self-controlled. When he spoke it was briefly, to the point and without elaboration. He seems to be a serious minded introvert in a society where it is usual for men to be excitable, exuberant, boastful and loquacious.

Having heard of his reputation as an honest and a reliable person, Khadijah, a wealthy widow, wanted Muhammad to oversee her caravan trade. She was so impressed with his management of her business that she offered him her hand in marriage.

His marriage to Khadijah gave Muhammad, for the first time, a taste of leisure and comfortable life. However, unlike most Meccan nobility, who would spend their wealth and time in luxurious consumption and materialistic pursuits, Muhammad preferred solitude and meditation—about creation, life, death, and the place of man in creation. He selected a small cave, Hira, near the top of a towering hill, *Jabl alNoor* (mountain of light) outside of Mecca. He would go to that cave for days at a time so no one would disturb him in his meditation.

One night, while in Hira, something happened that almost took his breath away. He saw someone coming toward him, completely unannounced, seemingly out of nowhere. He came directly to Muhammad and asked him to recite after him. Muhammad said that he could not recite. The visitor again asked Muhammad to recite. Muhammad again gave the same reply. The third time around, the visitor came forward, embraced Muhammad tightly and uttered the following:

> Recite in the name of your Lord who creates
> Created man from a clot of blood
> Recite for your Lord is most gracious,
> Who taught with pen
> Taught man what he did not know.
> (Qur'an, 96:15)

This was the first in a series of divine revelations that came to Muhammad for the next twenty-three years through an angel who was later identified as the archangel Gabriel. This was the year A.D. 612 and the last week of the Arabic lunar month of Ramadhan.

This encounter was so overpowering and so awe-inspiring that Muhammad fell sick. Much like the Hebrew prophets before him, he was scared and did not want to believe what had just transpired. Even so, he did not receive any more revelations for a while (for six months by some accounts) until he was awakened one night by the angel Gabriel, who delivered him the following divine message:

O you, keeper of the blanket
Get up and admonish
And glorify the name of your Lord
And keep your garments clean
And do not commit idolatry
And be patient in the cause of your Lord.
(Qur'an, 74:7)

This is how Muhammad, having undergone trials of growing up an orphan and finally settling down to relative comforts of life, became the prophet of God. As he began to prepare himself for further tribulations in life, he knew his future prospects were bleak. Soon he found himself struggling against a deluge of wrath, especially from the Meccan elites including many from his own tribe, the *Qureish*, who saw in him a great threat to their long established socioeconomic status. As he started gaining followers, mostly from slaves, servants, his immediate relatives, and close friends, the persecution by the Meccans intensified.

The initial appeal in the message of Islam, still more like a cult than a religion at the time, was vested first in the personality of the Prophet, who radiated truthfulness, patience, steadfastness, integrity, and promise. Secondly, there was the language of the revelation that attracted even his enemies. Lastly, his message, as Rahman (1966) stated, did not merely preach strict monotheism, it was full of a demand for justice for all, empathy for the poor, promise for orphans and slaves, and rejection of excessive materialism. Above all, the Prophet was becoming a threat to the status quo and vested interests in Mecca. As Esposito (1998) put it:

> For the powerful and prosperous Meccan oligarchy, the monotheistic Message of this would-be reformer, with its condemnation of the Socio-economic inequities of Meccan life, constituted a direct challenge not only to traditional polytheistic religion but also to the power and prestige of the establishment, threatening their economic, social and political interests. Evidently, Muhammad was not the first prophet to be persecuted by his own people. Noah, Abraham, Moses and Jesus had their own share of trials and rejection before him.

During ten long and trying years, Prophet Muhammad had two major preoccupations. First, with a succession of revelations urging nonbelievers to give up their pagan polytheism and treacherous way of life, he had to elicit a positive response from his audience and thus, gain converts to Islam. Secondly, the revelations in short, sharp, and beautiful verses were aimed at personal changes among his followers. The Prophet had the responsibility of promoting in them character of utmost truthfulness and piety, self-sacrifice and altruism, bravery, and patience, and a sense of mutual brotherhood and total commitment to the commandments of Allah (the God). Almost all Meccan revelation could be distinguished from later ones in this respect.

In this respect, Meccan Islam did not differ greatly in its objectives from those in other religions, for all religions put effort in character building among their respective followers. When he rings bells at the entrance of the temple and bows and sings a few hymns before a statue of his god, the Hindu Brahmin feels a bit transcendent. When a Christian goes to church on Sunday, he or she comes back feeling a bit holier than before. Likewise, a Sikh-reading Guru Garanth Saheb in a Gurduara, finds himself to be a bit above his or her selfish materialistic demands.

Likewise, the Prophet focused on retraining his followers, in addition to actively seeking converts.

But, then, what does it mean to be, nice, helpful, and charitable when the surrounding social order continues to function on principles which go against such traits? Indeed, if it powerfully defies such benign character traits by promoting more opportunistic, aggressive, self-centered, and self-indulgent personalities, then religion loses its energy to direct and shape the social order and is often reduced to meaningless rituals.

On the other hand, as we shall see below, the Islamic personalities that the Prophet was molding in Mecca were meant to become instrumental in creating a full-fledged Islamic social order, which could not be possible in Mecca. For this reason alone, Islam could not stay in its place of birth much longer. As persecution against the Prophet and his small band of followers became unbearable, and his enemies were now determined to kill him, it was time for him to go somewhere else.

THE MIGRATION

For ten trying years while still preaching in Mecca, the Prophet had made it a practice to talk to the pilgrims who used to congregate for *hajj* every year. During the *hajj* in A.D. 621, he visited the camp of a party of the pilgrims from Yathrib, an agricultural oasis about four hundred kilometers to the north of Mecca. Prophet Muhammad found them to be surprisingly receptive to his message. They returned next year and invited him to Yathrib as their leader, who would arbitrate among their almost unending tribal disputes. In A.D. 621, the Prophet made his escape and embarked on his historical journey called *hijrah*, or migration to Yathrib, which was later renamed as City of the Prophet (*alMadinat al Nabi*), or simply as Medinah.

Why were the people of Yathrib so receptive to the Prophet? The scholars (Armstrong, 1991; Haikal, 1985; Esposito, 1982) contend that this oasis was populated by three major tribes, who were mostly farmers and thus more peace loving than the very materialistically motivated and aggressive Meccans. Moreover, unlike in Mecca, they were hopelessly caught in an intertribal rivalry for which they were desperately seeking some solution. When the news of the Prophet reached them, perhaps, they saw in him the only solution to their problem.

Most other Meccan Muslims had migrated to Medinah before the Prophet, whose charisma arrived before he did. His arrival had been anticipated for days before he appeared on the desert horizon riding on a camel with his most trusted companion, Abu Bakr. It was in Medinah that the character of the revelations shifted from an exclusive focus on character building to institution building, including, primarily, economic, family, and political considerations. Now he was engaged in forging a new tribe, so to speak, based not on blood, kinship, and lineage but on ideology. The Qur'anic revelations were forthcoming as questions arose regarding behavior in war and peace with respect to the following: the defense of the community through proactive institution of *jihad*, especially against unforgiving and spiteful Meccans; the finality of consultation (*shura*) in decision making even at the highest level; to rules of marriage and divorce; and regarding inheritance, rights of women, widows, and orphans.

With Medinah as his capital, the Prophet was able to preach throughout Arabia. He even sent emissaries to the two superpowers—the Byzantium to the northwest and the Sassanid Persia to the northeast. Most importantly, after eight years of continuous warfare against the Meccans, he finally conquered Mecca in A.D. 630. Upon entering the city of his birth as a conqueror, his first act was to announce a general amnesty even for his worst enemies, who having escaped punishment, accepted Islam. Secondly, he cleansed the Ka'abah by destroying numerous idols placed inside it for centuries.

Thus, migration (*hijrah*) to Medinah is a milestone in the history of Islam. Neither the Prophet's birthday nor the day of the first revelation to him, but the event of migration marks the beginning of the Islamic calendar; A.D. 16 July 622 became 1 *hijrah* (Bloom and Blair, 2000:31).

A year after the conquest of Mecca, Prophet Muhammad performed the last *hajj* of his life. During this gathering of a few thousand Muslims, he gave his parting address, in which he re-emphasized rights of women and dropped hints of his departure from this world ("have I fulfilled my task?"). Only a year later, in A.D. 632 or 10 *hijrah*, he died after a brief illness. During twenty-three odd years of his career as a prophet, Muhammad wrote a chapter of world history that resonates even in modern times in many important ways.

THE FUNDAMENTALS

According to Muslim belief, Prophet Muhammad preached Islam following the directives of the Qur'an as it unfolded in Divine revelations over a period exceeding two decades. Together with the Qur'anic directives, his practice of these directives (*Sunnah*) forms the basis of the Islamic jurisprudence (*fiqh*) from which Islamic legal opinions (*Sharia*) is derived.

Before the Prophet died, his companions knew and practiced Islam in their lives under his personal guidance. He left a living tradition of compliance with the Qur'an in more specific as well as more general ways, the denial of which would constitute non-Islam. In practice, he broadened the very meaning of worship, which went beyond mere meditation or ritualistic prayers. It came to mean a total way of life in accordance with the Divine directives. The Qur'an (5:3) calls it *Deen*:

Today we have completed your deen for you.

To reiterate, Islam includes micro aspects focusing mainly on character building as well as macro aspect, such as institution building. It is these practices that we now turn to.

Micro Aspects: The Five Pillars

No discussion on Islam is complete without referring to the "Five Pillars," which many view as being the very essence of Islam. As mentioned earlier, they are not the only that constitute Islam. However, this is where Islam starts, there is no doubt about it.

The profession of faith (*shahadah*) is the very first pillar. It constitutes a declaration to oneself and if and when possible to others—I witness that there is no God but one and the only God, and I witness that Muhammad was His Prophet. This is the doorway to enter the fold of Islam. One does not have to go through any rituals, ceremonies, or priestly blessings. One has to only convince himself or herself about the existence of one and the only omnipotence God, called Allah in Arabic, and one has to be convinced that Muhammad was his Prophet. After all, acceptance of Muhammad's prophethood is at the very root of Islam.

Muslim scholars emphasize that the profession of faith (*shahadah*) implies that faith in Islam is not blind. The emphasis here is on conviction based on knowledge (Maududi, 1962). The Qur'anic revelations repeatedly address the polytheists in an almost unending discourse about the existence of Allah, the Creator and the Sustainer of the universe:

> The Compassionate
> He taught the Qur'an
> He created man
> And gave him speech
> The sun and the moon follow His measure
> And the stars and the plants bow to Him
> And high up there He created the sky in a balance
> ...and He created the Earth with animals and fruits wrapped in leaves
> How long are you going to deny your Lord's favors to you
> (Qur'an, 55: 1-11)

Or,

> Without doubt in creation of the heavens and the earth
> And the alternation of night and day
> There are signs for the more thoughtful
> Who remember Allah while standing, kneeling and prostrating
> And give serious thought to the creation of the heavens and the earth
> (and say) Our Lord, You have not created all this in vain
> Praise is for you, save us from the Fire.
> (Qur'an, 3: 190-191)

The Muslim scholars borrowed argument from the Qur'an and expounded upon it. In the following, we present an excerpt from a rather widely circulated speech by Maududi (1950) that he delivered to a mixed audience of Hindus, Sikhs, and the Muslims at Ludhiana, India, in 1946:

> Gentlemen, would you accept if one claims that in your city there is a shop, which does not have any owner; there is nobody in it, who brings things for sale, nor is there a person to look after the shop; and that the shop is running by itself; that things for sale in this shop are put in place and get sold by themselves.
>
> Suppose someone tells you that in this city there is a factory, which does not have an owner; there is no engineer or technician in it; and that it seems that the factory became established by itself; that all its machines were fixed all by themselves and that these machines are working and manufacturing things all by themselves.
>
> Would you not think that one who makes such a claim is out of his mind? Why go that far? Would you say that the light in this light bulb came all by itself? Would you agree even with a highly educated man that this chair came into being by itself? If you do not accept that this shop can run or function by itself, that this factory can operate without any one to operate it, then how can any one accept that this gigantic system of the earth and the heavens with all of its stars, suns, and the planets functioning like the hands of a clock came into existence without a maker and is running by itself?

It is evident from the above that the Muslims take existence of the omnipotent Almighty God rationally and seriously. Consequently, at least for knowledgeable Muslims, the existence of God is logical without any trappings approaching superstition. However, Islam is not the only monotheistic religion in the world. More importantly, one may ask the question: how could you accept Muhammad as a prophet? Recall that the prophethood of Muhammad is an indispensable aspect of the *shahadah*, or the profession of faith.

The declaration of Muhammad as a prophet is inescapably related with the Qur'an as a divinely revealed book. It is evident from the Qur'an that Islam, as a process of submission to God, progressed throughout a long history of creation. In this sense the whole creation is Muslim because all that exists in the universe obeys laws given by its Creator. God also created man but without any innate social laws. Instead, He sent directives that were transmitted through various prophets from time to time. The Qur'an claims that these divine directives to man constituted Books such as the Psalms (*Zobur*) as revealed to the Prophet Abraham (*Ibraheem*), the Torah (*Torait*) revealed to the prophet Moses (*Musa*), and the Evangel or the Gospel (*Injeel*) as given to the prophet Jesus (*Eisa*).

From the point of view of the Qur'an, there were two important reasons for the Divine messages to develop in a chain of succession of the prophets. First, the Divine directives progressed over time congruent with changes in human conditions due to expansion in human population, the growing complexity in human organization and emergence of trade and commerce along with nagging questions regarding private property, distribution of resources, status, and role of women in society and the like. Thus as human history took unforeseen turns, new Divine guidance was forthcoming in order to save mankind from making faulty and injurious decisions, which human beings are always prone to.

Secondly, new guidance was needed from time to time because Books given to earlier prophets were often destroyed by outside invaders and could not be properly reconstructed. Or, they were even distorted by the believers themselves for narrow, selfish reasons or due to widespread illiteracy in the population.

The chain of the revealed books finally culminated in the revelation of the Qur'an to the prophet Muhammad, the "seal of the prophets" as the Qur'an (33:40) calls him. As the last of the revealed books, the Qur'an informs about and certifies earlier books, and laying claims to finality, it contains directives, general as well as specific, which together address supposedly all essentials of societal living. This is how Islam is presented as containing rules for ritualistic worship or communion with God in addition to the code governing mutual social relationships including economic, family and political interaction.

But why should one accept the Qur'an, as a divinely revealed book? Although it does recognize earlier Books as being divine in origin, does it not make it clear that they were tampered with and interpolated, thus losing their original authenticity?

The question about the Divine origin of the Qur'an has been raised many times in the past. In fact this question was raised as it was in the process being revealed over two decades, and the Qur'an tackles this question squarely (see 2:23, for instance).

It is a well-known fact that the Qur'an can be singled out as an extraordinary book in Arabic, the language in which it was revealed. In fact, the Qur'an is a masterpiece and a milestone in Arabic literature, not only because of its literary beauty that has not been surpassed in fourteen hundred years, but also because of its tone and the imperative mood that pervades all its verses. According to Armstrong (2000:5), the Prophet:

> was also creating a new literary form and a masterpiece of Arabic prose and po-
> etry. Many of the first believers were converted by the sheer beauty of the
> Qur'an, which resonated with their deepest aspirations, cutting through their in-
> tellectual preconceptions in the manner of great art, and inspiring them, at a level
> more profound than the cerebral, to alter their whole way of life. One of the
> most dramatic of these conversions was that of Umar Ibn alKhattab, who was
> devoted to old paganism. . .

Like the Bible, the Qur'an contains ancient history, but unlike the Bible, it is not merely descriptive. History of mankind in the Qur'an is analytical, presenting dialectical patterns and the role of the elites, who, with their vested interests in status quo, try to resist reform and social change (see, for instance, 7:59-93). The Qur'an elevates history into a tool of law making—a practice, in which the Muslim scholars became adept so much so that history and law have to go hand in hand in Islamic jurisprudence (Al-Farouqi, 1974).

Speaking of law, not only are there laws to be derived from the history of mankind in it, above all, the Qur'an contains explicit laws, as mentioned above, governing family, economic, and interpersonal behavior. These laws form the outermost parameter not to be transgressed within the Islamic community. Finally, not only that the Qur'an provides a body of specific laws, it also outlines the basic process or the mechanism for making new laws, thereby allowing the Islamic society to embark on a dynamic normative and legal course. In short, one of the primary concerns of the Qur'an, like other religious books before it, is directing human behavior in society.

Most importantly, the Qur'an is considered to be the greatest miracle that Allah, God Almighty is supposed to have given to the Prophet Muhammad. This is so because all his life he remained an illiterate person. His contemporaries and his companions knew that during his unfortunate childhood he could not afford any schooling that could prepare him to read and write. This is an issue that did not go unnoticed by his biographers. For instance Armstrong (1992:88) writes:

> In the Qur'an, Muhammad is often called *Ummi*, the unlettered Prophet, and the doctrine of his illiteracy stresses the miraculous nature of his inspirations. There is no mention in the early sources of Muhammad reading or writing. When he needed to send a letter he would dictate it to somebody like Ali, who was literate.

His being an unlettered person (*ummi*) was not unusual in Arabia or in Mecca. In fact, literacy was a luxury not every one in Mecca could afford. It was, in general, limited to the more fortunate few, especially those engaged in international commerce. But none of those unlettered persons was expected to produce anything even remotely resembling the Qur'an. His being illiterate, then, was one of the major reasons why the Qur'an, with its literary beauty and its ideological, legal, and historical discourse, confounded the Prophet's fellow Arabs, some of them highly educated, into submitting to his invitation. Without the Qur'an, he was only one of the many ordinary citizens of Mecca albeit with a trustworthy character, but nothing else that would attract people's attention. With the Qur'an being revealed to him, he was charismatic and brilliant in war and peace. In short, what confounded his contemporaries was that the very beautiful words of wisdom, which defied the intellect of the educated and the very experienced, were being spoken by a confirmed illiterate, who lacked any kind of tutoring in what he was professing so eloquently and patiently.

Naturally, the Prophet did not just utter the Qur'anic revelations. As a husband, father, uncle, neighbor, guest, or host, he socialized with people. He discussed different strategies and listened to other people's advice. He shared his people's joys and sorrows. In his own simple ways, he showed his personal tastes in food, aromatic lotions, and choice of words. His sayings were recorded and compiled in a separate book of *hadith*. Any Arabic speaker who has some exposure to the Qur'an can easily distinguish between the Qur'an, the revealed word of God, and the the sayings of the Prophet (*hadith*), the man. In fact, the difference between the two is apparent on all counts—literary beauty, the imperative mood, and the normative character. The Qur'an commands. The Prophet puts it into practice.

In short, the Prophet's illiteracy elevated the Qur'an to the level of a miracle while the Qur'an declares the prophethood of Muhammad. To believe in the Qur'an and the prophethood of Muhammad means to believe in the existence of the one and only God (Allah) and follow His commandments. Thus, the very belief in the unity of God follows empirical belief in the Qur'an as a miracle given to the Prophet Muhammad. One enters the fold of Islam through the profession of faith (*shahadah*), the first pillar of Islam.

Formal prayer (*salat*), five times a day, is the second pillar of Islam. One may pray at home, in a mosque, or at any place, where he or she would not be disturbed. However, the most preferred way is to pray collectively in the company of others. This highlights the existence of a neighborhood mosque in easy walking distance. As soon as one hears the call to the prayer (*adhan*), one could walk to the mosque, perform ablution and join others in prayer—five times a day.

The call to the prayer (*adhan*) is not a part of the formal prayer. However, all formal prayers must start with the *adhan* even if one is all by himself or herself. Unlike other religions, in which bells, organs, horns, or music are used to call people to worship, Islam's call to the prayers consists only of loudly and melodiously uttering the fundamental declaration of faith:

Allah is greatest, Allah is greatest
Allah is greatest, Allah is greatest

I witness that there is no god but Allah
I witness that there is no god but Allah

I witness that Muhammad is Allah's Prophet
I witness that Muhammad is Allah's Prophet

Hasten toward prayers, hasten toward prayers
Hasten toward good, hasten toward good

Allah is greatest, Allah is greatest
There is no god but Allah.

Prayer (*salat*) itself consists of a few postures (standing with deference, kneeling, and prostrating) which depict submission to and humility before Him. More significantly, it consists of reciting verses from the Qur'an most important of them being the Opening (*al-Fateha*) often compared with the Lord's Prayer in the Bible:

All Praise is to Allah, Lord of the Universe,
Most Compassionate, most merciful,
Master of the day of Judgement.
Only You we obey and only You we seek for help.
Please guide us toward the straight path,
Path of those on whom You showered your bounties,
Not of those who received your wrath,
Nor of those who went astray. Amen.
(1:1-6)

The call to the prayer (*adhan*) and the Opening (*fateha*) set the tone for the prayers, which could be performed individually or, most preferably as mentioned above, collectively in the company of others. In the latter case, the *imam* leads the prayer, reciting the *fateha* and, as a matter of convention, a few other verses of the Qur'an while standing, kneeling, and prostrating. Others are supposed to listen to him attentively and follow his postures quietly until the prayer is finished.

The prayers must be performed five times every day—before sunrise (*fajr*), early afternoon (*zohr*), late afternoon (*asr*), or soon after sunset (*maghrib*), and late evening (*Isha*), before you retire. While prayer (*salat*) at any of these times takes only a few minutes to perform, engaging in it five times a day at proper time in the presence of others is supposed to wield a profound constraining impact upon the individual character. According to the Qur'an (29:45):

> Prayer (*salat*) rejects what is lewd and repugnant.

In short, *salat*, the second pillar of Islam, is generally recognized as being the first and the foremost step, which reinforces the profession of faith (*shahadah*) and which helps build Islamic character in the form of God consciousness (*taqwa*). Prayer (*salat*) serves as a medium to tell others as much as to yourself that you are in a state of submission to God's will. Especially when performed collectively with others or in congregation, *salat* is the very first step toward creating a feeling of community and equality—among the rich and the poor, the weak and the powerful, and people of all colors and ethnicity standing shoulder to shoulder next to one another and prostrating together in submission to their Lord.

Prayer (*salat*) has been emphasized several times in the Qur'an, signifying its importance as an Islamic practice. The Prophet regularly performed prescribed prayers at proper times, never missing any, and performed additional prayers, a practice which more dedicated Muslims try to emulate even today. According to the Prophet, *salat* is the primary fact of distinction between the believer and the nonbeliever. A number of Islamic scholars have interpreted this as meaning that a Muslim, who willfully evades *salat*, is equal to being a nonbeliever.

Zakat

Inasmuch as it has the function of reinforcing the profession of faith (*shahadah*) and building character, *salat* is not unique to Islam. Ritualistic worship, even in collective form, is performed in all major and several minor religions.

What is unique about it is that, except for a few instances, whenever *salat* is mentioned in the Qur'an, it is mentioned along with alms (*zakat*) which is money or property that is the right of the poor and the needy in your property that you rightfully possess. Giving alms (*zakat*), like prayer (*salat*), is incumbent upon the believer. Because they are almost always emphasized together in the Qur'an, they are considered to be closely related mutually reinforcing one another. Or, as the Qur'an (23:1-4) says:

Successful among the believers are the ones,
Who perform their prayers with full concentration,
Who avoid engaging in vain talk,
Who are quick in paying *zakat*,

It is emphasized (Murad, 1983) that while prayer (*salat*) makes it easier for you to detach a portion of your property for the sake of the poor, giving alms (*zakat*) as an act of sacrifice has the function of reinforcing the transcendental experience in *salat*. However, *zakat* is not an act of charity, as it has often been translated in English language, sometimes even by eminent Muslim writers. Charity is an act of goodwill. *Zakat* is a duty. Charity gives one a feeling of doing favors to others. *Zakat* is an act of helping yourself by cleansing your property. One may give any amount in charity. *Zakat* has a prescribed rate (2.5 percent of the accumulated property not in circulation in the previous year). *Zakat* must not be confused with a state tax on income either. Even if an Islamic state facilitates collecting it, *zakat* is not to be made part of the state budget.

One may give *zakat* to the needy in person. However, more preferably, it is to be given to a nongovernmental organization, to which a needy may contact without facing the *zakat* giver. A list of those who are deserving of the *zakat* is specified by the Qur'an. They are those in deep poverty (*fuqra*), those who are in need momentarily (*masakeen*), the orphans (*yatama*), and those who collect *zakat* (the *amileen*). If some money is still left, it may be spent for freeing the slaves and for the sake of teaching Islam to Muslims as well as non-Muslims (*dawah*).

In short, *zakat* is an act of worship with definite economic overtones. It may not eradicate poverty, but it has the function of easing pains of poverty. For those who are not in chronic poverty, it helps them make a fresh start. Sociologically, *zakat* means that your property is not just for you alone—it is a shared wealth. Psychologically, it means having a feeling for others in society.

Siyam

Fasting from dawn to dusk during the holy month of Ramadhan (*siyam*) is the fourth pillar of Islam. If giving alms (*zakat*) has the function of reinforcing prayer (*salat*) and the profession of faith (*shahadah*), fasting (*siyam*) has the function of reaffirming all these.

Physically speaking, one should stop eating breakfast and start fasting just before the early dawn prayers (*fajr*) and continue without any water, food, sex, cheating, lying, or purposefully deceiving for selfish reasons. Any persistence even in wrong thinking may automatically transform fasting into starvation. While he or she must engage in her normal routine of the day, the fasting person is supposed to continuously remain in a state of God consciousness (*taqwa*). Because it is an act of worship covering a relatively longer period of time (whole daylight hours), fasting (*siyam*) has to be performed with utter self-restraint. Knowing that this might not always be possible, many who fast prefer to spend their fasting time praying extra prayers, reading the Qur'an, and even trying to memorize it. For most *zakat* givers, Ramadhan is the time to give their yearly due. In short, during the *siyam*, the Muslim community is supposed to become an Islamic retraining camp. Thus, as a spouse or as a neighbor, as a businessman or customer, as a superior or a subordinate, as a political candidate or a voter, or as one who is about to enter a contract, one must be conscious of *siyam*, lest his or her fasting totter on the brink of becoming a futile exercise in mere starvation.

Fasting is not unique to Islam. Christianity, Judaism, Bahai religion, Hinduism, and Buddhism just to name a few have prescribed fasting in one form or another.

According to the Qur'an (2:183), fasting was prescribed even before Prophet Muhammad. However, *siyam* in Islam is definitely a more rigorous form of fasting demanding a greater amount of self-restraint on the part of the person who is fasting. Fasting in Ramadhan is performed in honor of the coming of the Qur'an with the very first revelation during the Prophet's heart-rending encounter with the angel Gabriel. *Siyam* is a sort of welcome given by the Muslim community to the book it so much reveres.

Hajj

The fifth pillar of Islam is pilgrimage (*hajj*), consisting of worship around the Ka'abah in Mecca and surrounding holy places. *Hajj* is incumbent upon all adult Muslims—men as well as women—who are healthy and can financially afford the travel to Mecca at least once in their lifetimes.

The Qur'an gives an eloquent historical account of the time, when under the Divine command, prophet Abraham (*Ibraheem*) took his wife Hager (*Hajirah*) and his baby son Ismail to the waterless valley of what is now known as Mecca and left them there all by themselves. As the baby was crying of thirst in the scorching desert sun, Hajirah, the mother, ran around desperately in search of water, but to no avail. As she came back to the baby, to her utter delight, she saw a spring of fresh water gushing miraculously from where the baby was kicking with his heels on the dusty floor of the valley.

Needless to say the two settled down in the valley of Mecca and in due time welcomed desert tribes and intercontinental caravans, which made the valley a more or less permanent station. Ibraheem, again under the Divine command, came back to see his wife and his teenage son. The father and the son together proceeded to build the Ka'abah, as a house of worship near the spring called *Zam Zam*.

Thus, it is clear from the Qur'an that the Ka'abah, the holiest mosque in Islam, was built by the prophet Ibraheem and his son Ismail. History tells us that in due course of time, the Ka'abah became the center of annual pilgrimage and attracted thousands of pilgrims mostly from the Arabian Peninsula. History also informs us that by the time Muhammad was born, Ka'abah, originally the center of monotheistic worship, was transformed into an abode of polytheism with 360 statues and idols placed under its roof.

After the conquest of Mecca, the Prophet destroyed the idols and the images, but continued the practice of annual pilgrimage (*hajj*). Muhammad as a prophet performed *hajj* only once. At that time, nearly all of the pilgrims were Muslims from Arabia. However, as Islam spread in the surrounding continents, the population of the pilgrims grew in size as well as diversity. It became heterogeneous in race, ethnicity, language, and nationalities.

In his last *hajj*, there were only a few thousand pilgrims who listened to his last sermon a few months before the Prophet died in Medinah. In February 2003, almost seventeen hundred years hence, there were more than 2.5 million pilgrims (almost 10 percent of the current population of Saudi Arabia), who came from eighty Muslim as well as non-Muslim countries, including a contingent of 1,781 from the United States (Center, 2003).

Pilgrimage (*hajj*) is aimed at recreating a feeling of unity and brotherhood in the heterogeneous mass of humanity. Logistical considerations do not permit the government of Saudi Arabia to allow more pilgrims than they can manage at present. Otherwise, given today's level of communications and transportation around the world, there would be a much larger mass of the pilgrims converging on Mecca each year. *Hajj* has had a rare attraction for Muslims all over the world for the past fourteen hundred years. Muslims from all the continents and of all races and nationalities, even if they do not practice Islam fully in their lives, long to go for *hajj* at least once in their lifetimes. In the past, they traveled for *hajj* on donkeys, horses, sailing ships, even on foot for days, weeks, months, and even for years. Today, of course, they use much faster and more efficient means to do so. There is little doubt that the *hajj* is the largest annual gathering of people—men, women, children, and the aged—at one place on earth.

Because almost every Muslim longs to go for *hajj* at least once in his or her lifetime, a set of preconditions are provided. For instance, one must not go in debt in order to pay for the *hajj*. One must not sell off all his property in order to go on *hajj*. Before one leaves for the *hajj*, it should be seen his or her dependents are left with enough living means until his or her return. One must be in good health to embark on this sometimes difficult journey. Save these preconditions, *hajj* is a duty on every adult and sane Muslim.

Pilgrimage (*hajj*) is a unique experience for the believer. Not only that one earns an honorific title *al-Hajj or Hajji* (*Hajja* if a woman) after he or she has performed the *hajj*, the very experience of seeing the *Ka'abah* with your eyes, touching it with your own hands, praying in front of it at very close distance, finding yourself among complete strangers who, "all with a common focus and united in complete submission and finding yourself in close vicinity of where the Prophet grew up as a child, where he first received the very first verses of the Qur'an, constitutes a living experience in self transcendence" (Mujeeb, 1989). It makes the believer feel in close proximity to God, not only when one is making his or her rounds around the *Ka'abah*, or tearfully asking the Lord to forgive his or her sins, but also when he or she is talking to others, sleeping, eating, or buying cold drinks.

"*Hajj* is an act of collective worship involving literally millions all around you. It goes on continuously for days and weeks starting when one leaves home to the day one comes back home" (Michaels, 2000). During the *hajj*, a man must be clad in a piece of white unstitched cloth wrapped around the waist coming down below the knees along with a similar piece hanging over the shoulders. Women are allowed to wear their usual attire meeting Islamic code of modesty.

While doing the *hajj*, one is not exempted from some other Islamic duties. For instance, he must utter the profession of faith (*shahadah*) loudly and repeatedly (women must do it quietly). One must join others in praying five daily prayers. Having already given alms (*zakat*) before leaving home, one is expected to give to charity generously.

It is not difficult to see the economic benefits that *hajj* brings to the host country. In fact, before the discovery of oil, *hajj* was the major source of revenue equally for the Saudi government as well as the public. Equally, it is not difficult to see the political potential in international affairs that *hajj* harbors as the fifth pillar of Islam. Beyond this, it is not difficult to see millions of Muslims in *hajj* from heterogeneous background making a formidable psychological impact of commitment to Islam upon one another.

MACRO DIMENSIONS

Mostly, Islam is remembered in terms of its micro dimensions, the five pillars, aimed mainly at personality building supposedly culminating in God consciousness or *taqwa* (often translated as piety in English literature). However, as mentioned earlier, in Islam *taqwa* is not an end in itself. It is the very first step toward building and maintaining a community of the believers with its own institutional structure consisting of economy, family, and polity (an *ummah*). Before the Prophet died, the Qur'anic rules of Islamic economy and Islamic family were already in practice. Structure of the polity was left to his surviving companions, who adopted a mode of election culminating in the *Khilafah al-Rashidah*, or the pious Caliphate.

Limitations of time and space do not allow us to deal with the details of these dimensions in these pages. Suffice it to say that Islamic economy respects private property and promotes open market with an explicit concern for those who are left behind in economic competition. Injunctions about alms (*zakat*), inheritance (*wiratha*), and prohibition of interest (*riba*) together put a greater emphasis on dispersion rather than accumulation of wealth putting Islamic economy between capitalism and socialism (Ba-Yunus and Ahmed 1985). Laws governing the formation of Islamic family make the publicly expressed consent of the marrying partners obligatory, make woman a property owner independent of her husband and other relatives, and gives woman the right to divorce. The system of *Khilafah* was based on the Qur'anic principle of mutual consultation (*shura*) allowing discussion, nomination, and dissent resulting in binding decision(s).

IDENTITY AND ETHNIC PRIDE

The history and the character of the Prophet and his companions have a profound impact on Muslim sentiments and conscience. Although the behavior of Muslims today may be farther from the ideals of Islam in many respects, and although this population of more than one billion Muslims may be divided ethnically, linguistically, and politically, the Muslims seem to harbor a relatively strong sense of community, a sense of belonging. Bernard Lewis, the Princeton historian, argues that whereas the West sees the world as being a system of nations divided in various ways including religions, Islam sees the world as being a system of religions divided in various ways including the nations. This makes the world of Islam as being one community—the *ummah*—among many other religious communities existing in the world (*The Economist*, 13 September 2003). Prayer (*salat*) as preceded by the call to prayer (*adhan*), five times a day, from a neighborhood mosque, communal fasting from dawn to dusk everyday for a whole month of Ramadhan (*siyam*), and especially pilgrimage (*hajj*) resulting in a mammoth gathering of Muslims from all over the world are primary cultural factors in shaping this entity. These are powerful elements of the Muslim personality reinforcing common identity, which transcends even sectarian differences among Muslims. They seem to have taken to heart the Qur'anic admonishment:

> O, believers, fear Allah the way He should be feared And do not die except in
> the state of Islam
> And hold steadfast together the rope of Allah and do not separate
> And remember the favors of Allah on you
> You were enemies to one another
> And He put love in your hearts
> And in His mercy made you brothers (sisters)
> (3:102-103)

Or,

> "Certainly the believers are brothers and sisters unto one another"
> (49:10)

This feeling of brotherhood standing for the Muslim nationalism was first inculcated by the Prophet in the city-state of Madinah fourteen hundred years ago. It served him well against his Meccan foes, and seems to have, in one form or the other, survived the onslaught of time. This "tribalism" is not unique to Muslims. Hindus castes, Jews, Catholics, Mormons, and a number of fundamentalist Christians seem to harbor strong community feelings. This sense of belonging or a common identity is usually heightened especially in times of a crisis, adversity, and defeat, or when a sense of helplessness prevails. In the United States, this must not come as a surprise especially to the Jews, the Mormons, and the Catholics. Present day adherents of Islam are no exception to this rule.

Moreover Muslims are heirs to a more than one thousand years' long mighty civilization, which almost looked invincible. Many Muslims, even educated among them, take pride in the past accomplishments of their forefathers, who gave to the modern world such sciences as numerals, algebra, logarithms, and decimal calculations, and whose military prowess once looked undefeatable. Basking in the past glory and gloating over the achievements of their forefathers seems to be yet another factor helping Muslims reaffirm their common identity.

Clearly, this sense of belonging implies that the Muslims, as the Prophet Muhammad once said, share the pains of other Muslims. This may explain why the Muslims, mostly experiencing defeat and dire circumstances these days, are easily excitable if and when they find a Muslim individual or a community in pain and suffering at the hands of the non-Muslims or even authoritarian Muslim rulers. This perception of Muslims, heirs to a once mighty world power, being under attack everywhere, even in the heartland of Islam, makes especially informed Muslims turn inward, which has meant Muslims reasserting and clinging to ethnic slogans more strongly.

As mentioned above, this ethnic pride is not peculiar to Muslims. Other groups, especially in minority situations often go back to their ethnic symbols and evoke slogans while struggling against perceived threats. However, when we are talking about the "Muslim World", we are not necessarily talking of ethnic minorities. The "Muslim World" consists of more than fifty-five independent states with overwhelming Muslim majorities. It is amazing to see how Islam continues to generate a sense of common ethnicity in such a large and a diverse population.

This ethnic pride among Muslims has in the past few hundred years gone through a few convulsions. First the Crusaders invaded and remained in occupation of Palestine and parts of Syria for almost one hundred years (1098 to 1187). Then in 1258 came the Mongols who sacked, raped, and burned Baghdad, the center and the symbol of Islamic prowess and civilization. Finally, starting in the 1700s, came newly energized Europeans, with new technology and newly earned economic prosperity, and turned tables by colonizing the Muslim lands. Each time freedom movements in Muslim lands could be fueled by invoking Islamic slogans, by reaffirming Islamic brotherhood, and by remembering the invincibility of the forefathers in order to beat back the intruders.

It was a combination of this sense of belonging and ethnic pride that propelled Muslims from nearly all over the world in fighting against a superpower—the Soviets—in Afghanistan for ten long years during 1980s. Again, this is what prompted them to fight against Serb atrocities in Bosnia and Kosovo, and against Russian excursion in Chechnya in the 1990s. This is how hostilities against Indian occupation in Kashmir (a Muslim majority nation) continue until today ever since independence of India and Pakistan in 1947. It may also explain why the United States, the only Superpower, is having such a hard time pacifying Iraq after overthrowing Saddam Hussein.

However, a few incidents enrage Muslim masses from Morocco to Indonesia as much as the problem and plight of the Palestinians. For Muslims the world over, Palestine seems to have become the symbol of gross injustice at the hands of the powerful West. "Palestinians are up against the might of the United States, which for its own internal political reasons, finds itself forced to support the Zionist state with all its most sophisticated weapons being used against rock throwing Palestinians" (Muhammad, 2002). It is one thing to come to the help of other Muslims in need, but Palestine is something else. Other than being the home to *alAqsa*, the third holiest mosque in Islam, Palestine hurts Muslim pride. Palestine provokes among Muslims a sense of powerlessness, which only enrages the more ethnocentric among them.

Few would deny that the Muslim World is, by and large, a part of the Third World today. It is economically depressed, technologically underdeveloped, and gasping mostly under the rule of dynastic, military, or dictatorial rulers with corrupt bureaucracies. Why so? What happened to that mighty civilization? The reason, we are told is that "We Muslims have given up Islam. We say that we are Muslims, but we are using our religion for our own short-sighted goals, the worst culprits being the ruling elite, who continue to cling to power with active help of powerful nations with neo-colonial designs of their own." (Ramadhan, 1965).

There must be different degrees of ethnic sensitivity among Muslims—from the very insensitive, the disillusioned, and the hopeful (those wishing somebody would do something), to the activists (those who would like to take initiative with whatever means available—speech, pen, demonstrations—not excluding armed struggle). The problem is that Muslim states in general are not "free speech states", most notorious among them being the ones ruled by "friendly tyrants" (Pipes and Garfinkle, 1993). This suppression promotes circumstance incubating conspiracies and violent action against corrupt ruling elite and their perceived supporters. Frequent military coups d'etat as exemplified by those staged by Jamal Abdul Nasser of Egypt, Momar Ghadafi of Lybia, Hafiz al Asad of Syria, and Saddam Hussein of Iraq on the left, and the emergence of Ayatullah Khomeini and Osama Bin Laden, on the extreme right, are examples. That this feeling knows no borders in the Muslim World is manifest from anti-Soviet struggle in Afghanistan and the entourage that gathered especially around Osama Bin Laden. However, everybody in the Muslim World is not Jamal Nasser or Osama Bin Laden. Most probably, most in the Muslim World belong to the two middle categories in the above—68 percent in terms of the bell curve. They are either disillusioned or they are optimistic hoping that somebody would soon do something in the name of justice, to restore the lost Muslim pride.

DILEMMA OF WESTERN LURE

Despite their ethnocentrism, which often erupts in mass hysteria, Muslims have generally remained enchanted with the glamour of the West. There are 6 or 7 million Muslims in the United States today (Ba-Yunus and Kone, 2004). Perhaps there are as many Muslims in Europe. While nearly all European Muslims (with the exception of those in the Balkans) are immigrants or children of immigrants, only about two thirds of American Muslims are of immigrant variety. These Muslim immigrants belong to the great wave of migration from the developing countries. This migratory episode started in the second half of the twentieth century and there is still no end to it in sight. Why do Muslims want to migrate to the West, especially to the United States? Perhaps their motivation to migrate is the same as that of other people from the developing countries—plenty of good jobs, higher wages, higher standard of living, quality of life including a democratic system of government, equality before law and freedom of speech, which are rare commodities in the Third World in general and in the Muslim World in particular. Those in the Muslim World, like others in the Third World, are obsessed with availing these opportunities by migrating to the West. They do all kinds of tricks, go to great expense, and take many risks in order to achieve their objective illegally if legal means are not available.

It must be emphasized here that most of these immigrants and would-be immigrants from the Third World including Muslims, are not all poor, uneducated, unemployed, or starving. Those who starve cannot spend thousands on their illegal journeys. In fact, evidence suggests (Newland, 1979) that most of these immigrants and would-be immigrants are not necessarily unemployed in their home countries. On the contrary, most of them are educated, skilled, or trained workers with some work experience in their home countries. Muslims are not an exception to this rule.

Then how is it that, if not compelled by poverty, they are so awfully eager to migrate to the "hated" West? How is it that as soon as they settled in the United States, they and their children are known as "model minorities?" Maybe their "hate" of the West is more apparent than real. It is instructive to see how most students in the Muslim World crave for entering Western universities for higher education and how after they finish their education in the West, most of them prefer to stay, rather than go back home. There is little doubt that there is a selective subterranean admiration for the Western ideals especially among the highly educated, many of them even practicing Muslims. It seems that the educated youth in the Muslim World, far from hating the West, are able to find Islamic ethos in such Western ideals as freedom of expression, equality before law, and educational and economic opportunities. On one hand, they may deride the West for excessive materialism, sexual laxity, and decline in family values. On the other hand, they admire economic and political opportunities available to the Western man. They revolt against the very idea of colonialism and neocolonialism on the part of the Western nations as they see it, and yet they may admire the Western system of governance. They are often puzzled as to why the champions of democracy have come to support some of the most authoritarian rulers in the Muslim world. Clearly, they see political opportunism behind tall claims of democracy and justice especially when it comes to Western policies toward the Muslim world. Conversely, they would welcome a democratic order, with all its imperfections, over the most benign authoritarian rule.

CHARACTER OF MUSLIM AMERICANS

Most Americans are hyphenated Americans: African Americans, white Americans, Italian Americans, Arab Americans, or Asian Americans, just to name a few. There are also Americans who are Catholics, but they are not known as Catholic Americans. Mormons are not called Mormon Americans and Buddhists are not addressed as Buddhist Americans. Among religious communities, this distinction, it seems, goes to the Muslims.

In the West in general and in the United States in particular, Islam has suffered from what Edward Said once described as "bad press." Although not a Muslim himself, in his *Covering Islam* (1981), immediately followed by his classic *Orientalism* (1982), Edward Said laments extremely biased and negative coverage that Islam generally received in Western academia, among policy-making elites and in the media.

But that was before 9/11. After that fateful day, like after the sneak attack on Pearl Harbor, a whole segment of American citizenship consisting of millions of Muslims—blacks, whites and browns—are marginalized if not criminalized altogether. This marginalization of the Muslim population has meant that all Muslims residing in the United States, citizens included, are suspect automatically. Even before 9/11, there existed legal provisions for racial profiling, which, more often than not, selectively apprehended and grilled "Middle Eastern looking" motorists and other travelers in the buses, trains and the nations airports. Immediately before 9/11, racial profiling had become such a serious issue in the Muslim American community that the presidential candidate who opposed it won the Muslim vote and presidency in the 2000 election.

Concerns about Muslims, especially in the wake of 9/11, living in the millions in the United States is understandable. Although, none of those suicide hijackers of 9/11 was an American citizen or even a legal resident (immigrant), all of them were Arabs and Muslims. Apparently, they seem to represent a deep anti-American resentment pervading the Muslim people especially of Arab origin. Hence the question: Why do they hate us?

There have been several answers to this question, mostly highly biased and partisan. What is serious is that "they" in this question is often meant to include Muslim Americans as well. For instance, in a widely circulated letter of appeal on behalf of the Heritage Foundation, none other than Steve Forbes writes (2003):

> ...Why is it so difficult to speak openly about the fact that many mainstream Muslim individuals and institutions, throughout the world and within our own country, give moral and financial support to their fellow Muslims who are waging terrorist war against us?

One answer to the above question and Steve Forbes' observation fits into it neatly, is that because they, not unlike the Jews and others, have a strong feeling of being one community or a nation so to say Muslims in the West strongly identify with other Muslims in the world. According to this view, their true allegiance is with the *ummah*, on whose behalf they will, if necessary, launch attacks on their host countries (see *Economist*, 2003).

Thankfully, not many in the West subscribe to this apocalyptic view of the post-9/11 world. Reuven Paz, an Israeli scholar, writing mainly about Muslims in Europe, argues that Islamic movements are taking advantage of growing alienation among the second and third generation Muslims. This alienation among European Muslims may often be traced back to the intractable government policies of host societies, France being most notorious among them (*Economist*, 2003).

However, the United States situation is considerably different from that in Europe. To begin with, a large proportion (about 30 percent) of Muslim Americans are of indigenous, mostly African American, origin. Even if they trace their origin to Kunta Kinte of *Roots* (Haley, 1976), they are no less American than a conservative like Steve Forbes himself. Moreover, whereas most Muslim immigrants to Europe have been from unskilled or semi-skilled working classes in their respective countries of origin, the United States has been blessed with Muslim immigrants belonging to educated, skilled, and well-trained professionals in medicine, law, finance, business, and similar high paying disciplines. Their American-born and raised children, contrary to that in many European countries, enjoy automatic citizenship by virtue of their being born on the American soil. These second generation immigrants could be characterized as the "yuppies" of the early twenty-first century for following the footsteps of their parents. They are becoming highly educated professionals themselves. Even Muslim American women, as we shall see in the following chapters, have an unusually high participation in elite professions in the United States. Often it may not be difficult to find that both Muslim husbands and wives are in the same elite professions.

In short, as Muslims, even as they harbor a feeling of belonging to the Muslim *ummah*, they have made heavy social and economic investment in the United States. Do they agonize over the plight of the Palestinians, the Bosnians, the Kosovars, and the Kashmiris? Yes, they do. Have they contributed to the charitable organizations with their *zakat* money and other charities? Most of them, perhaps, did. Did they knowingly break any laws in doing this? Most probably they did not. Not a single Muslim charity in the United States is found to have had any connection with or made any contribution to al-Qaeda, or, for that matter, any other organization with similar anti-American designs. None of the American Muslim charities now closed are convicted of any connection with terrorism (Lampman, 2004).

Also, it is instructive to read proclamations of national as well as local Muslim leaders, *Imams*, and other men and women of influence in the Muslim community: how vehemently they disavowed themselves with the 9/11 attacks as being un-Islamic; how out of the way they went in condemning Osama Bin Laden. Their ethnic pride notwithstanding, their Islamic sense of belonging to one community (*ummah*) is not ethnocentric. It could not override Islam's abhorrence to injustice and taking innocent lives: "one, who kills one innocent soul, kills the whole humanity unjustly" (Qur'an 5:32), we are reminded repeatedly.

Are all these utterances on the part of the Muslim leadership fake? If the answer to these questions is "yes," might not one be guilty of stereotyping them? If "yes" one would have to assume that this highly alluring American culture did not have much impact upon Muslims. It would mean that Americanization has somehow failed when it comes to the Muslims, many of whom have lived in the United States for decades, and most of whom are born and raised in this country. A tiny minority of them—those who are relative newcomers, those who have overstayed their visas, or who entered the United States illegally—are not awfully different from the parents or grandparents of millions of Americans. They are the ones who are driven by the American dream. Transient but upwardly mobile, they are not the ones who could be expected to bite the hand that feeds them.

The answer to the above question could be negative for another important reason. Like the followers of all other faiths in this secular society, Muslims have been able to practice their faith more freely than it is possible to do so in many Muslim countries. Islamic practice is, no doubt, more free in the United States than it is, say, in secular Turkey, or in conservative Saudi Arabia, or it was under the fundamentalist Taliban regime.

America is a place where you are free to go to the mosque. You are free not to go to the mosque. This is a society in which Muslim women observe modesty (*hijab*) out of their own free will. In the United States, Muslims live in a society in which they are allowed to march in protest in front of the White House. This is a polity that allowed Muslims (as they proudly point out) to put a president of their liking in the White House in 2000 and vote against him in 2004. No wonder millions of Muslims from all over the world want to leave their homes and make the United States their new home.

If one still persists in claiming that Muslims constitute a fifth column in the United States, the claimant might well be Islam-phobic. Moreover, it is not difficult to see that Islam is firmly rooted in American society. It is, by far, the fastest growing religion in the United States. Rather than looking at Muslims living next door with suspicion and insisting that they pay for the sins of others is like saying that all Americans are equal, but some of them are less equal than others.

REFERENCES

Al-Farouqi, Ismail R. "Nature of Islamic Jurisprudence." 1974. Presidential address given at 5th Annual Conference of the Association of Muslim Social Scientists, Indianapolis, Indiana.

Armstrong, Karen. *Muhammad: A Biography of the Prophet*. San Francisco: Harper, 1991.

Armstrong, Karen. *Islam: A Short History*. New York: Random House, 2000.

Ba-Yunus, Ilyas, and Farid Ahmed. *Islamic Sociology: An Introduction*. Cambridge: Hodder and Stoughton, 1985.

Ba-Yunus, Ilyas, and Kassim Kone. "Muslim Americans: A Demographic Report." In *Muslims' Place in the American Public Square*, edited by Z. Bukhari. New York: Altamira Press, 2004.

Bloom, Jonathan, and Sheila Blair. *Islam: A Thousand Years of Faith and Power*. New York: T.V. Books, 2000.

Esposito, John S. *Islam the Straight Path*. New York: Oxford University Press, 1998.

Haikal, M. H. *Prophet Muhammad*. Translated by I. R. al Farouqi. Plainfield, IN: American Trust Publications, 1985.

Lampman, Jane. "U.S. Muslims in a Quandary over Charities," *Christian Science Monitor* 96, no. 247 (2004): 11.

Maududi, Abul Ala. "On the Existence of One God." Speech delivered to a multi-religious audience at Ludhiana in 1946 (Lahore: Ashraf Publications, 1950).

Maududi, Abul Ala. *Toward Understanding Islam*. Lahore, Pakistan: Islamic Publications, 1962.

Muhammad, Mahathir. 2002. An interview with the author, Kualalampur, Malaysia.

Mujeeb, Ahmed. "Going For Hajj From Omaha to Mecca." *The Arabian Journal* (Spring, 1989): 17.

Newland, Kathleen. *International Migration: Search for Work* (Washington: Worldwatch Institute, 1979).

Rahman, Fazlur. *Islam*. Chicago, IL: University of Chicago Press, 1966.

Ramadhan, Saeed. "What do Muslims Have Against Islam?" A speech delivered to the Islamic Cultural Society in 1965, University of Minnesota.

Ruthven, Malice. *Islam in the World*. Oxford: Oxford University Press, 1984.

Said, Edward. *Covering Islam*. New York: Pantheon, 1981.

Said, Edward. *Orientalism*. New York: Vintage, 1982.

2

Estimating the Muslim American Population

How many Muslims are there in the United States these days? This is a question for which there have been no easy answers. In searching the literature on Islam in the United States, one is struck by the great interest that social scientists and other writers have shown in estimating this rapidly growing religion. It has been a matter of pride for some, a matter of curiosity for others, and a reason of concern for still others.

Contrary to what many might believe, Muslims are not strangers to American shores. Some speculate that the Muslim presence in the United States might have predated Columbus (Davidson, 1959; Quick, 1996; Nyang, 1999). What is quite certain is that Muslim names started appearing in slave records as early as the seventeenth century (Austin, 1984; Mehdi, 1978; Poston, 1992). Indeed, it is plausible that by the end of the eighteenth century, there have been more Muslims than Catholics and Jews in the United States. Alex Haley's *Roots* (1976) is based on similar folklore, especially among African Americans living in the inner city ghettos.

This chapter is based on the findings of a survey that we previously presented in *Muslims' Place in the American Public Square* (Bukhari, 2004), but this report also draws upon several other researches, surveys, and summaries. Some of these studies are extremely sketchy and speculative. They belie the difficulties involved in estimating a population not covered by the U.S. census. Others have focused on the Muslim population only tangentially while pursuing interests in some other populations. Still others have used more complex research designs in order to obtain information from immigration and birth statistics.

Because these studies were conducted with designs of varying rigor, the esti-mates of the Muslim American population also vary greatly—from about 10 million (American Muslim Council, 2001) to about 3 million (Smith, 2001). However, Muslim Americans are a fast growing population and thus, their esti-mation necessitates quick revisions. The reason the Muslim American popula-tion is growing so quickly (in addition to universal factors of growth, including natural growth and migration), is due to net conversion to Islam. Because of a convergence of these three factors of growth, it is not hard to arrive at overly ambitious estimations. On the other hand, this very conver-gence explains why the estimation of the Muslim American population cannot be too conservative. Also, what most of these studies suffer from is their near-exclusive focus on the size of Muslim American population. They generally ignore structural aspects, which might not only explain the division of this population in age, gender, educational, and professional categories, but also give us an idea as to the growth rate of this population. We would like to know not only how many Muslim Americans there are today, but also how many of them are males, females, children, and adults. We should also like to know projections for five, ten, to twenty years from now. Without such consid-erations, no demographic picture would ever be complete. We will try to address these considerations in this chapter.

ESTIMATION OF SIZE

Because the U.S. Census Bureau does not touch anything remotely resem-bling religion, estimations of the Muslim population is left to nongovernmental organizations and other interested groups whose studies, for understandable reasons, lack reliability in varying degrees.

The first attempt known to us so far has been in 1959 as commissioned by the Federation of Islamic Associations in America (FIAA). This study con-sisted of enumeration of the total number of households affiliated with the FIAA. The enumeration yielded a total of 187,112 such households. Due to the possibility of under-enumeration, this figure was rounded to the nearest whole (i.e., 200,000). Multiplying this by six, the average Muslim family size at the time, the FIAA announced an estimate of the Muslim population in 1960 at about 1.2 million (Alam, 1968). As is evident, this study was deficient in sev-eral respects. Most importantly, it ignored Muslim households which were not affiliated with the FIAA, leaving aside populations of Turkish, Albanian, Afri-can American, Pakistani (mainly Punjabi), and Bosnian origin. Evidently, this estimate deserved some serious upgrading, which, unfortunately was not done.

Ba-Yunus and Siddiqui (1998) estimated that this FIAA affiliate population had a natural growth rate (not considering migration) of 2 percent with a capacity to double itself in thirty years. This means that FIAA's targeted popu-lation alone was more than 2.5 million in the year 2000. This, we think, is an important factor to remember, for it means that the Muslim American popula-tion in the year 2000 was far greater than 2.5 million considering that the

FIAA study was an exercise in under-enumeration. Besides, large numbers of Muslims have migrated to the United States since the FIAA study was done.

This initiative by the FIAA was not followed by any other estimation attempts for another thirty years or so. We have discussed relative merits of these reports elsewhere (Ba-Yunus and Kone, 2004). Some of these studies aroused a great deal of controversy and debate (Phillip, 1980; Ghayur, 1981; Weeks and Siddiqui, 1993; Stone 1991; Ba-Yunus and Siddiqui, 1998; Kosmin, 1989; Bagby, Perl, and Froehle, 2001; and Smith, 2001). Some of these findings are poles apart. For instance, according to Bagby et al., the American Muslim population was around 6 million in the year 2000. According to Smith, on the other hand, the Muslim American population was less than 3 million at the same time. There is no doubt that the issue of Muslim population in the United States is a keenly discussed topic today.

SOURCES OF INFORMATION

Conscious of the pitfalls in previous studies, we proceeded step by step. First we aimed at preparing, as completely as possible, a list of Islamic centers and other Islamic institutions such as the mosques, schools, libraries, and central of fices of national and regional Muslim organizations. Major Islamic organizations maintain large mailing lists, which were made available to us. Additionally, annual reports, historically important old files, and interviews with the senior citizens, if and when available, provided further insight. Many of such listings are updated periodically and are now available for sale by some Islamic bookstores and publishing houses such as CAMRI, ISNA, and Soundvision, among others.

For the sake of this research, we distinguished among several different kinds of Islamic institutions in the United States. First an Islamic center or a Muslim community center was defined as a place in which its activity goes beyond the five times daily prayers and the *Juma'* prayers on Fridays. Most Islamic centers hold weekly Qur'anic study sessions, regular community dinners, women's programs, weekend classes for children, and various indoor and outdoor activities for the families, in addition to cooperating with local churches and temples, universities, and colleges. These centers, especially in large cities, can be old community homes, churches, or school buildings bought by the Muslims. Or, they can be newly built multipurpose mosques in the suburbs. Whatever the case, each center is supported by and betrays the existence of an expanding and relatively prosperous community in the surrounding territory.

Excluded from this definition are what may be called the *Masjid* or the neighborhood mosque, which holds five times daily prayers in addition to the *Juma'* congregation on Fridays. There are numerous such neighborhood mosques, especially in large cities. They are mostly unregistered and unlisted in telephone directories. These smaller grassroots institutions generally serve those who because of age, local business, new arrival, part-time jobs, or sickness stay home or in the neighborhood most of the time and are not always able to go to a major Islamic center far from home. Additionally, those who take advantage of and support such facilities could be transients, doctors in local clinics, taxi drivers, and day laborers who need and want to have a convenient place to congregate at prayer times. These religious structures could typically be basements of large apartment buildings, abandoned stores, and other unclaimed structures the city is happy to lease inexpensively. Most researchers have in the past showed little sensitivity to the existence of such neighborhood mosques (an exception being the *Center Finder*, a by-now suspended publication of the Islamic Circle of North America (ICNA), thus underestimating the fastest growing number of places of daily or weekly Islamic congregation. *Masjid Tahura* (Ch. 5) is an example of such growing in number of neighborhood mosques and the difficulty in finding them. Such mosques are difficult to locate because they generally are not registered and do not have any published address or a telephone number. They are quite cheap to start and maintain. Besides, they are much more convenient than the much larger, but usually distant Islamic centers. We used the "snowball" technique to discover these mosques in large and medium-sized cities. Moreover, Muslim taxi drivers/owners played an important role in locating them.

Also, in large cities, there are facilities established for the expressed purpose of holding especially *Juma'* prayers (Friday congregation). Let us call these part-time places of worship (*Musalla*). Usually such facilities, although they might remain open for five daily prayers, come to life on Friday afternoons (usually between 12:30 and 2 P.M.) when a large number of Muslims working in the neighboring district come for the weekly congregational prayer. Many of these worshippers may be members of major Islamic centers in the city. These part-time *Musallas* are relatively easier to locate because, in most cases, they are registered organizations for the purpose of raising funds.

Additionally, there are recently emerged educational organizations that mainly focus on the full-time education of Muslim children. They also serve as mosques and host a number of other activities typical of an Islamic center.

Last but not least in importance are Muslim Students Associations (MSAs) on several campuses. Some of the largest such MSAs, like the one at the University of Michigan at Ann Arbor or the University of Illinois at Urbana/Champaign, may have a few thousand Muslim students each. In general, on a campus where you may have around ten Muslim students on an average, you may find a functioning MSA, although it might not carry the name MSA. In cooperation with the local Muslim families, these local MSA organizations establish and maintain a place in which to perform, the weekly *Juma'* congregation on Fridays. The Muslim Students' Association of the United States and Canada (see chapter 4) is a national organization that has been in the forefront of most Islamic activity since its inception in 1963. Because there are no mosques on most campuses, Muslim students conduct their activity in houses that they rent or purchase near their campus. Or, they conduct their programs in interfaith chapels in gracious churches nearby or reserved rooms in campus student unions.

What is important about these local Islamic institutions is that most of them maintain a mailing or correspondence list in order to inform people of major events to be held but, most importantly, in order to raise funds. The correspondence or mailing list must not be confused with the membership list, which may be much smaller. For instance, the Islamic Center of Central New York at Syracuse only had eighty-five households as members in 2003, but it had a mailing list exceeding one thousand addresses.

The Islamic Center of St. Louis, Missouri had in the same year a membership of about eight hundred, while its mailing list contained more than eight thousand addresses. These lists are updated periodically. For the purpose of this study, names appearing on these lists with the same address and telephone number were defined as a household—a family or a few individuals living at the same address even if only for the time being.

Moreover, we made use of 1,550 informants (a number reduced to 1,315 in the end) who collected information as directed (collecting mailing lists and contacting families randomly chosen). We must mention here with gratitude that a number of Muslim taxi owners/drivers lent us their help in locating these Muslim institutions and collecting data from, in some cases, more than one of them. The method that we adopted in this research almost completely bypassed the method based on random sample surveys with very few exceptions. It was to prove that the Muslim American population despite its fast growth might still be reached by going into various places of Islamic worship and using the so-called snowball techniques. We do not know how accurate our findings are. Replications in future are clearly in order.

FINDINGS

Muslim Demographic History

As mentioned above, Muslims have been in the United States for a few hundred years. However, as surprising as it may sound, few authentic accounts of American Muslim history are available presently. The few who took time and effort to write on this subject mostly wrote about selected time periods. To date, Sulayman Nyang's *Islam in the United States of America* (1999) seems to be the only comprehensive historical work on this subject.

Nyang divides the Muslim history of the United States into four major periods: (1) pre-Columbian, (2) Antebellum America, (3) late nineteenth-century migration, and (4) late twentieth-century migration.

The Pre-Columbian Period

Nyang recognizes that writing about a Muslim presence in the pre-Columbian period is controversial, because the evidence is only sketchy and not universally accepted. In fact, the story of the discovery of America by Columbus is so widely accepted these days that any alternative account only generates yawns. No one, not even serious scholars, have considered any other alternative worth studying. He wrote, "But regardless of how one may feel about the evidence, the fact remains that Muslims or persons believed to be Muslims visited this part of the world in pre-Columbian past" (1999: 12). For instance, basing his view on a fourteenth century historian al-Omari's account of the sub-saharan Africa, Davidson (1959) concludes that in "1312 Mansa Abu Bakr of Mali is believed to have traveled from the Senegambian region of the African coast to the Gulf of Mexico." Harvard's Leo Weiner, in his book *Africa and the Discovery of America* (1922), seems to indirectly support Davidson's claim. Although this view continued to remain unpopular among the academics, Rutger's Ivan Van Sertima (1976) continued to remind his colleagues that there were others who came to America before Columbus.

As challenging as they are, these above discussions are mere speculations. They raise more questions than they answer. For instance, who was Mansa Abu Bakr? Was he an explorer, a maritime trader, or a navigator? Was Mali's culture in terms of its mode of economy, polity, or, say, family and religion conducive for such maritime explorations? Were Malians or West Africans known for transoceanic explorations? Even if answers to these questions are in affirmative, they could at best, provide a strong possibility of but not a certainty about trans-Atlantic trip(s) on the part of Mansa Abu Bakr.

Moreover, one may ask what happened to Mansa after he reached the New World? Did he settle down there? Did he come back? In all probability, he did not settle down there. Had he done so, he certainly would have implanted Islam in that part of the world and we do not have any trace of any such thing in that part of the world until the beginning of slave trade a few hundred years later.

Muslims in Antebellum America

Basing his view on the works of Allan Austin (1984), Nyang focuses on the involuntary migration of Muslims to America, mainly due to slavery. According to him, at least ten percent of slaves from Africa were Muslims. During the seventeenth century, when slave trade from West Africa was going on, Islam had already penetrated the Senegambia region. These Senegambian slaves were preferred in the American South because of their utility as farm and household workers. Because of very harsh treatment, few Muslim slaves were able to continue with their religion. Consequently, no Islamic institutions were allowed to appear. There were few "fortunate" slaves who were allowed to buy their freedom. After the American Revolution of 1776, some of these slaves, such as Yarrow Mamouth of Georgetown (who was called "Maryland Muslim" in one Smithsonian publication) appeared in a portrait by the celebrated Charles Wilson Peale.

Except for the figure of 10 percent of these slaves being Muslims, we are not provided with any other statistical information about the Muslims in America during this period. Because there were no mosques left by these slaves, it is also impossible to tell about the distribution of Muslim slaves in the region.

The Late Nineteenth-Century Migration

Contrary to what many believe, massive immigration to the United States began in the later half of the nineteenth century, especially in the post–Civil War period. The great Irish famine, political instability in Eastern Europe, and anti-Jewish programs prompted chain emigration from these regions. Most of these emigrants headed toward the United States where it was finally stopped by an act of Congress in 1920. Along with these Europeans migrants came the Muslims from the former Ottoman Empire in Eastern Europe and the Middle East. This may be regarded as the first period of voluntary Muslim migration to the United States. Also during this period, the British brought into Western Canada the Punjabi indentured labor from India. In time, these Punjabi workers, consisting mostly of the Sikhs and the Muslims, migrated south toward California, where their descendants thrived as inn and restaurant keepers and as the middlemen. Today they are found in large numbers in the San Francisco Bay area and the Stockton Valley.

In addition to these Muslim immigrants mainly from Albania, former Yugoslavia, Greece, Syria, and Lebanon came Muslims from as far east as the Ukraine and Central Asia. The immigrants settled mostly in large metropolitan areas of New York, Philadelphia, Boston, Detroit, Chicago, and Los Angeles. There they established their organizations, mosques, and schools, some of which have survived to today. In 1967 the Muslim Students Association of United States and Canada counted more than three hundred abandoned mosques along present day Route 80, which, joining the two coasts, cuts across eleven states (Ba-Yunus and Siddiqui, 1998).

These abandoned mosques speak of a number of things. For instance, most of them, built before or soon after 1920, show the extent to which Muslims had settled in the United States in numbers large enough to establish their own institutions. Often many of them were abandoned mainly because the townships in which they were built were abandoned due to the directions of the new roads, new railroads, or simply because the townships did not themselves remain self-sustaining. Lastly, many if not most immigrants during this period are known to have returned home in order to escape creeping secularization of their children, to raise them in Islamic environments among their own kith and kin, and, presumably, in order to retire in their home countries.

Muslims also had their own cemeteries often attached to these mosques or not far from them. In a study commissioned by the MSA, 208 cemeteries were counted. Most cemeteries along Route 80 were large (about five acres on average) relative to the number of graves in them (fifteen graves per cemetery). This shows two demographic factors acting together on this population—low death rate and high rate of regional mobility or return migration.

The Late Twentieth-Century Migration

Because it was officially stopped by an act of Congress in 1920, migration was reduced to a trickle in the third decade of the twentieth century. There was hardly any migration for the next twenty years because of the Great Depression during 1930s and because of World War II and its aftermath during 1940s.

It was only after the cessation of hostilities in Korea in 1955 that migration to the United States picked up as a result of the near relatives of the naturalized citizens heading toward the United States all over again. More importantly, this period saw the beginning of the entry of foreign students coming mostly from the Third World countries, often for graduate studies in prestigious American universities. Not only were various scholarships and fellowships now made available for foreign students, but the universities offered graduate research or teaching assistantships to all graduate applicants on a competitive basis regardless of nationality and the country of origin. The booming post-war economy could afford this generous posture on the part of the American government.

These new arrangements in American education attracted large number of students, especially from Third World countries that included Muslim countries, which were otherwise used to sending their talented students to their former colonizer countries. This deflection toward American universities meant a great loss of foreign students to the European universities and a great gain for American academia.

These new policies in the American education system did not only mean a great monetary gain for the American universities, it was considered to be a long-term gain for the United States as a nation. Foreign students would be returning home after spending a few years in the United States and would serve as defenders of the United States in their respective countries. Besides, they might provide future leadership in these countries that was oriented toward the United States. The new decade of 1960s was, perhaps, the best for foreign students seeking American financial help. A new batch of foreign students, including those from the Muslim countries, larger than that in the previous year, entered the United States every year until the unprecedented post-war economic expansion came to a sudden halt in the 1970s, followed by the problems associated with the oil embargo of 1973.

Not only were foreign students allowed to enter for education (and even for work experience for limited number of years after graduation), but, under pressure from the Johnson administration, Congress took the unusual step of reintroducing the immigration of foreign workers from all over the world on a first-come, first-served basis. The passage of this new immigration bill caused a deluge of immigrants, especially from Third World countries. The very first beneficiaries of this new law were foreign students residing in the United States on temporary visas. This gave these new immigrants as a whole a characterizing feature in terms of their education, professions, income, and prestige in this society. Although this law was withdrawn soon after the 1960s were over, these new immigrants became citizens in a matter of few years and started sponsoring their spouses (if they were not with them already) and their near relatives for immigration. As these new immigrants became citizens, they did the same thing. Thus, immigration to the United States became an almost unending process, which continues to this day. Like others, Muslim immigrants have been beneficiaries and some of the main actors in this late twentieth-century migratory episode.

In addition to an almost exploding immigration of Muslims, this period also saw conversion to Islam, especially on the part of African Americans, in significant ways. A number of indigenous groups and families were accepting Islam all throughout this period, but most important of these has been the Nation of Islam, which after the death of their leader, Elijah Muhammad in 1975, opted for orthodox *Sunni* Islam under the guidance of their new leader *Imam* Warith Deen Muhammad.

This period has, then, seen tremendous growth in the Muslim population size mainly due to immigration, but also due to conversion and, quite significantly, reproduction. With growth in Muslim population came Muslim institutions and organizations that we shall deal with in the following chapters. Suffice it to say that having rooted itself firmly in American soil, Islam is on the verge of making significant economic and political contributions to American society.

Where in the United States Do They Live?

Immigration to the United States in the latter half of the twentieth century has not been exclusively due to open immigration policy (short-lived as it was) of the Johnson administration. Concurrently the asylum seekers and the refugees from nearly all over the world have been and are being allowed entry into the United States. Although six hundred and fifty thousand immigrants are allowed entry each year, additionally a total of six hundred thousand refugees were also allowed to enter during the latter half of the twentieth century (Weeks, 1989:252). A majority of these refugees, as mentioned above, could have originated in Muslim majority countries. Besides, there has also been a substantial rise in work visas (in most cases changeable to immigrant status and eventually to citizenship) granted especially to the high tech specialists mostly from the Third World countries—overwhelmingly from India with a huge absolute volume of the Muslim population (almost 150 million).

However, more than half a million immigrants that are granted entry visas in this country are directly or indirectly related to the Johnson administration's open immigration policy during the later half of 1960s. In the five years before the decade was out, this open immigration policy yielded slightly more than three million immigrants (Weeks, 1989:205) before it was rather hastily withdrawn in 1970 under the Nixon administration.

The decade of the 1960s, then, could be taken as a turning point in the demographic history of Muslims in North America. Never before have Muslims been allowed to immigrate to the United States (as well as Canada) in such large numbers, in such a continuous fashion, and over such a long time (almost four decades by the time of this writing and still continuing).

Consequently, the Muslim presence in the United States and Canada is quickly becoming visible. In 1960, there were only one hundred and fifty Muslim students at the University of Minnesota in the Minneapolis and St. Paul area: the number of nonstudent Muslims was unknown. In the year 2000, there were more than three hundred Muslim students at the same university with about two thousand Muslim families living in the Twin Cities and surrounding suburbs. Like most other new immigrants and many African Americans, most

Muslims, individuals as well as families, prefer to live in or close to large metropolitan areas such Los Angeles, New York, Chicago, Detroit, Philadelphia, Houston, Boston, Dallas, St. Louis, Atlanta, and Washington, D.C. and their suburbs, just to name a few. Further, a quick telephone survey of fifteen randomly picked cities with more than one hundred thousand residents, conducted in August 2002, shows that each one of them has at least one Islamic center and two neighborhood mosques. This shows an overwhelmingly urban character of Muslims—immigrants or indigenous—in the United States.

Moreover, Muslims are spilling over into smaller towns in growing numbers lately. Utica, New York, with a population of fifty thousand, had less than ten Muslim families in 1970. Their number grew to around 250 families in 2002 (Omar, 2002). Furthermore, according to the Mohawk Valley Resource Center for Refugees, Utica was home to more than four thousand people of Bosnian origin in the same year (Hassett, 2002).

The second wave of migration to the United States starting in the latter half of the twentieth century yielded much more massive numbers of Muslim immigrants than was true of the first wave of migration of the latter half of the nineteenth century. This is so because in the "first wave" most immigrants to the United States came from Europe, very few of them from the rest of the world and the Middle East. Besides, most who migrated in the "first wave," as Smith (2001) pointed out, were minorities in their home countries (such as the Jews in Eastern Europe and Russia). The same could be true of the Middle East, which overwhelmingly contributed Christian Arab immigrants to the United States at that time.

However, in the "second wave," the situation changed drastically. For one, the people of the Third World, including the Muslims eager to migrate to the United States, dominated this wave. This resulted in massive immigration of people from Muslim majority countries.

A quick check of the membership lists of the Islamic Society of North America (ISNA) as well as the Muslim American Society (MAS), the largest body of African American Muslims, shows that Muslims as professionals— doctors, educators, engineers, computer scientists, and small businessmen— have begun to move and are now living in relatively smaller cities and towns such as Muncie, Indiana; Cortland, New York; Winona, Minnesota; Edmund, Oklahoma; Waco, Texas; Pullman, Washington; and Panama City, Florida, just to name a few. This spilling over of the Muslim population from major metropolitan areas into smaller cities and townships not only shows the ease with which Muslim individuals and families are able to move into small town America, but reflects the growing demand for Muslim talent across the board on this continent.

Not all of these Muslim moving in smaller towns are new immigrants or their offspring. Towns such as Lackawanna, New York; Dearborn, Michigan; Gary, Indiana; and Cedar Rapids, Iowa, have second and even third generation Muslims whose parents or grandparents worked in steel factories, farming, the import/export business, real estate, and the food industry.

Likewise, African American Muslims, who were concentrated mainly in large cities such as Chicago, New York, and Philadelphia, have more recently fanned out to relatively smaller places like Peoria, Illinois; York, Pennsylvania; Ponca City, Oklahoma; Joplin, Missouri; Tustin, California; and Gary, Indiana, just to name a few. They have established there own mosques either in cooperation with or in addition to other mosques or Islamic centers in their respective cities or towns.

HOW MANY AND WHERE?

In our estimation in this project, there are 5,745,100 Muslim men and women of all ages living in the United States today. Of these, only 3,953,651 or about 69 percent were born as well as naturalized citizens. Of the rest, a total of 1,321, 011 or 23 percent were legal immigrants. Of the rest, there were foreign students as well as those on professional and business visas. Their numbers were derived mainly from, as mentioned earlier, the mailing lists of various Islamic centers, neighborhood *Masajid* or mosques, the *Musallas*, full-time schools, and various MSAs. We were able to locate a total of 1,751 Islamic institutions. However, because of nonavailability or disarray with respect to mailing lists, we were able to use information only from 1,510 or 87 percent of them. Of these, 801 (53 percent) were Islamic centers; 194 (13 percent) were neighborhood *Masajid* or mosques; 101 (7 percent) were *Musallas;* 199 (13 percent) were full-time schools, and 215 (14 percent) were MSAs. Of these 437 or 29 percent were run by the people of Arab background, 392 or almost 26 percent were run mainly by the African American Muslims, and 379 or about 25 percent were administered by the South Asian Muslims. The mosques or *Musallas* run by the MSAs were comprised of 187,015 college students (including foreign students) constitute a little higher than 3 percent of the total Muslim population. They were typically multiethnic. The Turks, the Bosnians, the Malaysians, and the Somalis, among others, ran the rest of the institutions.

Overall, there was an overlap of 14,487 names that we took care of. Most of this overlap was detected in the listings of the *Musallas* where people mostly go for the *Juma'*, or the Friday congregation only. The total number of households attached with all Islamic institutions in this study was 1,149,100 yielding an average of close to 766 households per institution.

Further, our informants collected data from a total of 2,852 households picked randomly from the correspondence lists. From these, we randomly picked a subsample of one thousand households. Our computations show that the average size of Muslim households attached with these institutions is a little more then five.

The distribution of the Muslim population in the United States is far from being uniform. We found that 774 or slightly more than 50 percent of the institutions of Islamic worship comprising almost 3 million Muslims live only in eleven states (see table 1), with an average of about 260,000 Muslims in each

Table 1.
Concentration of the Muslim Population

State	#Islamic institutions	Population
New York	126	579,152
Illinois	112	381,155
California	143	310,538*
New Jersey	105	208,210
Pennsylvania	61	281,455
Michigan	51	272,380
Massachusetts	48	272,273
Maryland	25	251,185
Texas	63	211,031
Georgia	25	121,379
Florida	15	105,101
Total	774	2,893,849

*Data from two Islamic centers and eleven mosques was lost. The above figure was computed by missing data technique.

of these eleven states. It means that in the rest of the forty-one states, there are only about seventy thousand Muslims each. A majority of these eleven states of relatively higher Muslim density (New York, New Jersey, Pennsylvania, Massachusetts, Maryland, Georgia, and Florida) are on the East Coast. Three of them (Illinois, Texas, and Michigan) are in the Midwest. All of them except two (Texas and California) are to the east of the Mississippi River. Only California, with largest number of Islamic institutions, is on the West Coast.

Household Size and Structure

Out of a total of close to 1 million, our informants were able to collect most information requested of them from 2,852 households. Because of time constraints, we drew a sample of 1,000 from these for further analysis as mentioned earlier. We found that the overall average size of the Muslim household was around 5.1, including all adults as well as minors of both sexes using the same address and the telephone number (710 or about 70 percent of them had more than one telephone or at least one cellular telephone).

Because many of our subjects did not remember or were reluctant to show real ages of their dependents, we used broader (20 year) age categories than usual. Table 2 shows that the Muslim population in the United States as a whole has a pattern of a newly immigrant population with largest concentration (54 percent) in the working age categories (21–60). However, it seems to be assuming a youthful character with an expanding base (25 percent under age 20). Table 2 also shows substantial numbers (20 percent) in the pre-retirement and retired age categories. This seems to be a bias due to the broader-than-usual age categories that we used. We believe that a fine-tuning would have shown that a majority of those in these categories would be closer to 60 than 80 years of age.

Table 2.
Age/Sex Structure in the Sample

Age	M/F				Total		Sex Ratio*
	N	%	N	%	N	%	
1–20	658	51	630	49	1,288	25	104
21–40	532	48	585	52	1,117	22	92]
41–60	739	50	746	50	1,485	29	100]
61–80	562	50	558	50	1,120	22	101]
80+	64	58	46	42	110	2	152]
Total	2,555	50	2,565	50	5,120	100	100

* Rounded to the nearest whole.

Table 2 also shows that the males and the females among Muslims in the United States are almost equally divided with a total rounded sex ratio (number of males per 100 females) at 100, although a closer look shows that overall females outnumber males by a slight margin. Males conspicuously outnumber females in the youngest age category (1–20), yet in the next two age categories, when combined together, females seem to outnumber males (a combined sex ratio of 96). However, when the next two age categories are combined, there are conspicuously more grandfathers than grandmothers in the Muslim households, with a sex ratio of 126, meaning that there are 126 males for every 100 females in this advanced age group.

Ethnicity

Muslims in the United States are ethnically a highly diverse population. Indeed, the ethnic composition of this population shows the extent to which Islam spread in the world during the past fourteen centuries.

The largest single group in our sample (close to 32 percent) consists of people of the Arab origin. On the whole it may translate to 1.8 million Arabs or their first and second-generation descendants. They are followed by the American Muslims (mostly African American) with 29 percent in the sample or 1.7 million on the whole. A close third are South Asians (from Pakistan, India, Bangladesh, Ceylon, Afghanistan, and Maldives) with 28.9 percent or 1.6 million on the whole. Then, there are 5 percent (close to 290 thousand) Turks, and 2 percent (115 thousand) Iranians and Bosnians. The rest of them are Kosovars, Malays, Indonesians, and others.

Profession

According to Table 3, 2,606 or about 51 percent in our sample are in the middle of working age. There are some who must have been left unaccounted for because of the age category 61–80 which includes more than mere retired persons. Likewise, some who are working full time do not appear in category 1–20

Table 3.
Muslim Males and Females in Professions*

Profession	M		F		Total	
	N	%	N	%	N	%
Engineering, Electronics	866	28	744	24	1,610	52
Computer Sc. Data Processing	435	14	371	12	806	26
Medicine, Doctors, and Others	122	4	126	4	248	8
Business and Finance	125	4	92	3	217	7
Self-employed	94	3	60	2	154	5
Professor/Teacher, Imam	19	.6	12	.4	31	1
Lawyer/Police/Politics	13	.4	6	.2	19	.6
Other	9	.3	6	.2	15	.5
Total	1,683	54	1,417	46	3,100	100

*percentages are rounded to the nearest whole

either. If so, we think we found these invisible data, for in our subsample we found a total of 3,100 of our respondents were working full-time (see table 3).

As is evident, professional distribution of Muslims betrays their high level of education and income also. Most of them (86 percent) are concentrated in three professions: engineering and electronics, computer science and data processing, and medical doctors and various related professions. Teaching and law are not the most favored professions yet. On the other hand, there are substantial numbers in business and finance professions (7 percent), as there are a few who are self-employed (5 percent). The category "other" includes such professions as journalism, social work, taxi driver, and auto sales.

What is significant is the relative visibility of the females in the full-time work force, especially so in elite professions (40 percent). Still the work force sex ratio (119 males for every 100 females) favors the male worker. Presumably, even here in the United States, quite a few Muslim females enjoy being homemakers.

Growth

Our efforts to find historic correspondence lists from several Islamic centers proved to be unreliable or too few from which to draw conclusions. Also because we did not have specific data on birth, death, migration, and conversion rates, we had to estimate growth of the Muslim population mainly through our respondents in our sample. However, in our sample, we could not get reliable information on these households beyond five years in the past. Table 4 shows that thirty-two of these one thousand households in the year 2000 did not exist in 1999. Likewise, there were only 855 households in 1995 giving us an overall 30 percent increase in the five-year period. It is also evident from this table that as the number of the Muslim households increased, so did their population. Eight hundred and fifty-five households that existed in 1995 had a total population of 4,260 with five members per household. Their number has

Table 4.
Growth Rate of the American Muslim Population

Year	Number of Households	Total Population	Growth Rate*
1995	855	4,260	–
1996	877	4,385	3
1997	883	4,416	3
1998	929	4,646	4
1999	968	4,836	2
2000	1,000	4,936	3

*Rounded to the nearest whole.

been growing with an overall rate of 3 percent per year, giving us a total of 4,938 for 1,000 homes in the sample in the year 2000. With this rate, this population promises to double itself in less than twenty-five years. Thus, although it may be risky to do so, one could expect that soon after 2020, the American Muslim population would be substantially in excess of 11.5 million, or more than 3 percent of the projected national population about that time.

SUMMARY AND CONCLUSION

It would be much nicer if someday the U.S. census would start asking questions regarding religious affiliation, for the American religious landscape has changed drastically, especially since the beginning of the 1970s. A population that was used to having immigrants mainly from European countries is now facing a huge influx of people migrating from Third World countries. In just about two decades after new immigration policy was instituted in 1965, the Asians dominated this new immigration, with 48 percent, followed by the Latin Americans with 35 percent. In between the two, then, these two sender regions totaled more than 80 percent immigrants to the United States (Bouvier and Gardner, 1986:17)

These new immigrants have contributed to religious diversity as never experienced before in the United States. Nowadays we find Americans who pursue, in addition to the traditional Protestant, Catholic, and Jewish denominations, religions such as Islam, Buddhism, Hinduism, Sikhism, Taoism, Bahaism, and a score of other previously rather unknown faiths. Apart from purely academic curiosity, this new religious mosaic should surely be of great political and economic significance in the near future.

Among these new American religions, it seems, Islam stands out as being the object of exceeding interest, scrutiny, and scholarly pursuits. However, above all what this report brings about is that, while the census is not perfect in itself, a population, which is not covered by the census, is difficult, if not impossible, to estimate with accuracy. This is so because none of the alternative methods are perfect. While "guesstimates" may often be beset with subjective biases and selective perceptions of their authors, most rigorous of all attempts at estimating a population, the census seems to undershoot the target. Even the U.S. census cannot claim an exemption to this rule.

Thus, while the estimates of the Muslim population in the United States standing at about 10 million cannot be substantiated, the claim that the best estimates put it between 1.9 and 2.8 million seems to be equally untenable. Simple calculations support our claim. Let us take the higher of these two figures and round it out to the nearest whole, that is, 3 million. Should this be true, how many of them are foreign born? If we assume that of these 3 million Muslims, native born (indigenous as well as children born to immigrant Muslims) constitutes only 1 million (which seems to be gross underestimation), then we are left with only 2 million foreign-born Muslims. Considering that since the 1960s, the United States has admitted around 30 million immigrants, this figure amounting to less than 7 percent of the total immigration since that time looks awfully low. This is especially true in view of the fact that Asia, with largest concentrations of Muslim population in the world, has been in the leading regions sending migrants to the United States. If we assume that of these 3 million Muslims, one half or 1.5 million are native born, then the proportion of immigrant Muslims is reduced to only 5 percent of the total migratory volume in the United States during the period under consideration. It is like saying that while the people of the whole underdeveloped world in general are seeking an opportunity to migrate to the United States the Muslim people of the world remain tied to their homelands. The "push-pull" hypothesis would not support this assumption. This is so because most Muslims in the world are living under some of the most dictatorial or oppressive regimes; and contrary to what many might believe, Muslims are some of the most literate people in the Third World and may, therefore, be relatively more knowledgeable about and more prone to the lure of better prospects in the United States.

Data that we gathered shows that there may not be less than 5,745,100 Muslim men and women of all ages in the United States today. With a 3 percent growth rate it may double itself in a little more than twenty years, provided the present trends do not change.

However, not surprisingly, this seems to be an underestimation, although we cannot say by how much. As mentioned above, we received information from 1,510 or only 86 percent of 1,751 Islamic institutions due mainly to disarray or absence of the mailing lists. This lack of information from more than two hundred Islamic institutions must have a downward effect on our findings. Other than most MSAs on our list, a number of small city Islamic centers, as well as a few neighborhood mosques, are responsible for this deficiency in our report. Besides, it is almost certain that some Muslim individuals, as well as households, might not have appeared in the mailing lists of these institutions. Also the large number of Muslim inmates, who live behind bars, could not be included in this research. Moreover, there is a strong suspicion that in this study we must have undercounted the number of MSAs, thus grossly underestimating the Muslim population on college campuses.

Lastly, the large number of Muslims belonging to sects other than the dominant *Sunni* also escaped notice, for a great many of them rarely participate in *Sunni* institutions. According to the latest estimate, the *Shia* Muslim community in the United States comprises of 157,238 households (Hussein, 2002). If their average household size is also around five, then their total number may be in the neighborhood of 786,000. It means that the total size of the Muslim population in the United States must exceed our estimate by a wide margin.

Other than these two sects of Islam in the United States, there are many who claim to be Muslims, although they may not be recognized as such by the two dominant sects in Islam. For instance, the *Ahmedies*, an offshoot from the *Sunni* sect, and the *Aghakhanis*, from the *Shia*, are considered to be beyond the outer fringes of Islam (although they claim to be Muslims). Likewise, in this report we could not include the followers of the Nation of Islam, led by minister Louis Farrakhan, who declared his adherence to the mainstream (presumably *Sunni*) Islam soon after this project was initiated. Thus, it seems that our findings as to the number of Muslims in the United States are closer to the estimation by Bagby, Perl, and Froehle (2001) than to that by Smith (2001).

REFERENCES

Alam, Mahmoud. "Muslim Organizations in America." 1968. Paper presented at the 6th Annual 1968 Convention of Muslim Students Association of U.S. and Canada, Green Lakes, Wisconsin.

Austin, Allen D. *African Muslims in Ante-Bellum America: A Sourcebook.* New York: Garland Press, 1984.

Bagby, Ihsan, Paul M. Perl, and Bryan T. Froehle. *The Mosque in America: A National Portrait.* Washington, D.C: Council for American-Islamic Relations, 2001.

Ba-Yunus, Ilyas. "Muslims of Illinois: A Demographic Report," Special issue, *East West Review (*Summer 1997):1997 Special Supplement.

Ba-Yunus, Ilyas, and M. Moin Siddiqui. *A Report on Muslim Population in the United States of America.* New York: Center for American Muslim Research and Information, 1998.

Bouvier, Leon F. and Robert W. Gardner. "Immigration to the U.S.: The Unfinished Story," *Population Bulletin* 41, no. 4 (November 1986).

Davidson, Basil. *Lost Cities of Africa.* Boston: Little, Brown, 1959.

The Economist. "A Year of Living Nervously." September 17, 2002: 29–30.

Ghayur, Arif. "Muslims in the United States: Settlers and Visitors," *The Annals of the American Academy of Social and Political Sciences,* 454, March, 1991.

Haddad, Yvonne. "Muslims in America," *The Muslim World* 76, no. 2 (1986).

Haley, Alex. *Roots.* New York: Doubleday, 1976.

Hassett, Kelly. "E. Utica Becomes a Heaven for Bosnians." *Observer-Dispatch.* 2002.

Hussein, Adil S. *Shia Muslims in America.* Toronto: Annual Report of the Shia Institute, 2002.

Isbister, John. *Immigration Debate.* West Hartford, CT: Kumarian Press, 1996.

Kosmin, Barry. *Research Report: The National Survey of Religious Identifications.* New York: The City University of New York Graduate School and University Center, 1989.

Mehdi, Beverlee T. *The Arabs in America, 1492–1977*. New York: Oceans Publications, 1978.

Newland, Kathleen. *International Migration: The Search for Work*. Washington, D.C.: Worldwatch Institute, 1979.

Nyang, Sulayman S. *Islam in the United States of America*. Chicago: ABC International Group, 1999.

Omar. M. 2002. Interview by the author. Utica, New York.

Phillip, Thomas. "Muslims." In *The Harvard Encyclopedia of American Ethnic Groups*, edited by Stephen Rhornstorm. Cambridge, MA: Belknap Press of Harvard, 1980.

Poston, Larry. *Islamic Dawah in the West*. New York: Pantheon, 1992.

Quick, Abdullah H. *Deeper Roots of Muslims in the America and the Caribbean from Before Columbus to the Present*. Boston: Taha Publications, 1996.

Rumbaut, R. "Origins and Destinies: Immigration to the United States since WW II," *Sociological Forum* 9, no. 4 (1994): Table 1.

Smith, Tom W. Estimating the Muslim Population in the United States. An unpublished report prepared for the American Jewish Committee. Chicago: National Opinion Research Center, University of Chicago, 2001.

Stone, Carol. "Estimate of Muslims Living in America." In *The Muslim America*, edited by Yvonne Haddad. New York: Oxford University Press, 1991.

Weeks, John R. *Population: An Introduction to Concepts and Issues*, 4th ed. Belmont, CA: Wadsworth, 1989.

Weeks, John R., and M. Moin Siddiqui. *The Muslim Population of the United States: A Pilot Project*. San Diego, CA: International Population Center, San Diego State University, 1993.

3

The Muslim Activist: Organizing Islam in America

American Muslims are divided into at least ten major easily identifiable groupings embedded in racial, national, linguistic, and sectarian characteristics. It might not be incorrect to say that Islam in the United States reflects the extent and the scope that Islam has acquired in the world during the last fourteen hundred years. With so many different kinds of Muslims present in a relatively limited corner of the world, each Muslim group generates activity furthering its cause with respect to its socioeconomic, political, family, and even literary concerns. It must not come as a shock if you come across Muslim groups such as the Malaysian Study Group, Aligarh Old Boys Association, or the Hyderabad Memorial Society of America.

But these are small associations of American Muslims operating alongside the larger Islamic activity of national and, sometimes, international scope. Larger organizations present in North America today started a few decades ago with almost a defensive posture—to keep the Muslim identity intact and save the fundamental Islamic character of the next generation. Very early Muslims, brought in slavery, were forced to quit Islam and assimilate into a biracial American society. However, those who came to the United States voluntarily were also prone to assimilation simply because they were so few in the beginning and lived so far apart from one another in different corners of the continent. Typically, Muslim immigrants of the late nineteenth and early twentieth centuries tried to "save" their children from complete Americanization by going back to their homelands after having generated enough resources with which to create a respectable living for themselves and their families back home. Because their children, who were born during their stay in the United

States, were American citizens, they immigrated back to the United States after growing up, only to repeat the cycle all over again.

Thus, voluntary Muslim migration to the United States was transitory in its early days. This explains an almost complete absence of Muslim neighborhoods, while other immigrant groups such as the Irish, Jews, and Italians were busy expanding their ghettos. Because of emigration back to their homelands, Muslims generally remained few and far between during the first major American migratory episode of the late nineteenth and early twentieth centuries. Also, it seems that during those early years there were few divisions among American Muslims. African Americans were almost invisible. Arabs, Turks, Eastern Europeans, and a few South Asians, especially on the West Coast, were just about the only groups represented among these immigrants.

Being so widely dispersed and always thinking of migrating back home, Muslims in the first major migratory episode to the United States, remained, by and large, on the sidelines. It seems that they did not feel the need for any activism other than finding ways to get rich as quickly as possible and going back before their children grew up. Whatever its merit, this strategy among those early Muslim immigrants betrays their concern for their religion. Whether or not they were good practicing Muslims is beside the point. They did share the same sensitive concern for Islam with subsequent Muslim immigrants, who came in droves almost one hundred years later.

Those who chose to stay had to create symbols of their religion in the form of mosques or places of Islamic worship, just as the Jews and the Christians did in their communities. Some of those early mosques still dot the American landscape. Muslims of Cedar Rapids, Iowa, claim that their mosque, dating back to 1886, was the very first on this continent. The Muslims of Edmonton, Alberta, challenge this claim. Their mosque is now dedicated as a national historical marker by the Canadian government. It was here, they claim, that the late Abdallah Yusuf Ali started his now widely circulated translation of the holy Qur'an. There are other claimants to having the very first mosque built in this country. But this is beside the point. What is important is that by the late nineteenth century, Muslims in the United States were numerous and settled enough to establish their mosques, which also served as their community centers with weekend schools, social activities, periodic dinners, and other programs for children. According to Elkholy (1966), most of these mosques were in and around large metropolitan areas such as New York, Philadelphia, Boston, Detroit, Chicago, St. Louis, Los Angeles, and San Francisco. Naturally, they showed larger concentrations of Muslims in those days. Some industrial towns like Quincy, Massachusetts; Buffalo, New York; Gary, Indiana; and Dearborn, Michigan also had enough Muslim populations to justify establishing mosques.

NATIONAL ORGANIZATIONS

Appearing on the map like isolated dots, these communities along with their mosques remained dispersed until 1952, when Abdallah Igram, a successful

Muslim entrepreneur in Cedar Rapids, Iowa, wrote letters to the presidents of individual mosques emphasizing the need for unifying existing Muslim communities under one organization. He seems to have hit a responsive chord. Four hundred delegates attended the first national Muslim conference (Mahdi, 1991), representing more than two hundred communities. The main theme of the conference was unity and coordination among these otherwise isolated and dispersed communities. A motion was passed and Abdallah Igram was requested to form a committee to act upon this motion.

Federation of Islamic Associations in the United States (FIAA)

A year later, in the second conference, held in Toledo, Ohio, a motion for creating a national organization called the Federation of Islam Associations in America (FIAA) was passed, and Abdallah Igram was elected its first president. The role of the federation was basically educational—spiritual, cultural, and social development among Muslims, children in particular, and promoting better understanding of Islam and Muslims in American society.

The FIAA held annual conventions and rotated them in different cities. In 1955 Canada hosted the first FIAA convention in London, Ontario, (Mahdi, 1991), thus signifying that the Canadian Muslim communities could also be counted under its umbrella. This was a major step, which made the FIAA the only Muslim organization of international stature in United States and Canada.

However, the FIAA could do little more than hold annual conventions, which, otherwise, were gaining more participants every year. For instance, the ninth annual convention held in Indiana City, Michigan in 1959 was attended by more than one thousand participants. The size of the convention is significant. It gave a rough estimate of the number of Arab-Muslim communities affiliated with the FIAA, which also undertook the very first count of Muslims in the United States, however deficient it may look today (see chapter 1).

It seems that the main effort of the FIAA has been to create a sense of unity and maintain Islamic identity of North American Muslims, especially those of Arab decent, many of whom were by then second or even third generation Americans. Other than not being able to go beyond merely holding annual conventions, what FIAA could not do was attract Muslims of non-Arab origin. From its inception, FIAA remained an Arab Muslim organization. Other communities such as those of the Turks, Bosnians, and the Punjabis of the West Coast remained conspicuous by their absence from the membership of the FIAA. This gave a false impression to many, who had a hard time distinguishing between the Arab and Islam. However, the FIAA succeeded in attracting American born and educated professionals—those in military service, business, education, and industry—to regularly participate in its activities.

The Muslim Students Association of U.S. and Canada (MSA)

Already, by the time Abdallah Igram had begun to unify Muslim communities in the United States, students from the Third World countries, including the Muslim countries, were entering American universities under various post-World War scholarship programs. These students entered the United States on temporary visas, which allowed them to stay in this country as long as they fulfilled college requirements. A new visa category, the F.1, was created to serve this purpose (F.2 was reserved for the dependent[s] of these students). Apparently, the idea behind this program was to educate promising students, who could help their respective countries after they would return home. An underlying and an unspoken intent, however, was to create pro-American elite in different countries, which were until then mostly tied to their former colonizing states of Europe.

Whatever its underlying objective, the program also allowed twenty-four months of stay for practical training beyond the college degree. It allowed an extension of the visa after the first degree if the student was admitted for a higher degree program or was admitted for another degree with a different major. One could apply for a permanent residence (immigrant) visa if the student got a job and his or her employer sponsored him or her for permanent employment. Change from a student visa to a permanent resident visa signified a permission that the student could, in about five years' time, apply for a change to a citizenship status. The only other way to change student visa status to a permanent resident status was to get married to an American citizen. Rules of the Immigration and Naturalization Service (INS) have changed several times, but its overall strategy has remained the same over the years.

Many foreign students, not excluding Muslim students, profited from these immigration rules. A number of them would go home after finishing their degree program, but often it took a long time to finish a degree program in an American university (five years after a college degree on an average to finish a doctoral program). If they worked under a practical training program, it would take even longer. Most foreign students preferred to stay beyond receiving their degrees if only to make some money before returning home for good.

Thus, introducing the F.1 visa presumed that an overseas student would stay in this country for a number of years while simultaneously a batch of new students entered every year. This resulted in a relatively high rate of entry and a low rate of departure on the part of these students in any given year. Consequently an explosion of the foreign student population on American campuses got under way starting some time in the late 1950s.

Thus, the FIAA was not even ten years old yet when students from Muslim countries became visible especially on large state university campuses all over the United States. Soon they formed local Muslim student organizations chartered under the rules provided by each university campus. It was quite an enthusiastic activity. For the first time in his or her life a given Muslim student came in close contact with Muslims of other countries—an opportunity he or she could hardly afford before coming to the United States. Muslim students of Arab, Pakistani, Indian, Iranian, Turkish, African, and Southeast Asian origin came together. As soon as they arrived, their first concern was to make arrangements for the weekly congregational prayer on Fridays. This provided them an opportunity to come together at least once a week. These organizations also generated intellectual activities such as symposia, debates, and conferences that included professors, students, and interested citizens in the area. These activities naturally focused on problems of the Muslim world. Local media picked up and generated a great deal of interest and curiosity in the campus and local population.

These Muslim student organizations, spread all over the country, were invited to join together through an initiative by the Muslim students association at University of Illinois, Urbana/Champaign in the winter of 1963. This resulted in a new organization named the Muslim Students Association of U.S. and Canada (MSA), which held its first annual convention in Urbana attended by less than a hundred Muslim students representing less than twenty local organizations. In spite of its humble beginning, the formation of the MSA was a historic event in Islamic activity in North America. Although it affiliated itself with the FIAA, the MSA quickly overshadowed every other organized Islamic activity in North America. As more local Muslim student organizations joined the national MSA as affiliates, its annual convention, held regularly over the Labor Day weekend, became an eagerly awaited event. Because of its leadership and student membership, MSA conventions had an intellectual flavor articulating Islamic traditions with modern social, political, and economic circumstances. In short, the MSA conventions became known for dealing with problems of modern living in the light of Islamic injunctions.

Because of the rapid increase in the number of affiliates in different regions of North America, the MSA also introduced regional conferences in relation to its three regions in United States and two in Canada. This brought huge numbers of Muslim students and others who, otherwise, could not afford the expense of the journey to the national annual convention. Naturally, what transpired in these conventions and conferences focused on the Muslim world in a highly informed manner. Reputable professors, journalists, ambassadors, and other political personalities, plus non-Muslims from North American institutions and overseas, came to address these gatherings. This opportunity could not remain hidden from Muslim businessmen, who started renting space for their shops to sell books, rugs and carpets, jewelry, formal and informal attire, canned fruits and juices from Muslim countries, and many other things that attracted Muslim students from overseas. As conference attendance grew into the thousands, shops in the "bazaar" became numerous and competitive.

Most importantly, these conventions became like large-scale classrooms, which interactively informed and taught their participants about their individual homelands and the Muslim world as a whole with regard to its political and economic status in the world. Initially, expenses of the MSA were born by the members. Everyone paid membership dues; heavy registration fees and the donations were also made at conventions and conferences. All traveled on their own and paid for their own meals and accommodations. Consequently, the MSA conventions and conferences not only paid for themselves, they also generated lucrative surpluses, which were used to pay for other activities such as paying for the publication of *Al-Ittihad*, a monthly magazine and a biweekly newsletter. Mail and phone expenses were also covered by these surpluses. Many Arab students, who went back, became another source of donations, especially after the substantial increase in oil money beginning after 1973.

A new development had taken place in the ranks of the MSA. In 1965 President Johnson signed a bill opening immigration to United States from all over the world on a first-come, first-serve-basis. Some of the very first beneficiaries of this new law were Muslim students, who had been in this country on F.1 visa for some time. Many of them were still in college. Others were working as professionals under the practical training provision. Still others, having finished all visa provisions, were preparing to leave when this new bill was signed. Most of them decided to take advantage of this new law and opted to stay in the United States while keeping open the option to go back home. But the longer they stayed, the longer they hesitated to go back. Finally, when the time came for them to apply for citizenship, they opted for it and most of them became naturalized American citizens. This opened the floodgates.

Although the law itself was repealed by an act of Congress in 1970, newly naturalized citizens, a great majority of them, curiously enough, not from Europe as expected, but from the Third World, including Muslim countries, started using their privilege as citizens to sponsor close relatives (parents, siblings) so they could come to the United States as immigrants on a permanent residence visa. These immigrants eventually repeated this cycle when they became citizens. Until today we see no stoppage in this flood of immigration to the United States. So far, this is the second largest migratory episode in this country and shows the promise of surpassing the first such episode of the late nineteenth century.

How did this impact the MSA? Around the beginning of 1970s, its ranks were swelling with the professionals who were no longer students, with the new immigrants who had not seen a single day on an American university campus. The latter were mostly living in communities and not necessarily on or near university campuses. They were married, had children (some of them grown up), or were about to be married. In short, by the beginning of 1970s, it was becoming apparent that the demographic character of the MSA rank and file was changing from nearly all of them being students to most of them being nonstudents. Already voices were being heard in annual conventions and regional conferences that the MSA could not handle the problems of nonstudent communities. Many were asking that another organization be created that would cater to the needs of the families living in communities. The debate continued within MSA leadership and the rank and file until 1982 when at the nineteenth annual convention in Bloomington, Indiana, it was decided to work on the formation of a broad-based organization in addition to the MSA (later named the Islamic Society of North America).

Before this new organization was commissioned, however, the MSA had done a great deal of groundwork for meeting the needs of its constituency and for generating an Islamic identity among Muslims of diverse national origins coming to the United States in droves. In addition to its conventions and regional conferences, the MSA also arranged and provided for annual trips to Arabia for *Hajj* or the annual Muslim pilgrimage to Mecca. It established a *waqf* or a trust (North American Islamic Trust or NAIT) to look after its assets and those of local Muslim communities. It also established a publishing house and an Islamic book service. It started a program of a dialogue with the churches and maintained a list of able speakers and writers on Islam with deep insights into contemporary Western civilization. The MSA was also instrumental in creating sister organizations at the professional level, such as the Association of Muslim Scientists and Engineers (AMSE), the Association of Muslim Social Scientists (AMSS), and the Islamic Medical Association (IMA). More than this, the national MSA encouraged its local affiliates to get Muslim students involved in Islamic work while keeping in close contact with non-Muslim friends and sympathizers. In short, the MSA during its first twenty years of existence remained active nationally as well as locally, bringing together Muslims of varied racial, ethnic, and national backgrounds while keeping its doors open to the non-Muslim for dialogue.

Islamic Society of North America (ISNA)

Judging from its membership and the level of participation in its annual convention, the ISNA is by far the largest organization reflecting the diversity of Muslims in the United States and Canada. After it took over from the MSA, more than four thousand attended its first annual convention in Louisville. At its annual convention held in Washington, D.C., in 2002, close to fifty thousand people came to take part in its activities and to listen to and to enter into discussions with numerous Muslim and non-Muslim scholars, imams, priests, ministers, and rabbis. For those still around who participated in the first annual convention of the MSA in 1963, the 2002 convention of the ISNA represented a world of difference.

The ISNA provides the only forum for bringing together the diverse constituency spread over a very large continent. The ISNA seems to satisfy the intellectual curiosity of almost every Muslim living in American and Canada. In its annual convention and its regional conferences, the ISNA offers special sessions on women, children, professionals, communities, and especially political problems in the Muslim world. Its bazaar, a busy market place, sells anything from raw dates to book titles ranging from commentaries on the Qur'an to scholarly books on the Muslim World dealing with economics, politics, family, population, war, and peace.

ISNA is often described as an umbrella organization. It is governed at the top by the consultative assembly (*majlis al shura*), which directs, makes, and reviews policies to be executed by the Executive Council. The *majlis* is composed of, other than members of the Executive Council (elected directly by the membership), representatives of the five sponsoring organizations (MSA, AMSS, AMSE, IMA, and NAIT). In addition, heads or representatives of the

Muslim Youth in North America (MYNA), the Muslim Arab Youth in America (MAYA), and the Muslim American Society (MAS) headed by Imam Warith Deen Muhammad also sit in the *majlis* as voting members. The president of the ISNA, elected directly by the membership, presides over the Executive Council as well as the *majlis*. However, the president of the ISNA, who must otherwise be obeyed in all organization matters, has only one vote when he presides over the *majlis* deliberations. This means that the ISNA's consultative assembly (*majlis al shura*) is not merely a consultative body. While in session, it can overrule the president by a majority vote in its deliberations. Far from being the chief decision maker, then, the ISNA president has the status of being the chief executive officer, who is supposed to execute the decisions made by the *majlis* with the help of members of the Executive Council.

This model of decision making followed by the ISNA is unique in the history of Islamic organizations, political or otherwise. It is also unique in its democratic deliberations. It follows a presidential form, in which the president, however, runs the risk of being overruled like a prime minister in a parliamentary system. It utilizes a collective decision-making process at the top. It follows a deliberate interpretation of the Qur'anic injunctions.

AND CONSULTATION IS THE BASIS FOR DECISION MAKING AMONG THEM...

Evidently, both the ISNA and the MSA borrowed the convention and conference format from the FIAA. However, whereas the FIAA conventions had increasingly become occasions for entertainment—singing, dancing, dining—with free mixing of men and women, the MSA introduced, and the ISNA followed, a more serious and ideologically committed format for its gatherings. ISNA conferences and conventions start on Fridays after the weekly *Juma'* congregational prayer. Throughout the conference, Islamic manners, dress codes, and ways of greetings are followed. Arrangements are made for all five daily prayers, which are heavily attended. Themes and topics of discussion are chosen carefully to reflect the ongoing concerns of Muslims all over the world, including North America and Europe. *The Islamic Horizon*, a monthly periodical of the ISNA, reflects the same ideological commitment, as do the publications of its affiliated organizations.

The ISNA is considered a national organization that claims to be representing the Islamic mainstream in the United States. In doing this, however, ISNA leadership, unlike the FIAA, deliberately promotes among its members as well as its affiliates, an ideological approach to Islam as a *deen* or a total system of life not to be confined to the mosque or formal daily prayers only. In short, the ISNA does not merely aim at reflecting Muslim behavior in the United States. Through its annual convention, regional conferences, publications, and speakers that it provides to the mosques or the churches, it deliberately serves as a reminder to those who go astray. Consequently, ISNA forums often include discussions on economics, politics, education, family, community, and

Islamic jurisprudences as articulated with modern living. These discussions have become significant on their own because of the continuous influx of new immigrants as well as new converts to Islam in the existing population. Because there is no priesthood in Islam, the ISNA program committee carefully selects those who are generally recognized authorities in their legal specialties. Because the ISNA has been successful in attracting a diverse Muslim population, no one school of thought in Islam dominates its activities (although one might detect that the middle of the road *Hanafi* approach of *Sunni* Islam is being generally subscribed to).

Evidently, ISNA's success lies in that it has thoughtfully avoided extremes, for example, Wahabism, Sufism, or liberalism. Being highly educated professionals in the modern sciences, ISNA leadership centers on the least common denominators among Islamic belief and practices. However, ISNA has the potential to do much more. It could, for instance, introduce programs more attractive to indigenous Muslims, most of whom embraced Islam only recently and have a history different from the histories and cultures of most who are relative newcomers to the United States. Immigrant Muslims are more interested in political and economic problems in the Muslim world. Indigenous Muslims, who are mostly African Americans disappointed by a long history of slavery and racial discrimination, are more interested in abolition of racial prejudice and civil rights in the United States. Although some notable African American Muslim leaders, Warith Deen Muhammad being the best known among them, have served and continue to serve in ISNA's decision-making bodies, most indigenous Muslims continue to feel more comfortable in their own national organizations.

Likewise, although the main reason for ISNA's birth has been the conspicuous emergence of the Muslim population in noncampus communities, ISNA has yet to attract Muslim communities to its governing structure. Of approximately twenty-five hundred registered Muslim community organizations, only a handful are formally affiliated with the ISNA at this writing. Although the NAIT holds the titles of around four hundred mosques, which profit by investing in the NAIT's business, the ISNA has only one vote in NAIT's deliberations. Because it lacks control over the NAIT, it is hardly in a position to exert any control over community organizations affiliated with NAIT. ISNA has yet to call itself a community-based organization.

Because all Muslim talent, resource, experiences, and the next generation exist in communities spread like mushrooms all over American landscape, the ISNA, which is autonomous and answers only to the local benefactors, donors, and long-time Muslims, can better serve American Muslims as well as benefit by making itself more attractive to individual Muslim community leadership.

Moreover, ISNA's main strength, which lies in its appeal to diversity among Muslims in the United States, has shown a tendency to recoil upon itself. Two main constituencies within ISNA—Urdu-speaking South Asians and Arabs—have often found the ISNA to be overextended in addressing their specific questions and needs. This resulted in the formation of the Islamic Circle of

North America (ICNA), composed mostly of South Asian Muslims, and the Muslim American Society (MAS), composed mainly of those from Arabic speaking Middle East. Recently, the two joined hands and held their first annual convention together in Philadelphia during the weekend of July 4, 2003.

This convention, which looked more like a younger sister of the ISNA annual convention, nonetheless showed less timidity than ISNA does when it comes to political processes in the United States. All three organizations (ISNA, ICNA, and MAS) are registered as educational and religious organizations. Hence, they cannot participate in political activities in this country. However, the ICNA/MAS convention in Philadelphia showed what most Americans otherwise know quite well, namely, that criticism and commentaries on American political processes does not mean politicking. For instance, this convention highlighted the Arab and Muslim experiences in the United States since the 9/11 attacks and the passage of the USA PATRIOT Act, that "made our own government the great purveyor of discrimination against Muslims at this time" (Bahadur, 2003). In his opening remarks, the ICNA president (once a long-time ISNA activist) pointed out, "We are coming to Philadelphia because Philadelphia stands for the ideals of American liberty and freedom. The whole convention will focus on how far the United States has really drifted away from these ideals." Speakers in a panel discussion criticized President Bush's trying of six terror suspects from Afghanistan before a military tribunal, an extraordinary step that has not been taken since World War II (Bahadur, 2003). A guest speaker pointed out: "When the government acts secretly, we lose the ability to ensure that it is acting properly" (Siegel, 2003).

Compare the performance of these younger offshoots with ISNA's more recent conference and convention themes and, "ISNA is beginning to look more like a good old grandmother who cares for you, but cannot do much for you." There is no doubt that these days when so many Muslim individuals, families, and communities are under the gun in the United States, the ISNA has to show a greater political sensitivity to its constituency's current problems.

In fact, the ISNA has a history of being politically timid since even before 9/11, when the whole Muslim community in the United States woke up to the possibility of serious recriminations if not anti-Muslim pogroms or Japanese-style internment. This gave rise to two small organizations gaining in stature quickly across the United States. One of them is the American Muslim Council, which, although not registered as a political action committee (PAC), does nearly all those things that a lobby in Washington does—dealing with politicians (including the White House), inviting them, working with them, and keeping up with the media. The AMC also conducted two major surveys regarding the Muslim population and Muslim communities in the United States.

The other organization, which is spreading fast with chapters everywhere, is the Council on American-Islamic Relations (CAIR). The main objective of the CAIR is to keep track of the events involving encroachment on the rights of Muslims as citizens and residents of this country. It also keeps an eye on the misrepresentation of Islam in the media, textbooks, and in the acts and words of political and religious leaders. Both the AMC and the CAIR are based in Washington. Lately, they are gaining a reputation as the primary defenders of Islam and Muslims in the United States.

Muslim American Society

The Muslim American Society (MAS), formerly known as the American Muslim Mission (AMM) and, before that, as the World Community of Al-Islam in the West, is the largest Muslim organization of indigenous American Muslims of African American heritage. Headed by Imam Warith Deen Muhammad, son of the late Elijah Muhammad, the MAS has a long history in the United States. It may not be wrong to claim that the MAS is not merely an organization; in fact, it represents an African American movement aimed at recapturing, rebuilding, and rejuvenating Islamic identity, which was destroyed by the institution of slavery in the United States.

Muslim slaves had to go through almost complete identity change after coming to the United States. Initially, they were addressed by the numbers assigned to them. Then, they were given new names. Their family life and religion were destroyed. Treated like animals, they survived only at the mercy of their masters. It is surprising that after going through such unfortunate circumstances through several generations, these slaves were even able to remember their Islamic roots. It seems that Islam survived at least in a folkloric sense among African slaves. However, it was only after emancipation that the former slaves could actively try to rebuild their lost identity as different from that given to them during the days of slavery. Judging from Alex Hailey's *Roots*, no doubt, Islamic folklore played a crucial role in rebuilding African American identity.

Historically, we know of one major early Islam-centered movement among African Americans: the Moorish Science Temple. The Moorish Temple was established by Noble Drew Ali, born in 1913, and emphasized the West African Islamic background of blacks and gave them some rudimentary principles of Islam.

These two movements form the backdrop of the Nation of Islam, which became a more intense rejectionist movement among African Americans starting in 1930s. Elijah Muhammad (born Elijah Poole) seems to have embodied both Noble Drew Ali and Marcus Garvey in shaping his Nation of Islam movement, although he claimed to have received his religion from Fard Muhammad, a god incarnate, who appointed Elijah as his prophet.

The charismatic appeal of Elijah Muhammad lay in his categorically rejecting not merely the religion of the whites—Christianity—but also their culture and replacing it with Islamic injunctions. First he tried to cleanse "the spirit, mind and body" of his individual followers by prohibiting alcohol, gambling, usury, and sex outside of marriage. Dietary restrictions included the prohibition of pork and other meat over which the name of Allah was not recited at the time of the slaughter. Change in appearance and behavior involved emphasis on loose attire not exposing body contours, frequent washing and bathing, respect for women, prohibition of lying, cheating, and seeking handouts. The followers of the Nation were encouraged to become self-sufficient by buying farms, pursuing small business including clothing stores, restaurants, grocery stores, slaughterhouses, and schools of their own.

At first, the Nation of Islam looked like a direct challenge to Christian establishments in the black ghettos. However, the Nation was not seen as a threat to the general population and the social structure of the black community. In fact, people admired the uprightness and cleanliness of individual members of the Nation (McCloud, 1995).

However, the Nation aroused widespread suspicion in the white community. The FBI, white Christian churches, and the press were deeply irritated by the Nation's rhetoric. As if the use of Islam as an insignia of the movement was not enough, calling whites "green-eyed devils" only managed to anger many. At the same time, the civil rights movements headed by Dr. Martin Luther King was joined by a number of whites. The Nation was regarded as a racist and a radical movement preaching black supremacy.

Above all, what Elijah Muhammad wanted was recognition of the Nation of Islam by the orthodox community of Islam in the world, and this was not forthcoming. From established *Shia* as well as the *Sunni* point of view, Elijah Muhammad proclaiming Fard Muhammad as a god figure and himself to be his prophet was nothing less than an innovation or heresy. From the Islamic point of view, calling whites green-eyed devils was a racist claim that denied the universality of Islam. Elijah Muhammad showed a great deal of sensitivity to this discrepancy between his movement and orthodox Islam. In defense of his movement, once he was quoted (McCloud, 1995:32) as saying:

> My brothers in the East were never subject to conditions of slavery and systematic brainwashing by the slavemasters for as long a period of time as my people here were subjected. I cannot, therefore, blame them if they differ with me in certain interpretations of the Message of Islam.

It was not until Malcolm X joined it in 1952 that the Nation of Islam started to gain stature and attract media attention. Before his untimely assassination in 1965, Malcolm X (renamed Malik Shabazz), was also beginning to give a more universal direction to the Nation by accepting Islam after having performed his pilgrimage to Mecca in 1965.

Malcolm was in prison when he accepted the mission of the Nation. Then, as a free man he climbed the leadership hierarchy of his newfound religion, in which "he found a space where an African American could be a subject, rather than an object" (McCloud, 1995:36). What characterized Malcolm was that he believed in Elijah passionately. He was a voracious reader. He was articulate and charismatic. Elijah found in Malcolm a gifted and useful servant. Soon Malcolm became the tutor of his mentor's sons. Elijah sent all three of them to Egypt and then to Mecca for a pilgrimage. It was in Mecca that Malcolm reached a turning point in his view of Islam. In doing this, Malcolm came face-to-face with the dilemma that had troubled Elijah for so long—how to reconcile his Nation of Islam with the larger community of Islam in the World. Or, as McCloud (1995:35) put it, the question was how to resolve the tension between *asabiya* (concerns of the local community building) and commitment to *ummah* (identifying with the larger Muslim community).

The day Malcolm and his two companions (Elijah's sons) accepted Islam brought about a new dawn in the several centuries long African American Islamic movement, for Islamic faith that he found in Mecca was not only the religion of his slave ancestors. The Islamic faith was a significant player in and a maker of world history—a world melting pot in which each individual Muslim community maintained its essential character. Changing his name to Malik Shabazz, he thought he could resolve the dilemma that plagued his mentor for so long. He could go beyond racism, act against injustice rendered his people in the United States, and champion historical Islam at the same time. However, to do so he had to change the direction of the Nation as set by its founder Elijah Muhammad. A new tension arose.

Accustomed to making unquestionable proclamations and in frail health a few years before his death, Elijah Muhammad was not ready to be dictated to by anybody in his movement that he singlehandedly created. He snubbed his sons. He deposed Malik Shabazz, who was soon assassinated while addressing a meeting of his admirers in New Jersey.

On his deathbed in 1975, Elijah Muhammad nominated his oldest son Wallace D. Muhammad as his successor, knowing fully well that Wallace had accepted orthodox Islam along with Malcolm or Malik Shabazz. Thus, before he died, Elijah knowingly paved the way for the new direction his movement might take in the near future.

As soon as he took over the Nation, Wallace D. Muhammad declared that he subscribed to orthodox *Sunni* Islam as laid down in the Qur'an revealed to the Prophet Muhammad fourteen hundred years ago. He changed his name to Warith Deen Muhammad. He preferred to be called an *imam*, which has several leadership connotations, but which does not mean a prophet by a long shot. He declared that his father did not consider himself to be a prophet in the same sense as the prophets of the Qur'an. Then trying to quickly set the controversy aside, he emphasized institution building in families, mosques, schools, and businesses. Thus, rather than becoming bogged down with the theological issues of yesteryear, he took practical steps. The Nation of Islam was to be called the World Community of Islam in the West. *Muhammad Speaks*, the Nation's periodical, was renamed *The Bilalian News*, named after Bilal, an African companion of the Prophet Muhammad. Members of the World Community of Islam in the West (changed to the Lost-Found Community of Islam in the West), had to drop "X" from their names and replace it with usual Muslim names. Particular attention was paid to the schooling of children. Clara Mohammad Schools is perhaps the largest school system of Muslims in the United States. Classes in this system remain segregated by sex. The system maintains a high standard of education and scholarship. Places of worship, known as temples under the Nation of Islam, were now called mosques. Members and their families were encouraged to learn Arabic and abide by Islamic duties and observances. A closer cooperation was deliberately sought between the World Community (now renamed again as the Muslim American Society) and other national, regional, and local Muslim organizations. Imam Warith Deen was offered and he accepted a seat in the consultative assembly (*majlis al shura*), the highest policy-making body of the Islamic Society of North America. A Muslim-Christian dialogue program was initiated, whereby the Muslim community leaders would visit churches and synagogues in order to give lectures on Islam trying to create mutual understanding among these religions. A major offshoot of this program has been the *Dawah* (invitation) program whereby the followers of the World Community would visit the homes of non-Muslims. There they would explain Islam and give people copies of the *Bilalian News* and the English translation of the Qur'an by Abdallah Yusuf Ali—the most widely read translation in the United States for more than a century—and invite them to visit their mosques and schools.

Imam Warith Deen's divergence from the direction set by his father was not easy, especially in the absence of his former mentor, the charismatic Malik Shabazz. Some in the Nation of Islam did not universally accept this divergence. Of the several who challenged Imam Warris' leadership, the most well known has been Minister Louis Farrakhan.

Based in Chicago, Minister Farrakhan was a gifted speaker and organizer, who often walked in the shoes of Malcom X if not those of the late Malik Shabazz. Unlike Malik Shabazz and Imam Muhammad, Minister Farrakhan continued to enthusiastically preach late Elijah Muhammad's program of racial separation and loudly championed the cause of the African American people. Claiming to believe in the Qur'an as the revealed word of God and the prophethood of Mohammed, he however continued to preach the divinity of Fard Mohammed. Minister Farrakhan gained notoriety especially in the media because of his passionate and vocal rhetoric resembling that of the late Elijah Muhammad before him. Not the least significant among African American leaders, Minister Farrakhan, however, finally came to embrace Imam Muhammad and in the year 2000 declared himself to be a follower of orthodox Islam "as practiced the world over."

Though the largest and best organized among African American Muslims, the Muslim American Society is not the only organization among indigenous American Muslims. According to McCloud (1995), there are at least sixteen other African American Muslim organizations operating in the United States. Most of these organizations sprouted in the late 1960s and early 1970s. They reflect not only the influence of the late Malik Shabazz, but also the *Sufi* influences and the civil rights movement among African Americans, including the former Black Panthers. Most of these organizations are found in small communities functioning around their respective mosques in inner cities mainly on the eastern seaboard. These organizations are well known for their clean living, small business enterprise, and successful campaigns against street crimes and illicit drugs.

SUMMARY AND CONCLUSION

Muslims have been present in the United States at least since the days of slavery. However, because of the very nature of slavery, no Muslim organizations or mosques were established during that early period. Indeed, under slavery Islam was reduced to a cherished but distant memory. It was not until at least the second decade of the twentieth century that organizations invoking the name of Islam appeared in the United States. Even so, the descendants of former slaves, many of whom migrated to the northern cities after emancipation, knew little about the basic principles of Islam. These early movements drawing on Islam continued to address the plight of African Americans, who although slaves no more, continued to suffer from racial injustices and other forms of social and economic inequality in American society. However, these very movements gradually gave rise in less than one hundred years to organizations which are following Islam as it is practiced in the world today.

The movements toward Islam among African American communities were paralleled by similar movements among Muslim immigrants, who successfully created some of the largest and most visible Islamic organizations in the United States.

Thus, there seem to exist two major strains among Muslims in the United States these days. One of them is what may rightly or wrongly be called "indigenous Muslims" and the other "immigrant Muslims." Both groups follow the fundamentals of the same *Sunni* sect to which most Muslims subscribe in the world. An "immigrant" Muslim visiting for prayers a mosque run by an African American community, say, the Muslim American Society, may not find himself or herself at odds with his or her beliefs and practices. The same is true for an African American Muslim going to a mosque run mainly by an immigrant community. Indeed, mosques run by African American Muslims in inner cities often attract immigrant Muslims who work in nearby downtown districts as professionals. Likewise, it is not uncommon to find African American individuals and families to attend and serve in mosques run mainly by immigrant groups. However, this bifurcation of Islam is more apparent than real in that the immigrant Muslims themselves are not one ethnic, racial, or national group in themselves. As we shall see in the following pages, ethnic and nationality differences among immigrant Muslims are often reflected in the way mosques are run in different places in the United States. Moreover, immigrant Muslims also include large number of men and women who were born and raised in the United States. It may not be fair to call them immigrants any longer.

What really makes the difference between these two groupings of American Muslims is their history and culture. African American Muslims share with African Americans in general a long history of slavery and racial discrimination, which affects their psyche profoundly. No African American organization, Muslim or non-Muslim, can afford to ignore the civil injustices they have been subjected to. Race, then, is an inalienable aspect of African American activism, religious or otherwise. Muslim African Americans, justifiably so, are no exception to this rule. Very much like the minister in an African American Christian church, the Muslim African American cannot afford to deliver a sermon without directly or indirectly alluding to the injustices of the past and the present as suffered by his kind.

However, for most so-called immigrant Muslims, even if they are sometimes subjected to ethnic prejudice in the United States, the most important preoccupation has not been economic or with respect to jobs. Most of them have been able to find stable jobs sooner or later and settle down in the suburbs or small towns in good school districts. Many, if not most of them, contrary to their fellow Muslims in Europe, are well educated and trained professionals or self-employed. Their above-average education explains the better-than-average performance of their children in schools and colleges.

A primary concern of the Muslim immigrant parents has been the future adherence to Islam and the moral character of their children. They have generally looked at the high rate of crime, drugs, and sex in the United States with great concern, lest their children fall prey to the highly permissive culture. Besides, there has existed among American Muslims long before 9/11 a sense of widespread misunderstanding of Islam and hostility to Muslims in American society. A Muslim response to all of this has been to hold on to Islam ever more tightly. As their children grow up, suddenly Islam looks like a necessary tool against the lures of American culture. Perceived hostility against Islam makes them take steps to further strengthen Islamic fiber of future generations.

Secondly, having settled down comfortably in the United States, many American Muslims now feel more concerned about socioeconomic and political problems that beset the Muslim world. Now that they are so well settled in life, the plight of their fellow Muslims in Palestine, Kashmir, Chechnya, Afghanistan, Iraq, and elsewhere pricks their conscience and motivates them as American citizens to help alleviate the problems of Muslim people.

Thus, indigenous and immigrant Muslims seem to have slightly different social and political priorities rather than other theologies. These differences become visible in sermons on Fridays and in different conferences and programs that individual mosques and national organizations initiate from time to time. These differences are often reflected in the way Muslims become politically involved. African American Muslims, for instance, are almost to the core supportive of the Democratic Party. Immigrant Muslims, at least in the first generation, are neither Democrat nor Republican. They are more pragmatic. They would ordinarily favor the party, which seems to support their cause in relation to the Muslim world. They may support Republicans in one election, but may change their support to the Democrats in the next. In the same election year, they may support a given political party in a national election, but may support a different party candidate at the state level. In short, immigrant and indigenous Muslims in the United States have different political party preferences. In this respect, while indigenous Muslims are more predictable as to their voting behavior, immigrant Muslims remain an unknown quantity.

Because immigrant Muslims are more numerous and because they are more resourceful as to their income, education, and professionalism, they represent a much greater political potential. However, as a group, they have been somewhat slower than other immigrant groups at learning the tricks of American political trade.

American Muslims, indigenous or immigrant, are already beginning to play the American political game locally and at the state and national level. However, they have carefully kept their mosques, schools, and national organizations from any political involvement. At present there are only a handful of Muslim individuals occupying state assembly positions. In the near future one may expect to see an increasing number of them running for local and state positions. Most of these are individuals who have succeeded economically, and have political ambitions that have little to do with Islam and Muslims overseas or here in the United States.

On the other hand, it is interesting to watch individual Muslims of repute in the Muslim community getting together, discussing, and making recommendations with respect to politics at the national and state levels. E-mail and online communication has made it possible to contact thousands of Muslim individuals and families across the nation. This is a relatively newly acquired capability, which has made it possible for American Muslims to stage huge demonstrations in Washington, D.C., New York, and other major cities with respect to Bosnia, Kosovo, and especially Palestine. Often non-Muslim friends and political leaders are invited to participate in and address such large gatherings.

These activities among Muslims may or may not have a direct impact on national elections. However, they are becoming big media items and help create an exposure of Muslim causes. They also enhance the visibility of the Muslim community in the United States. For instance, as reported by the media, in the election of 2000, Muslims overwhelmingly voted for Mr. Bush. Muslims themselves took pride in the fact that were it not for their vote, Mr. Bush would not have been elected president of the United States the first time around. More than 70 percent of 60,000 Muslim voters in Florida are believed to have voted in his favor. The only exception, as expected, was the African American Muslim vote, which went to the Democratic candidate.

However, the American Muslim vote must not be taken for granted. If we measure Muslim attitude by the pronouncements of the speakers in Muslim conventions and conferences, as well by the opinions of writers in several Muslim magazines and newspapers, immigrant Muslims have become ambivalent toward the Bush administration over the years. The main reason for this is the perceived mistreatment, detention, and deportation by the Department of Justice, Immigration and Naturalization Service, the Internal Revenue Service, and other major federal agencies. This reaction to 9/11 on the part of the Bush administration resulted in stereotyping of Muslim people by ordinary American men and women resulting in the extreme sufferings that many Muslim individuals and families are presently experiencing. This will be further elaborated on the following pages.

REFERENCES

Bahadur, Ahmed. "The Arab and Muslim Experiences in America since the 9/11 Attacks." *Message* (Fall 2003), 11–15.

Elkholy, Abdu A. *The Arab Moslems in the United States: Religion and Assimilation.* New Haven: College and University Publishers, 1966.

Mahdi, Gotbi A. "Muslim Organizations in the United States," in *The Muslims of America*, edited by Yvonne Haddad. New York: Oxford University Press, 1991.

McCloud, Beverly Thomas. *African American Islam.* New York: Rutledge, 1995.

Siegel, John. Reported in Bahadur (2003).

4

Minarets on the Skyline:
The Culture of the Muslim
Community

UNITY IN DIVERSITY

At the crossing of Damen and Devon Avenues on the north side of Chicago, just above the sign of Devon there is another sign that reads "Mohammad Ali Jinnah Way." This sign is present at every crossing for six blocks as you go west on Devon from that point on. Now, what on Earth, one may ask, is the name of the founder of Pakistan doing on Devon in Chicago? The logical answer is that it must have some thing to do with Pakistani American voters of Chicago. An empirical search shows much more than that. The population on this street is overwhelmingly Muslim (although not all of them are originally from Pakistan). Bangladeshis, Afghans, and especially Hyderabadi Muslims from India are to be found almost everywhere. For nearly ten blocks, it looks as if you are not in the United States so much as you are in a South Asian Muslim city with numerous restaurants serving such South Asian delicacies as *mutton pilaf, nihari, paye, shish kabob*, and *matka chicken* along with hot, fresh, out-of-the-oven *nan* (flat bread). Then there are stores selling properly slaughtered meat (*halal*), South Asian spices, tropical fruits, books in Urdu, Pakistani television shows on tape, and South Asian Muslim attire. In between these are offices of immigration lawyers, alternative medicine shops, and a branch of the National Bank of Pakistan, American Express currency exchange, photo studios, and travel agents. There are few indigenous or Arab Muslims to be seen. Mohammad Ali Jinnah Way is basically Muslim South Asia transplanted in the United States.

The signs on the shops are in English as well as in Urdu, Persian, and Arabic with a touch of calligraphy. In almost every restaurant, there are four newspapers, printed in Urdu as well as in English. You could pick one or all of them—for free. Extending quite a few blocks on either side of Devon, it is not easy to ignore Pakistani women clad in *shalwar, qamis*, and *dopatta*, and men, some old, some young, taking their families out. Others are rushing for prayers in a nearby mosque while children on their push-scooters are playing with their friends, some of them non-Muslims.

One block to the west of Damen on Devon is Seeley. You turn right on Seeley and two blocks down the street on your left you find yourself staring into a sign on a wall in a back alley. It says *Masjide Tahoora* or sacred mosque, but the "mosque" is nowhere to be found at first. There is no dome, no minaret, and hardly an *adzan* or a prayer call to be heard. In fact, the "sacred mosque" is in the basement of a four-storied building whose owner converted the basement into a place of Muslim worship. The floor is covered in numerous oriental rugs and several copies of the Qur'an and other Islamic literature are on the tables along the walls. A few minutes before a given prayer time, the *Muezzin* comes, turns on the microphone, and gives the *adzan*—loudly. As mentioned above, you can hardly hear this *adzan* outside of the basement, but seemingly mysteriously, people soon start flocking in sizeable numbers before the *imam* starts the prayer, with a few dozen devotees standing quietly in straight rows, facing Mecca, behind him. Soon after the prayers are over, children start their class, sitting on the rugs in a semi circle (*halaqa*), learning how to write and recite the Qur'an along with a few lessons about the history of the Prophet Muhammad and his companions.

Over the weekend, you can see many more rows in prayers (five times a day), many more children in attendance in class, and many other programs on contemporary topics of interest to those who come to the mosque. *Juma'* (Friday) is the day for weekly congregation prayers. Because it is a working day, many adults pray somewhere else. Many children are absent too for the reason of being in school. The old and the feeble outnumber others in the *Juma'* congregation.

Ramadhan, the Islamic month of fasting culminating in the celebration of *Eid al fitr* (followed by *Eid al Adha* in two-and-a-half months' time) attracts a much larger attendance. On these occasions, most people living on Seeley would like to go for a prayer in the main mosque (*Juma' Masjid*). A much larger place six blocks to the west on Devon may be used depending on the weather when older men fresh out of the shower and children enjoying their new suits would pray in their small but convenient sacred mosque. Women clad in their colorful attire mostly wait at home for their men to return so they could go for *Eid* visits or to eat out on Devon. It is a day of feast, not only among Muslim Americans, but also among all Muslims all over the world. It is a day of great business on Devon. It is the day when the whole Muslim community along Devon is out.

Prayers and shopping are not all that people do along Devon in Chicago. Away from the main shopping district, small town atmosphere prevails.

Business is all of a sudden somewhat slower and life is a bit easier. People talk of good old days "back home," Pakistani television dramas, cricket, and field hockey. As newcomers keep coming from overseas, old timers subject them to solicited or even unsolicited advice. There is a great deal of "back alley" politicking going on, especially among senior and not-so-senior citizens, who apparently afford some time to socialize. Half a block to the west of Seeley is a small shop selling, among household items and stationery, telephone cards. Qamruz Zaman Khan, a very pleasant seventy-year-old Muslim gentleman from India has more visitors than customers, who recite poetry, tell jokes, sip hot, thick, milky, sweet tea brought from the street corner Ghareeb Nawaz Restaurant. This crowd eagerly gives their opinion on Palestine, Kashmir, Pakistan, Afghanistan, India, Britain, Russia, and the Bush administration. Everyone speaks with the confidence of a professor in a classroom. "I tell you, Bush did not have much of a chance but for those sixty thousand idiots (Muslim voters) in Florida." A rather sober looking gentleman in his sixties thinks about the future Muslim vote in the United States. He says, "You know there are ten million Muslims in this good old U.S. of A., but we still have to learn so much. American politics, you know..." Into the shop comes a customer, who wants to know which card to buy in order to make the cheapest call to Mir Pur Khas in Pakistan. Zaman Khan talks to the customer and politicking takes a pause.

Come August, which is increasingly becoming a holy month for Pakistanis on Devon, politics takes a noisy turn. Pakistan gained independence from the British *raj* on 14 August 1947. Things start moving in the first week of August—a spicy hot dinner given to the Pakistani community by the Irish American mayor of Chicago, a march on Devon by thousands of Pakistanis on or around 14 August, and lots of Pakistani flag-touting teenagers stuffed into pickup trucks driving very fast and shouting "Pakistan Zindabad"—Long live Pakistan!—up and down the whole length of Mohammad Ali Jinnah Way and beyond. A great deal of this noise, it seems, is not so much to celebrate the birth of Pakistan as an independent nation as it is to dare the neighboring Indian community along the next door, Gandhi Marg, a supposedly enemy turf that could be violated with impunity. It is interesting to see how the great South Asian rivalry is recreated thousands of miles away on Devon every August.

Devon seems to be on the verge of bursting at the seams every evening, but much more so on *Eid* and around Independence Day. Cars horns blow, men laugh loudly, women clad in colorful attire and twenty-one carat gold jewelry talk incessantly while trying to control their unruly children eager to dive onto the busy street, while young men run across the street, daring slow moving cars with angry drivers cursing. Here customers stand shoulder to shoulder waiting to be seated at crowded restaurants and stewards shout orders to the cooks in the kitchen. But there is no pushing and shoving, no purse or jewelry snatching, no street fighting, no drag racing, and not a police officer present on the scene either. It seems that the law is by and large alive on Devon supported by the citizenry and the mores in tow. This is a community where millions of dollars change hands every day.

By far Devon Avenue is not the only area of Muslim presence in "Chicago Sherif" or noble Chicago, as the city is sometimes referred to among its Muslim residents out of devotion or a sense of belonging. There are a number of large, very prosperous Muslim communities with spacious mosques, especially in the Western suburbs where Muslims live much farther apart and are thus diluted in the larger non-Muslim population. Muslims associated with the Islamic Foundation live in five adjacent Western suburbs, from where they drive in their Mercedes, Jaguars, Subarus, and other foreign-made cars every Friday for the *Juma'* congregational prayers. The foundation has a brand new multi-million-dollar mosque with a full-time school and a huge parking lot. The clientele of the foundation is in the thousands, about a third of whom, we are told, are in medical and related professions. Others are in finance and banking. Still others are computer scientists or electronics engineers. Some are successful small industrialists or are otherwise self-employed. Here, unlike on Devon, politics is more a function of high level of education beside having lots of spare dollars to boot. They donate heavily to charitable causes, but there seem to exist many who can afford to spend on their political ambitions. We spoke to a number of them who are active in both national political parties. Some favor a third party or speak of new parties. Their children go to private suburban schools, as well as to the weekend school at the Foundation, thus receiving some of the best secular and Islamic education.

The foundation is run by a privately registered board, firmly in the hands of a very well-respected, soft-spoken retired engineer, who prefers to run the foundation without much noise and criticism. Perhaps it is due to his more authoritarian bent that the foundation functions like an efficient machine with only muffled words of criticism heard once in a while. Devon is only a short distance away, but a far cry from the foundation community in size, available funds, in the stability of the community, in average educational level, and resourcefulness of its constituents. The Islamic Foundation depends upon as much as it benefits a settled community. Devon is where the transient and upwardly mobile Muslims are still trying their luck in the United States. The foundation has college-educated professionals in surrounding suburbs. Devon is like a busy downtown, which has taxicab owners, small shopkeepers, those in the restaurant business, and the suppliers who did not necessarily come to the United States for the sake of higher education. Residents of the foundation community like to drive down or ride in these taxicabs in order to go to Devon to eat out, buy attire and jewelry, and take their guests for an evening treat. It may not be too surprising if Devon might soon have its first cinema running full-length imported Pakistani and Indian films. Those around the foundation watch these in the warm comfort of their spacious basements.

Almost two hours by plane to the south takes you across the Mississippi to Dallas, Texas, home of Southern Baptist ideology, oil-related industry, and college and university campuses. It looked prosperous even in the middle of the price of oil and housing bust a few years ago. Few realize that it is also one of the busiest hubs of Islamic activity in the Southwest. The focal point is the

Muslim community (the Islamic Association of North Texas), which runs the Dallas Central Mosque in Richardson, Texas.

Dallas Central is a big mosque. A very prosperous community of Muslim professionals and businessmen supports it. A very articulate and active *imam* with a doctoral degree in Islamic studies, Yusuf Zima Kavakci, runs the mosque. Mr. Kavakci is long-time Turkish immigrant whose daughter, Merve Safa, an elected member of the Turkish Parliament, gained fame for refusing to take off her *hijab*—long scarf covering her head and shoulders. For this "crime" she was deprived of her seat in the Turkish Parliament.

Imam Yusuf runs the mosque as, in his words, a "real mosque," which means that it is not merely a place of formal five times a day prayers, but also a school, center of regional conferences, and home to an outreach program with Christian and Jewish churches. With more than seven hundred people of all colors attending daily prayers and more than three thousand people coming to the weekly *Juma'* prayers, the parking lot of the mosque overflows. Imam Yusuf made arrangements with the neighboring churches—North Dallas Community Bible Church and Christian World Church—on a reciprocal basis to use their parking lots. The Dallas Mosque also sponsors two overseas mosques, one in Mexico City and one in Belize. It also has two satellite mosques in the greater Dallas area. Although children receive full-time education from fifteen teachers hired by the Mosque, their real Islamic education comes from their involvement in conferences, conventions, and other activities run by the mosque.

There are many other large mosques west of the Mississippi (such as the Islamic Society of St. Louis, the Islamic Center of Houston, the Islamic Society of Southern California, and the Islamic Society of Orange County, California). But Dallas Central is becoming famous for the regional conferences and out reach programs in the Southwest.

Almost eight hundred miles to the east of Chicago in Syracuse, New York, each Friday between 1 and 2 P.M. the huge cemetery on Comstock Avenue is left with hardly a single parking space on its winding walkways. This is so because the Muslim worshippers are praying *Juma'* in a mosque across the street, and the parking lot of the mosque is much too small for the number of cars. Additionally, about one-mile long stretch of Comstock is open for car parking on both sides for the benefit of *Juma'* worshippers. The mosque was built to accommodate at best three hundred people in the main prayer hall with a corner reserved for women. Twenty years hence, the mosque got an upper floor built for women only in addition to the basement, which is also filled on Fridays. Thus the *Juma'* population of the mosque has more than doubled during the past twenty years. The mosque presently cannot accommodate the total worshippers at the occasions of *Eid al Fitr* and *Eid al Adha*. The community has to make special arrangements for these prayers, most of the time downtown.

Syracuse is home to Syracuse University, the State University of New York (SUNY) Medical School, and a number of other smaller colleges and numerous industries, which together have attracted large number of Muslim students, American as well as foreign, and professionals. A city of nearly two million including its suburbs, Syracuse is one of the three largest cities in upstate New York. According to the latest count, the Syracuse mosque serves nearly six hundred families, which live within a radius of approximately thirty miles from the mosque. The Syracuse Muslim community, then, extends beyond the city limits of Syracuse itself. Although there is an active chapter of the Muslim Students Association (MSA) on the Syracuse campus, the Syracuse mosque (Islamic Society of Central New York) serves students as well as nonstudents. In fact, long before there were any Muslim professionals in appreciable numbers in the Syracuse area, the MSA represented practically the only Islamic activity in town. It was mainly through the efforts of the MSA that the land for the mosque, at a walking distance from the campus, was bought in 1979. Then the community pitched in and built the mosque, and a few years later completed a small symbolic minaret on one side.

Before the mosque was built, the MSA used to hold *Juma'* prayers in a big hall in the student activity center reserved every Friday for that purpose. All other functions such as weekend Qur'an studies and occasional symposia used to be held in different halls on the campus. However, as the number of nonstudents increased in the community and the mosque was built, most MSA activities shifted to the mosque. Soon the mosque became an Islamic community center as well. Families with women and children, who were hardly ever seen on campus before, now come to the mosque regularly. A women's committee was formed with a responsibility especially to cater to women's concerns. A local activist, Diana W., started a group called Women Without Boundaries, which invites women of all faiths and color to discuss national and international issues. Soon arrangements were made for the weekend school for children. A session was added for a Saturday morning Qur'an reading. With the families and students from Syracuse University and the Medical School crowding it, the mosque becomes a lively place starting Friday afternoons through Sunday evenings. Besides, the mosque also became a place for occasional wedding ceremonies, weekly community dinner, as well as occasional funeral prayers.

The mosque's constitution and the bylaws, borrowed from the MSA, are simple. They provide for an executive committee (*shura*), which is elected every two years. The president (*ameer*) is the head of the executive committee. However, the *ameer* has only one vote when the *shura* is in session. The bylaws of the mosque also provide for a salaried *imam*, who, because of being paid by the mosque, cannot participate nor vote in any decision-making sessions of the executive committee.

The present *imam*, Ahmed Nazar of Syracuse, is a graduate of the famous Al-Azher school established in a mosque in Cairo in 1458. Moreover, after coming to Syracuse, he also enrolled for and received an M.A. and a Ph.D. degree in counseling. Having received traditional Islamic as well as secular university education, the *imam* gives enlightening *Juma'* sermons, in which he tries to come to grips with economic, political, family, and psychological problems of modern day living in the light of his Islamic training. Likewise, his advice on Islamic rulings (*Sharia*) does not always follow the traditional course. Being an *imam* in the mosque while being a graduate student on the campus, he was also able to work closely with the professors and university administration for the sake of the local MSA and for Muslims and Islam in general. He became instrumental in securing holidays for *Eid al Fitr* and *Eid al Adha* at Syracuse University. He arranged symposia and debates in the mosque involving reputed American and Muslim professors, writers, and intellectuals. He successfully started a dialogue with various Christian and Jewish organizations in the area, while at the same time overseeing the weekend school and adult classes in the mosque. In short, the present *imam* of the Syracuse mosque, far from pursuing the course of traditional run-of-the-mill *imams* of the mosques in the Muslim world, preempts the role Islamic leaders might play in the United States in the near future. Naturally, he could not have done all what he did without the active support and encouragement from the executive council (*shura*), which is often composed of graduate students from Syracuse University and highly trained professionals working in the Syracuse area.

Except for the students, who live on or around the campus, most Muslims in Syracuse live in the outer suburbs and beyond with spacious homes belying their higher socioeconomic status. A few African American Muslim families, much more highly educated and with a conspicuously higher income than their non-Muslim African American neighbors, prefer to live closer to the mosque and the university campus. Lately, an influx of a few hundred Bosnian and Kosovar refugees further contributed to the overall size and ethnic diversity of the Syracuse Muslim community.

If the community along Devon is mostly composed of transient upwardly mobile Muslims and that of the Islamic Foundation is made up of mostly settled professionals, the Syracuse community is a mixture of the two. Those in Syracuse—of indigenous as well as immigrant origin—have already raised at least one generation of children who grew up to become high earning professionals following the footsteps of their parents. However, since 1999 the resettlement of almost five hundred nearly non-English speaking Bosnian and Kosovar refugee families has changed the structure of the Syracuse Muslim community. Whereas "old" Syracuse Muslims had already achieved a stable pattern of relationships and were successfully pulled in the activities of the Islamic Society of Central New York, the "new" immigrants are visible by their mostly remaining aloof. Of course language is the greatest barrier between them and other Muslims. Even so, as their communication skills improve, more and more of the newcomers gradually appear in the mosque regularly. There is little doubt that the established Syracuse Muslims went out of their way to help Bosnians and Kosovars during the Balkan crisis. Now with these newcomers living in their midst, the mosque has developed different charitable and educational programs for them.

What is significant about Syracuse is that there is no equivalent of Devon Avenue. Most Syracuse Muslims live in distant homes in the outer suburbs.

Yet, distinctly among Syracuse Muslims there exists a high degree of mutual familiarity and a sense of belonging characteristic of smaller towns. Most people know one another by their first names. Children have developed their own friendship cliques. Outside of the mosque activity, people may gather informally at numerous occasions over dinners, wedding parties, or picnics, whereby children have fun running around in the park or the lakeside. Despite great distances between homes, ethnic backgrounds, and racial histories, Muslims of Syracuse share with one another their joy and sorrow together. When Diana lost her daughter in a car accident on an icy road, about a hundred "sisters" of all colors gathered to give a ritual bath to the body and pray for her salvation before she was buried. When Ba-Yunus' mother died in Texas after a long illness, the whole *Juma'* congregation prayed for her in Syracuse. Almost half of the Syracuse Muslim community, we are told, was present at the wedding dinner of Tanvir's daughter.

But, Dr. Rafil's case (see chapter six) touched deeply almost every one in the community. One dark, snowy day in February 2003, Dr. Rafil was stopped and arrested by the FBI at five in the morning while on his way to join the *Fajr* prayers at the mosque ten miles away. Three other individuals were also apprehended (but later released on bail). A general feeling of resentment and helplessness took over the whole population, we are told. It was like a pall hanging over the whole Syracuse Muslim community. The FBI also interviewed three hundred families, some several times. Several people, including those released on bail, were fired from their jobs. Whatever the outcome of the case, "everyone was in a state of shock and disbelief. It was like it happened to my own brother," said a local Muslim. For months, prison officials could hardly cope with the influx of visitors who wanted to see Dr. Rafil and assure him of their help. The Muslims of Syracuse offered their properties to raise bail worth three million dollars. So far, he has been denied bail four times. It seems that as long as the Iraq war does not settle one way or the other, prosecutors are in no hurry to start proceeding against him and the judges continue to treat him as a flight risk, denying him release on bail. Ironically, Dr. Rafil was once treated as a flight risk while behind bars under Saddam Hussein's regime whose grips he escaped only to become a respectable oncologist trying to save and comfort hundreds of women suffering from cancer. Trying to comfort was Dr. Rafil's mission, whether they were cancer-stricken women in upstate New York or starving children in Iraq—a mission for which he is being disgraced and penalized like an ordinary hoodlum.

To the southeast of Syracuse, in the nation's largest city, a small street crossing at Fulton and Bedford in Brooklyn is overwhelmed with the Muslim worshippers on Friday afternoons. In a small house turned into a mosque at this crossing, Imam Siraj Wahaj leads the *Juma'* congregation. He has been doing this every Friday for the past twenty-five years or so. Siraj Wahaj started his Islamic career as a follower of the late Elijah Mohammad. Just before Elijah's death in 1975, Siraj Wahaj, along with few others, broke away from the Nation of Islam movement. They moved to Brooklyn and declared Sunni or the mainstream orthodox Islam as their religion. Soon after their arrival in Brooklyn, they bought a run-down structure, renovated it, and established their mosque—*Masjid al Taqwa* (mosque of piety)—in order to conduct regular prayers in it.

They lived in Brooklyn cleanly, kindly but firmly. They cleaned the street everyday themselves because no one else did. They chased the drug traffickers out of the neighborhood. They married destitute girls and saved them from becoming prostitutes. They hired neighborhood toughs to work in the mosque and in their local small businesses, thus saving them from the world of crime and delinquency. They started a full-time school in the mosque. Jalal, an accountant with the Islamic Media Foundation in northern Virginia, fondly recalls the days when as a child in *Masjid al Taqwa* school, he, along with twenty other children, used to learn the Qur'an in the morning and mathematics and English in the afternoon.

The community of *Masjid al Taqwa* is African American. It is growing fast due to reproduction and conversion. It is a part of an overwhelming African American neighborhood. The school that the mosque runs is all composed of African American (some of them non-Muslims) children. Yet this community is as thoroughly Islamic as any in North America. Their mother tongue, English, is heavily laden with Islamic vocabulary and expressions. Men are generally clad in lose attire characteristic of Pakistanis or the Arabs. Their women never come out of their homes except in *Hijab* from head to toe. The *Juma'* sermons by the *imam* are often attended by several non-Muslims from the neighborhood and even beyond. His sermons are recorded and the tapes are sold even in non-African American Muslim communities. He is a regular speaker in national and regional Muslim conventions and conferences. In short, the *al Taqwa* community is a testimony as to how a single determined individual could create a whole community out of scratch by sheer persistence and the strength of his character. Siraj Wahaj leaves you with the impression of being a well-balanced leader who can discuss issues more with reason than emotion. He remains at home with all kinds of people, including Muslims and non-Muslims, indigenous or immigrant.

A similar community was in the offing in the slums of Atlanta, Georgia, under the leadership of Imam Jamil al Ameen (former H. Rap Brown of the Black Panther fame), whose charismatic career was interrupted by a court conviction on a charge of manslaughter. His case is still pending in an appellate court. In the meantime, the *imam* is doing what he is supposed to do—preaching Islam to his fellow inmates. Speaking of Islam in the prison, there is a high-walled, maximum-security so-called correctional facility at Auburn in the beautiful Finger Lakes region in upstate New York. The facility is one of the first and one of the most infamous state prisons in the United States. Under training, guards and other prison officials from other states are sent to Auburn to learn their trade. This is the place where they are supposed to learn it well.

The prison is overcrowded. Each day there are so many visitors: parents, wives, children, and friends coming to see the loved ones behind bars. It seems at first impossible to get an entry permit even for research purposes. But, as a Muslim chaplain, Sami Khalifah had done his homework. He had arranged a function celebrating *Milad al Nabi* (the Prophet's birthday) in the prison and had thus secured special permission for this event. The program of the *Milad al Nabi* was arranged under a big tent. There were close to two hundred inmates attending, including around fifty or so non-Muslims. Fifteen of these, including Imam Abdallah al Kareem Mohammad Farouq (otherwise Michael Roberts), were serving life sentences without parole. Imam Abdallah, a soft-spoken gentleman of likeable manners with a handful of beard, was sixty-three years old. He had already served thirty-nine years of his sentence. Showing few signs of aging, the *imam* behaved like being a charismatic leader of his flock, which had expanded over the years mainly through conversion to Islam. He was a follower of late Elijah Mohammad before he was convicted on a charge of killing a white couple in Chicago. After Imam Warith Deen Muham-mad took over the movement and declared himself to be a *Sunni* (or orthodox Muslim), Michael Roberts followed him and became a *Sunni* Muslim himself.

In 1975, when Michael opted for the main stream orthodox Islam, there was only fifteen of his kind in the prison. Very few of the followers of Imam Warith Deen would end up in jails. However, those of his followers who were at Auburn developed strong group relations and solidarity among themselves. This is how they provided security to each other within the group—a rare attraction for the weak and the newcomer, who would be looking for strong patronage in the dog-eat-dog world of inmates. This is how Imam Michael's group gained in size and stature. Those who would join his group would have to openly declare Islam as their religion, take a shower, and take an oath of brotherhood.

Imam Abdallah or Michael Roberts is an authoritarian, a totalitarian but a seemingly benign ruler of the Muslim inmate population. He has the last word in the internal matters of the group as well as outside the group such as com-municating with prison authorities as well as other similar groups in the prison. His understanding of the Qur'an, as limited as it might be, is preferred over that of even chaplain Sami Khalifah, who wisely prefers not to interfere in in-ternal matters of the group. However, Sami's role as a chaplain is crucial as a bridge between the inmates and the outside world, especially when it comes to arranging various functions and festivities, making contact with various educa-tional institutions and, not least, considerations for parole.

There are several other groups among Auburn inmates. Most of them are race-based, but, perhaps, none so strong and expanding as Imam Abdallah's "Black Muslim group" as the prison officials often call it. Life in Auburn prison is a big mess for most inmates for a number of reasons. One of them is a hateful feeling of being confined behind high walls all the time and a state of continuous bore-dom that accompanies the inmates like their shadows. Secondly, often tough and repeat offenders end up in this facility. They are quite capable of doing serious harm to one another if not kept under control. Thirdly, the prison officials at various levels engage in at least making a show that they are quite tough. They are quite capable of making life miserable, especially for a weak character without much social support. Perhaps the lower level officials, mostly those under training, are under pressure to prove themselves.

However, accepting Islam as his religion makes the life of an inmate at Auburn quite a bit easier and more secure in a number of ways. He is safe from random attacks by other tough characters in the prison. He himself becomes more disciplined. At the time of this study, a number of them were preparing for high school equivalency and, even, college- level examinations. More importantly, the prison officials may look at him with a bit of grudging respect and trust him more than they would.

The program of the *Milad al Nabi* started with the recitation of *Surat al Fatiha* or the introductory chapter often described as the Lord's Prayer of the Qur'an. A relatively young inmate, John Maldoun, otherwise known to his fellow Muslims as Abdur Rahman bin Auf al Madani, did a reasonably good job of recitation, which was followed by *tafseer* or explanation of these verses by the *imam*. Everyone listened to the *imam* quietly without any interruption. Next, one of the guest speakers spoke about on the life and the career of the Prophet Muhammad, stressing brotherhood (how would you like to see your brother put down on the floor and beclubbed by a few burly guards, or how would you feel when your own brother is lying in dust with a knife in his belly?) and not to despair, to remain steadfast in their newly found faith For a Muslim, he explained, there is always light at the end of the tunnel. Toward the end of the function, the group gained 6 new converts, increasing the Muslim population in the prison to 177.

The group is short on rituals but jealously guard the rules of Islamic conduct— brotherhood, sharing and mutual care, respect for one another, and prohibitions against talking on the back of a fellow Muslim, being disrespectful to the *imam* in public, and using obscene words in general. Arabic is difficult to learn. But among themselves, the Muslim inmates use usual Islamic expressions such as *Asslamo alaikum* (peace be on you) rather than saying good morning or good evening, *Subhan Allah* (praise be to God) when something good happens, or *Insha Allah* (If God so wills) when they expect or hope for something good in future.

It is evident that the group life among Muslim inmates at Auburn revolves around concerns for security and the personality of Imam Abdallah. He is not going to be freed from the prison. But what if and when he dies? There is no council of elders in the group, although there are a few who are closer to the *imam* than others. They are his confidantes. However, few in the group, which has substantial turnover, ever raise this question. The *imam* is getting old, but he is still relatively young and most in the group hope to be free eventually. The group, then, would continue one way or the other; it seems, at least out of necessity for security and survival.

THE STRUCTURE OF THE MUSLIM COMMUNITY

As mentioned earlier, there may be in the neighborhood of fifteen hundred, even more, registered Muslim communities, and their number continuously increases. Besides, there are numerous large and small unregistered communities like the one on Seeley, but they have roughly the same functions to perform as registered communities, that is, establishing a regular place for worship, education, and mutual discussions on matters of concern.

Although the term "community" has been in use by Muslims in the United States for a long time, it was deliberately used and popularized by the national organizations in order to distinguish between students and nonstudent Muslims residing in the United States. Students mostly live on or around college campuses. Their lives revolve around courses, classes, libraries, professors, and examinations. More importantly, for a long time, until the late twentieth century, Muslim college students remained synonymous with foreign students, who were in the United States for a temporary stay and who would go back home once they finished their education. Community, on the other hand, was initially used for all others who are not students but permanent residents or citizens of America. Community referred to those who worked for a living, lived in their homes with their own families.

This is such a broad definition that a Muslim community may not necessarily have to refer to a well-defined neighborhood. Muslim communities are often described as Muslim ghettos such as Dearborn, Michigan, or Lackawanna, New York, but newly emerging communities such as the one along Devon Avenue in Chicago are more an exception than the rule. This is so because Muslim immigrants to the United States, especially those who arrived in the second half of the twentieth century (Syracuse community for instance), did very well educationally and economically in a few years after their arrival. Indigenous, mostly African American Muslims also, given time, have fared much better than their non-Muslim brethren as a whole.

Improvement in socioeconomic situations brought about improvements in the standard of living. It may not be incorrect to say that the Muslim population in the United States as a whole enjoys middle- to upper-middle-class status. This becomes clear when you look at these communities' pecuniary consumption patterns, as reflected in their homes, the way their homes are furnished, the automobiles they drive, and the schools and colleges that their children attend. In short, Muslims in the United States have few "China Towns" of their own. Those that exist are relatively small, far in between, and almost exclusively inhabited by African Americans or the newly arrived, upwardly mobile transient population. By far most Muslims, whether in large or small cities, generally live dispersed and diluted in different neighborhoods where they mostly remain invisible as Muslims, except when some of their women (usually relatively younger in age) start taking *hijab*. Even African American Muslims tend to follow the same pattern with rise in socioeconomic status.

Muslim community in the United States, then, does not necessarily mean well-defined townships or suburbs. At best, it may be described as a population locally organized in order to avail itself of Islamic services asserting its Islamic identity. A mosque or an Islamic center is soon established for this purpose. Not all in a given area are *bona fide*, fee-paying or card-carrying members of the organization of the mosque or the Islamic center, but most of them, in many ways, benefit from and contribute to the organization of the mosque.

It must be evident by now that a primary function of a Muslim community has been to establish a facility for the *Juma'* (Friday congregation), in addition to five times a day regular prayers. If there are children in the community, then the mosque also provides them with at least weekend schooling in Islamic sciences, mannerisms, and character. Whatever you may call it—a *masjid* (mosque) or an Islamic center—the place where Muslim community members gather for prayers regularly betrays the existence of a sizeable Muslim population in the adjoining territory. Like the "sacred mosque" on Seeley in Chicago, the place may not have a dome or a minaret. The place might not have been built as a mosque to begin with. Such places that still exist especially in large cities mainly serve a transient population as mentioned above. However, as Muslim populations grow in strength and prosperity, new and more expensive structures following the traditional structure of a mosque along with a dome and the minarets are appearing on American horizons. One of the most visible of such mosques is the one just outside of Toledo, Ohio. Driving on Route 80 in either direction—east or west—one cannot miss the minarets gradually emerging out of the flat black earth of the Midwest. A closer look at the mosque would reveal that the structure of the mosque is a copy of the famous *Aya Sufya* mosque in Istanbul, Turkey, although most Toledo Muslims, who financed it, are not Turks. They are very successful first or second-generation immigrant Muslim businessmen and professionals settled in and around Toledo for more than fifty years.

Not all mosques with traditional designs are new. In fact, some of them, such as the ones in Gary, Indiana, and the one in Cedar Rapids, Iowa, were built in the late nineteenth or early twentieth centuries.

There are three types of mosque organizations. Most mosques are run by their governing boards or executive committees, which are elected by the general membership. The president is the chief executive, who runs the mosque in consultation with the members of the board or the executive body. Issues are discussed and voted upon among the executives more often than not leaving only one vote for the president. Some large national organizations such as ISNA, as mentioned before, function on the same interpretation of the concept of *shura* as laid down in the Qur'an. In case there is a serious issue to be discussed or there is serious disagreement within the governing body or among the executives, a general body meeting is called to vote on the issue in order to resolve it.

Secondly, there are mosques run by groups subscribing to specific ideologies. The most important one of such groups operating in the United States is the *Tablighi Jamaat*, a staunchly apolitical group, which has its origin in nineteenth century India under the British rule. The group started mainly with purpose of taking Islam to illiterate and undereducated country folks, who had become prone to superstitions and were contaminating Islam with Hindu practices Muslims perceived as pagan. *Tablighi Jamaat* has not gone through any significant change during the past 150 years. Its main focus has been the development of personal character along Islamic prescriptions, that is, being nice, helpful, self-sacrificing, righteous, soft-spoken, nonargumentative, and so on in addition to always observing daily prayers, fasting in the month of Ramadhan, and never evading paying alms (*zakat*) or the poor due as prescribed by the Qur'an and the Sunnah of the Prophet. As a member of the *Tablighi Jamaat*, one has to pledge a few days in a year that should be devoted for going with a group of fellow members spreading the word of Islam.

Mosques run by the *Tablighi Jamaat* must always remain under exclusive control of the *Jamaat*. Others may come and pray with them. They must be encouraged to do so, but while in the mosque must follow the rules laid down by the mosque administration without question.

On West Foster Avenue in Chicago, the Khan Palace, an apartment complex, houses a small mosque run by the *Jamaat*. The basement of the Khan Palace is at the street level and the mosque is an enclosure on one side of that basement. It is easy to ignore this mosque because there is nothing that betrays its existence as a place of Islamic worship. However, once you enter it you may know right away that you are in a mosque. There is a place to do ablutions. There is a small stand for storing your shoes. Then there is a large room with the floor covered with white bed sheets and the prayer rugs. In a corner there is a small table with a few copies of the Qur'an and other Islamic literature, but no newspapers or news magazines. A large sign on the nearby wall indicates that because this is a House of God, politicking is prohibited.

Thirdly, there are privately owned mosques. A person or his family, who runs the mosque, might own it. People are encouraged to pay donations, which may or may not be tax exempt. Or, the mosques could be registered as private enterprise registered under the name of a group, which functions according to certain bylaws agreed upon by the group. The head or the president of the mosque is elected within the group. When there is vacancy in the group, it is filled by nomination and appointment by the group.

Whatever the nature of the mosque administration, most mosques in the United States have a very limited membership—only a fraction of all who live in the adjoining territory—although the number of those benefiting from its services may be quite large. Limited membership often creates a host of problems for the mosque and, indeed, for the community as a whole. Foremost of these problems has been that of insufficient funds with which to run the mosque. When the community is small, the problem may not be awfully serious. A smaller community has a smaller mosque and fewer functions to perform. Some smaller mosques, for instance, do not even hold *Juma'* congregation. Moreover, smaller mosques, often-improvised apartments or basements, require fewer expenses for their maintenance.

It is the larger communities that often suffer from a perpetual problem of scarcity of funds for the mosque and its related facilities such as schools, although the community as a whole may be quite prosperous. Mosques with insufficient funds have tried several ways to raise funds. They hold regular fundraising dinners with professional fundraisers invited to motivate the audience. They try calling as many big donors as they know in the nation. They try to borrow from other larger and more prosperous communities. Some have tried to advertise their needs repeatedly in multiple Islamic magazines, newspapers, and journal shopping to reach a large audience and consequently get a large response. Yet another strategy, especially in the 1970s, was to appeal to the charitable trusts in oil-rich Gulf states, which could satisfy their pricking conscience by giving funds for the establishment and upkeep of the mosques all over the world. A number of former American graduates from the Gulf countries went back home and occupied important positions in their respective countries. Initially, they played an important role by serving as contact persons and helping to raise funds for these newly emerging mosques in the United States. But soon these overseas funds proved to be undependable, irregular, and sometimes even disappointing.

A story, which we could not authenticate, circulated widely in Islamic circles in the United States in 1987. One of the fundraisers of a major American Islamic organization was, after a great deal of effort, able to have an audience with the Saudi king Fahd, who gracefully ordered a donation of twenty million dollars to that organization. The following day, this award became a headline in Saudi press to the dismay of other competitors of such awards from the Saudi court. However, this award never materialized because the secretary of the court (*wakeel*) was not consulted before such a request was made. Consequently, the secretary of the court blocked the award and the king could not be reached again so he could be reminded of his generous but unfulfilled offer. Whether or not this incident was real, the story shows the Muslim American belief that you cannot depend upon Arab bureaucracies, which could easily destroy your designs for Islamic development in the United States.

Saudi Arabia is not the only country which was approached by the American Muslim fundraisers. Kuwait, Qatar, Bahrain, and other Gulf states also put aside from their oil money substantial sums for the religious purposes (*awqaf*), mainly for the mosques all over the world. Because the *awqaf*, like the *zakat*, is a purely religious fund, it is given without any strings attached. However, this money did not last very long. Soon there were too many contenders for this money, which, anyway, gradually lost much of its value due to the negative impact of the 1973 oil embargo in this interconnected world economy.

However, as sources of funds from the Middle East were drying up, the per capita income in the ever-expanding American Muslim community was rising. The decade of 1980s saw a distinct movement of Muslim population into the suburbs, and the appearance of the minarets began on the American skyline as never before. According to a survey done by the Islamic Resource Institute of Tustin, California, almost half of twelve hundred registered Islamic centers or mosques in the United States were built between 1969 and 1983. Initially, overseas funds helped, but only a handful of them. In fact, all major mosques or Islamic centers serving Muslim populations in large metropolitan areas, were started somewhat before the oil producing sheikdoms of the Middle East had their oil bonanza in early 1970s. By that time, most of these mosques were receiving major portions of their funds from prospering individual Muslims: high ranking executives or self-employed professionals.

A prospering Muslim community population does not mean that their mosques are also prospering. Over the past three decades, Muslim populations in the communities have been expanding as never before. Thus, more people come to pray in the mosques. More children are coming to pray as well or at least attend the weekend school. More social functions such as wedding ceremonies, community dinners, and children's programs are held. Consequently, the mosque administrations are under constant pressure to expand mosque premises and their facilities by buying adjoining properties, moving to new and much larger facilities, buying old church or school buildings. But these moves for expansion need more funds and the ratio of members of the mosque to the nonmembers has not changed much over time. Consequently, most mosques in the United States are undergoing a chronic need for a continuous supply of funds. Even the most active and the prosperous-looking mosque, when you look at it closely, is run by a rather anxious executive board indeed. Because a church-like organization does not exist among mosques, each mosque is like a mushroom—fat or small—tending to its own needs.

The *Imam*

Almost every mosque in the United States and, for that matter everywhere, has a person who leads the daily prayers. He is called the *imam*. Generally, he also leads the *Juma'* or the Friday congregation as well as the prayers at the occasions of *Eid al Fitr* and *Eid al Adha*. You do not have to have a formally designated person with the position of an *imam* to lead in prayers. Any person who is considered to be "the best among you" may be requested to do so. Who is going to be your *imam*, then, may vary in time and space. However, in the United States as elsewhere, the mosque administration tries to make sure as to who is going to be the next *imam*. For practical considerations then, each mosque designates a person who is given the responsibilities of making arrangements for the prayers, leading the prayers, as well as taking care of the weekend school and any other responsibilities as deemed necessary by the executive board of the mosque. Because this is almost necessarily a full-time job, most mosques hire a person to perform these jobs. Far from being a priest, a divine or a spiritual leader, a typical *imam*, then, is generally a paid employee of the mosque with certain designated duties.

However, the *imam* must have certain qualifications, the most important of which is that he is a *hafiz* (one who put the whole Qur'an to heart). He should be a one who can recite the Qur'an with beauty (*quari*). He must have a good working knowledge of the Islamic law (*Sharia*). He may or may not be a graduate of an Islamic college. If he is, it is most desirable. He may or not be a graduate of an American college. If he is, it is an additional qualification. Most importantly, he is expected to be a good speaker so that he is able to

deliver the sermon in *Juma'* prayers (*khutba*). Because he is not a spiritual figure, regard and respect accorded to an *imam* depends primarily on his charisma, which is partly a function of his ability to deliver the sermon
(*khutba*)—not only what he says but also how he says it.

Khutba dates back to the Prophet Muhammad. It precedes but is considered
to be an integral part of the ritual *Juma'* prayers. The one who leads the *Juma'*
prayers is expected to give a sermon, however briefly, even if he is not a recognized *imam*.

In their *khutub* (plural of *khutba)* the Prophet and the four pious caliphs
(*khulafa*), who succeeded him, generally spoke on topics of great concern to
the community or the larger society (*ummah*) of the believers. Topics such as
war and peace, politics and economics, marriage and divorce, and crime and
conformity were always mixed with belief in Allah, the One God and His
Prophet, along with topics of morals, manners, devotion, and piety, with a
great emphasis on life after death. After the system of elected *khilafah* or the
caliphate was abolished and the dynastic rule set in, the *imams* had to restrain
themselves and avoid speaking on topics of larger societal affairs lest they
would go overboard and be punished by the agents of the dynastic rulers.

This became a fourteen-hundred-year-long tradition. The *khutba* assumed a
structure—profusion of praise to Allah and prayers for Prophet Muhammad
and all other prophets before him with great emphasis on being good. There
are two parts to the *khutba*. The first part usually revolves around the benefits
and advantages of good manners and morals, which are considered to be
socially beneficial. The sermon has to be reinforced with quotes from the
Qur'an, the sayings of the Prophet (*hadith*), and the Prophet's practices
(*sunnah*). This pattern became so pervasive that even in countries not under
dictatorial monarchial rule, emphasis in the *khutba* remained limited to these
topics. Recently Sakr (1998) published a book presumably in order to help the
imams in the United States to pick their *khutba* topics. A cursory look at the
table of contents shows an array of topics, such as belief in Allah and his
prophets, best manners, guarding the tongue, repentance, forgiving, cleanliness,
truthfulness, and so on. Not a single topic in this book deals with the status of
Muslims as a minority in the United States or their social, economic, and political concerns. In many contemporary Muslim countries, as well as in Europe
and the United States where few such restrictions on *khutba* exist, *imams* (or
whomever lead the *Juma'* prayers) have often taken the liberty of discussing
socioeconomic and political issues in the light of Islamic injunctions.

The *imam* would sit down for a minute or two at the end of the first part.
The second part would mostly consist of praying—for the poor, the needy, the
sick, the Muslim community, and humanity as a whole. At the end of the second part, the *imam* would start the formal collective ritual prayers, whereby
those attending the prayers would stand behind him in rows and engage in prescribed form of the prayer after him.

Because each sermon (*khutba*) is supposed to be punctuated with a profusion
of references to the Qur'an, *hadith* and the *sunnah*, the *imam* has to have some

education and training in using these sources of Islamic discourse, as well as in the art of addressing people.

Evidently, not every Muslim can do this. Thus, over the years being an *iman* became a calling. Just like people aspire to become engineers, doctors, or lawyers, some choose to become *imams*. However, there have been few schools around that would give you a degree that would qualify you to work as an *imam*. One may only have had a chance to attend a school and put to heart portions of the Qur'an, *hadith*, and the *sunnah*. Or one may go to an Islamic college of repute and graduate from there. One may go to any college offering concentration in Islam. Or one may receive private tutoring in the Qur'an, *the hadith*, the *sunnah*, and maybe Islamic history. In the end what counts is the reputation of the place where you received your education and how you are able to use your training. In the United States, there is a whole spectrum of the *imams*, from those who were educated in local schools to the graduates of such reputable institutions as al Azhar of Egypt, Ummul Qura of Saudi Arabia, or Darul Ulum of Pakistan. Some of them also went to American universities and received their doctoral degrees, often in Islamic studies or related social sciences. On the other hand, there are *imams* who received their informal education through their party affiliations such as *Tablighi Jamaat* in India or *Jamaat Islami* in Pakistan. Also there are a number of American Muslims, mostly African Americans, who received scholarships to study Islam in an Arab country or other Muslim country. They came back with working knowledge of Islam that could be used in the *Juma' khutba* in their communities. At the bottom of the scale, one may also find *imams* who were practicing their trade in small towns in the Muslim world by virtue of being able to recite the Qur'an melodiously and remember it by heart.

It must be evident that the sermon (*khutba*) as delivered in American mosques must vary in sophistication from mosque to mosque depending on whom the *imam* is. A great exception to this almost universal pattern of the *Juma' khutba* is the one given by the leader of the prayers on college campuses. College students cannot afford to and generally do not care to have a traditional *imam* come to their campus for the exclusive purpose of leading the *Juma'* congregation. Students on campuses generally take turns leading these weekly prayers. Although often being relatively deficient in their vocabulary of the Qur'an and the *sunnah*, these students have shown an exceptional ability to articulate Islam in relation to the problems of contemporary societal and international affairs.

Usually, an *imam* of a mosque is supposed to assume additional responsibilities such as managing the weekend school and, sometimes, as Zoll (2003) pointed out, taking care of the mosque as a whole. He must also perform weddings. People may come to him for counseling. He should also be available in the mosque most of the time. If so desired, he should also be able to answer questions or give advice on the application of Islamic law in given situations. He is often, depending on his qualifications and reputation, expected to represent the mosque and its community in local, regional, or national Muslim or non-Muslim gatherings.

These are seemingly clear and simple expectations from an *imam*. These make him look more like a pastor of a modern day church (Zoll, 2003). However, in practice, his position is often quite precarious. For instance, because the *imam* is an "expert" in the Islamic law, he may give or reserve an opinion as to what is Islamic or un-Islamic in a given situation—a ruling that the president or the executive board of the mosque may find disagreeable or undesirable momentarily. When such a situation arises, the mosque administration may seek opinion from some other experts of equal or better reputation living in and even serving some other community. There may also exist in the community other experts who may not always agree with the opinion of the *imam*. Moreover, being in paid service of the mosque or the community, he is not in a position to participate in any decision making or otherwise make and try to impose his decision. The community may, because of his reputation and respect for him, request his active participation in decision making. Occasionally, even the bylaws of the mosque may have formal clauses to this effect, but not necessarily. In fact, in most cases, the *imam* knows his place quite well. One who has serious reservations of his own regarding this arrangement runs into trouble with the mosque community or its administration quickly.

However, there are also powerful *imams*—eloquent, appealing, and charismatic—who, like Siraj Wahaj, become almost indispensable for their communities. Or who, like Abdullah al Kareem Mohammad Farouq (Michael Roberts) of Auburn prison, have been able to create and enlarge their flock of followers by providing them group solidarity and personal security. There are few precious such *imams* in immigrant communities. African American *imams*, on the other hand, generally enjoy powerful positions in their communities; most reputed among these is Imam Warith Deen Muhammad, whose community is truly a national community of African American Muslims.

Muslim Community Education

As mentioned above, Muslim communities in the United States established their mosques partly as defensive mechanisms against the perceived onslaught of non-Islamic influences in American society. Thus, other than facilitating regular prayers, mosques became, at least, part-time schools trying to inculcate and preserve basic Islamic belief and character of the next generation. It is out of such activities that full-time schools, initiated by the mosques, developed over time. There are about three hundred full-time schools operated by Muslim communities across the country. Many of them, especially those run by the Muslim American Society headed by Imam Warith Deen Muhammad, have already graduated a whole generation of students, some of who went on to reputable universities and are now working as respectable professionals.

Thus, there are two kinds of schools that are initiated by the Muslim community in the United States. First, there are weekend schools. These schools have an exclusive focus on teaching fundamentals of Islam, including the ritual prayers, recitation of the Qur'an, the *sunnah*, the *Sharia* or the Islamic law, and morals and manners. In addition, a number of programs for children including indoor and outdoor games and hiking (when and if possible) are important parts of the curriculum. In a number of mosques, adult classes, separately for men and women, are also an important aspect of weekend schooling. Consequently, establishment of mosques has meant that whole families are involved in Islamic activities over the weekend. Evidently, the *imam* alone cannot shoulder all what the mosque is performing without active involvement of the volunteers in the community.

Weekend schools have played an important role in the continuation of Islam through generations in the United States. Most weekend schooling is carried out within the premises of the mosque. It often does not have or need qualified teachers, only highly motivated volunteers, who often teach without any salaries. There are few standard textbooks available for children or even adults. Classes are held in the main prayer hall, in women's section, or in the basement with the help of collapsible partition walls if and when available. Children's classes are generally graded by age. Typically, only two or three grades are formed in the weekend school.

Although it generally goes unnoticed, one of the major consequences of weekend schooling in the mosques has been the formation of selective friendships. These grow across racial and nationality backgrounds and between children, who are students, as well as adults, who are teachers. These informal relations among children and adults have given rise to broader family circles that deepen community relations across ethnic lines, especially in the younger generation.

Beside being relatively inexpensive, weekend schooling in the mosque also consists of informal ways of learning Islam through games, picnics, plenty of home-cooked food, the practicing of the Islamic code of conduct, and group prayer in the park at prayer time. Weekend schooling, in short, is a small and isolated Muslim community's dream come true. It serves as an effective tool in inculcating Islam in the next generation and presumably "saves" them from perceived immorality and crime in the larger society. Besides, it serves an additional function of promoting internal solidarity in the community, as mentioned above.

The weekend schools run by most mosques generally do not hold any tutorial classes involving courses taught in full-time schools during the weekdays, although some weekend schools are known to have offered help in preparing students for the SAT or other college entry exams. However, full-time schools in a controlled Islamic environment, directed by Muslim staff, and run by Muslim administration, have been one of the cherished desires of most Muslim communities.

Running full-time schools is an expensive proposition. How can communities, which cannot satisfy the bottomless needs of their mosques, contemplate opening their own full-time regular schools? Full-time schools mean following government guidelines with respect to space and building codes, qualified teachers, standard texts, accounting, and auditing. Thus, the talk of having full-time schools of one's community often sounded like an exercise in futility. However, full-time Muslim schools, imparting most modern education, are now appearing in increasing numbers. According to the latest count kept by the National Association of Islamic Schools (NAIS), there are close to three hundred such schools in operation. Best organized among these, with the best results thus far, have been Aunt Clara Schools under the trusteeship of Imam Warith Deen Mohammad. Efforts are under way these days to standardize curriculum in all schools run by the Muslim communities across the United States.

Muslim schools do not face the problem of school prayer, which haunts so many other community schools in the country. Muslim schools also do not have the controversy regarding the validity of the theory of evolution. All students are supposed to pray together when it is time for the prayers. Students are given heavy doses of Islamic morals and mannerism. Even non-Muslim students (some schools have reserved a few seats for non-Muslims) are given time for their prayers.

However, full-time schools, even those run by the Muslim communities, have to provide at least minimum amount of purely secular education, including mathematics, physical and natural sciences, and geography. So far, Muslim schools have done a considerably better job of this than many other schools in the nation. On average, Muslim schools give twenty days less vacation time than other schools in the nation. Seventy Muslim schools that have granted high schools degrees for the past ten years have sent nearly all their graduates to colleges and universities (Shehan, 2002).

What is noteworthy here is that the aspirations of Muslim students (even those going to secular schools) as to their professions in future are considerably higher than those of non-Muslim students. In her study of seventeen schools in California, Shehan (2002) found that while 87 percent of students from Muslim schools and Muslim students in secular schools are aspiring to become doctors, business and finance executives, computer scientists, engineers, and lawyers, most (76 percent) non-Muslim students prefer professions such as primary and high school teaching, nursing, and sports. From this Shehan concludes that the next generation of Muslims is getting a better orientation as to how they could be more successful in this material world by entering into highly paid and more prestigious professions.

However, Muslim schools are still in their infancy. They suffer from a chronic shortage of funds and teacher retention problems. The school staff is underpaid. Schools charge high tuition fees (higher than even some of church-operated boarding schools). Most well-to-do Muslim families do not send their children to their community schools, although these schools are now becoming known for giving better secular as well as religious education. Other than the prestige of having their own full-time school, most Muslim communities insist on doing this because American schools in general have a bad reputation these days for substandard education, rampant juvenile delinquency, drug use, and sexual laxity. Hence, the justification for establishing Muslim community schools despite all their other problems.

Despite these problems, Muslim educators have an optimistic view of their enterprise. In his paper, Mahmati (1996) notes:

> Whatever their problems, Islamic schools produce students who show a well-rounded capacity to work successfully in this technologically advanced, post-modern society. Because this generation of Muslims is born and raised in the United States, it does not show the same timidity that characterizes immigrants in the parental generation. Members of this generation are as American as apple pie. They do not have any place else to go, and their sense of history is substantially different from that of their parents. This brought this new generation born to the immigrant parents and those born to indigenous parents, closer together in their outlook as being American Muslims.

It is not difficult to see the final product of these schools. Graduates of Islamic schools are the best students in mathematics and sciences. They have much less incidence of sexual promiscuity, drug addiction, alcoholism, and juvenile delinquency in general. But they are poor students of Western civilization, American history, and American political system.

Weekend schools, full-time schools, and even colleges and universities run by the churches are not uncommon in the United States. Muslim communities are just now learning how to run full-time schools with great effort and difficulty. Few in the Muslim community gave serious thought of taking the next logical step—establishing an Islamic college or a Muslim-run institution of higher learning. There have been few attempts, not initiated by the communities, and they have been a disaster. The American Islamic College, next to the scenic Lake Shore Drive in Chicago, has been one such casualty of inexperience, inefficiency, and outright theft of funds. The beautiful St. Mary's Seminary was sold in the early 1980s to the Organization of Islamic Conference (OIC). The church needed funds and the OIC was awash in petrodollars. Somehow the OIC came to believe that African Americans were turning to Islam in large numbers and that there was a great need for the *imams* in the black community. Hence, the need for an institution of higher education in Islam became obvious. Such an institution was conceived of as a degree-granting college, which would offer courses in Arabic language, the sources of Islamic law, recitation and explanations of the Qur'an, and Islamic history. Instructors and professors were to be recruited from a pool of learned scholars in the Muslim world, in Europe as well as in North America.

Evidently, the American Islamic College had a rather limited scope. It was conceived mainly in terms of an Islamic "seminary," the likes of which are only rarely found even in the Muslim world today. The college was conceived on the pattern of traditional medieval *madrasa* and not a modern college that offers programs in sciences and arts as well. No feasibility study was done. Was there a demand for such an institution? It seems that the whole effort was justified on the basis of a small research report (Abugudeiri, 1980), which, evidently, needed replication. After a million dollars were spent on remodeling the seminary building and gathering staff and expensive faculty, it was found that there were few buyers of the idea. A few students who enrolled in the college expected tuition wavers and subsidized boarding and lodging in the dormitories on the campus. Soon it was found that at American Islamic College, staff and faculty outnumbered students by a wide margin and the gap between the two showed little prospect of shrinking. In three years, the OIC was in no mood to continue with this venture. The college campus was leased to a private party with even less experience in running an institution of higher learning and a greater interest in using the campus as a piece of strategically located real estate. There is no doubt that the American Islamic College has been a sad experience in Muslim inefficiency and yet another example of how petrodollars could be wasted without much accountability.

About the same time that the American Islamic College was started with great fanfare and surplus funds, an unemployed Pakistani with a Canadian citizenship came to Chicago in 1979. After receiving his doctoral degree in educational administration from Indiana University, he drove a taxi in Indianapolis for a while before he landed a position as an academic dean at Daniel Hale Williams, an undergraduate college run by an African American group in Chicago. At Daniel Hale Williams, Wasi Khan came to understand how to run a college on a tight leash with the help of state and federal tuition grants reserved for minority students. In the two years after Daniel Hale Williams folded in scandals, he conceived of starting his own East-West University following what he called the tuition-driven-model.

At East-West, Wasi Khan brought with him a few of his colleagues from the now-defunct Daniel Hale Williams. He rented a few rooms in a four-storied building south of the loop, resting his hopes on African American students disillusioned and disappointed with Daniel Hale Williams.

As soon as tuition grants for minority students arrived, his East-West University also expanded, eventually buying the whole building across the street from Chicago Hilton on Michigan Avenue overlooking Lake Michigan. Having formed a governing board consisting of people of repute and influence in the Muslim community of Chicago, Khan meticulously followed all intricate legal details necessary for keeping his university afloat, though barely.

East-West started by offering general education courses for the first two years of its existence. For the third and the fourth years, it offered majors in areas more economical to teach, but in greater demand such as civil and structural engineering, industrial engineering, mathematics, statistics, business administration, and finance. In order to teach these courses, the university hired from the nearby loop in downtown Chicago, where a number of professionals were ready to moonlight on a part-time basis.

Almost a quarter of a century hence, East-West University is a story in personal and institutional success. It is still small, but the university's name appears in the listing of accredited colleges and universities in the United States. It is an expanding college aspiring to introduce graduate programs in business administration and Islamic studies.

The failure of American Islamic College and success of East-West University are intimately related with the Muslim community of Chicago. In the case of the former, the experiment failed because the Muslim community of Chicago, an amalgamate of several ethnically diverse groups, was never consulted or taken into confidence. In the later case, despite initial misgivings, East-West University aspired to and remained a part of the Muslim community of Chicago. Not only are the members of its governing board some of the influential Muslim elites of Chicago, the university is a member of the prestigious Islamic Council of Greater Chicago. Most importantly, the university is, for all practical purposes, part of the African American neighborhood from where it draws most of its students and staff. Being in close vicinity to the loop, the university is able to recruit professionals as teachers for very economical salaries. There is little doubt that East-West University reflects ingenuity, hard work, and resourcefulness of the Muslims of Chicago.

Lately, two other institutions started functioning. One of them—the American Islamic University—is already offering off-campus correspondence courses. Located near Detroit, Michigan, the university is like any other church-sponsored school with a secular program. A glance at the courses being offered shows that the university is simultaneously aiming at Americanizing new Muslim citizens while exposing them to the essentials of Islam.

Another school, located in Queens, New York, offers computer-generated teaching presently limited to Arabic language and understanding of fundamentals of Islam. Both are relatively new institutions, not unlike many church-related schools of nineteenth-century America. Their success or failure is still too soon to predict. What is important is that both are deeply couched in and dependent upon the larger Muslim community in the United States.

THE MUSLIM COMMUNITY IN POLITICS

"Dear Professor, we got to go for a brunch today," so informed Arshad. He thought we had to be there at 10:30, but Sabri Nihari was still closed on that hot Sunday morning when he parked his car along the curb. The occasion was a reception given to Jan Schakowsky, a congresswoman from the ninth district in Illinois.

Tip O'Neill, a very well-known former speaker of the U.S. House of Representatives, once observed that all politics is local politics. As mentioned earlier, the Muslim community is not an exception to this rule. Political commentaries, partisan debates, and frequent discussions—written or otherwise—are as common in the Muslim community as they are in any community in the United States. Hailing mostly from countries where democracy is more talk than reality, most immigrant Muslims are, nonetheless, slowly but surely learning the tricks of American political trade. The following advice a Muslim gave to his brothers and sisters in Islam makes this clear:

> "Do not be ethnically offensive, always remain open for a compromise, support Jan in her bid for re-election and Jan would support your cause as a community! The very fact that she agreed to come means that she knows you are worth her distended belly after consuming hot Sabri spices. A gift of a few thousand

dollars is always a big help despite the fact that she would have to later face some angry questions from her own Jewish community on Golda Meir Boulevard only a few blocks down."

All charm and smiles, Jan was given a warm welcome. The function started with the recitation of a passage from the Qur'an 49:13:

> He created you in communities and tribes
> So you could identify yourself
> Surely the best among you is the one who is God conscious.

Jan was admired for her fight in the Congress for the right of the minorities and the elderly (there was no elderly present in the meeting though). A Democrat, she attacked President Bush for his invasion of Iraq. Would she support repealing the USA PATRIOT Act? "Yes" she said, "when it would be on the floor in the Congress." So the sponsors of the meeting later declared that they won a point. She went home happy that a few thousand votes in her district were in the bag come election time next year.

In a similar meeting in Ithaca, New York, Congressman Maurice Hinchey blasted the ruling party in Washington. "They think God is Republican and that He talks to them every day before they leave home in the morning." He criticized the Bush administration for the invasion of Iraq. "Where are those weapons of mass destruction?" he asked and chastised the administration for patting Israel on the wrist for defying the rules of the Middle East Peace Road Map. He received a standing ovation from the audience—professors from Cornell, doctors from Ithaca, engineers from Corning—Muslim as well as non-Muslims.

Apparently, Muslims are cultivating close contacts with their elected representatives, their neighbors, and their coworkers. Muslim college students are known to be working in election campaigns for candidates of their choice. The local Muslim community does not have to initiate such moves from the mosque, although politicians as well as other well-known non-Muslims are invited to give talks in the mosques on topics including local or national affairs. Many local community leaders often with positions in their mosques condone such activities. This is not denying the fact that there exist in the United States mosques, which would not permit anything even remotely resembling politics.

However, there is a difference between Muslims going to the mosque for, say, *Juma'* prayers each Friday and going for a political brunch or dinner held only occasionally in a nearby club or a hotel. Going for *Juma'* prayers on Fridays is a duty that no adult Muslim should ever forego. A gathering with a political candidate as guest speaker is a privilege that you may choose not to exercise. You do not have to put any money in the donation box when you go to the mosque for prayers on Fridays although most people donate some money anyway. At political meetings, as infrequent as they are, sponsors of the meeting have plates for sale in order to make campaign contributions for the candidate. The reason for mosque gatherings is definitely more sacred than political gatherings, which are more mundane and secular. However, it is important to note that almost the same people present in political gatherings are the ones who go to the mosque frequently. In the Muslim community of the United States, it seems the more religious one is, the more political he or she is.

Still, the *imam* gets a much wider audience than the political candidate in the Muslim community. The reason for this is that prayers are mandatory and group prayer is the preferred form whenever possible, giving the *imam* a large and consistent audience. The *imam*, if educated and eloquent, commands greater respect and moves many more hearts than a political candidate.

On the other hand, the *imam* does not have to talk politics from the pulpit. He only has to ask you to join him in prayers for the innocent victims, say, in Bosnia, Kosovo, Chechnya, Palestine, and Kashmir. Prayers in the mosque, especially on Fridays, provide an occasion for Muslims to gather at one place in large numbers. As long as they are praying for their brethren under hardship, a political act may be in the offing. Thus, mosque gatherings, far from being political, are nonetheless potentially political crowds. It only takes a smart political candidate to keep his or her eyes open looking for such crowds of the faithful, which are swelling by the day.

Still, there is an element of political refrain in the Muslim community, whether indigenous or immigrant across the United States. Muslims associated with the *Tablighi Jamaat* are strictly apolitical ideologically. Also, there are influential leaders and the *imams* in immigrant as well as indigenous communities who look at American political system as being "un-Islamic," that is being full of lies, deceit, and double-talk. They would not like to pollute their religion with this kind of politics. Lastly, because most immigrant Muslims do not have any background in politics of democracy in countries where they came from, they are not sure that their political efforts would ever be fruitful. So, why bother?

However, as more Muslims have become educated, as more Muslims have become professionals, as more of them have become economically secure, more of them are looking at themselves as being Americans. Moreover, the second generation of immigrants—born and raised in the United States—is already in college or in professions. Members of this generation are already showing signs of political maturity. Many of them like the much-admired Afeefa Sayeed in Virginia (Schumitz, 2003; Shulman, 2003) would rather run for political positions themselves. With an increase in numbers, education, and economic power, can political power be too far behind? At least this is what Muslim community elders are hoping for.

In short, there are signs that the Muslim community is slowly but surely becoming politically conscious and active. There is little doubt that it has the educational, economic, and demographic potential to do so. As areas of Muslim concentration are becoming more visible, as mosques are growing in size and becoming more numerous, and as more educated Muslims, men as well as women, are entering prestigious professions, their political activity has to take off. There seem to be two political forces acting in the Muslim population in

the United States these days. One is the political inertia with increasing resources within the Muslim population. Another is the political candidates and
hopefuls, not necessarily Muslims, actively trying to seek Muslim political
capital.

However, at the national level, there are still too few Muslims at present to
affect the course of national election in a significant way. There are around six
to seven million Muslims present in the United States these days. Despite the
birth rate going above the national average, these six to seven million Muslims
may not be in a position to register more than one or two million voters. The
Islamic Society of North America (ISNA) was more realistic when in its forti-
eth Annual Convention (Labor Day, 2003); it resolved to raise the number of
registered voters to one million. Evidently, one million voters are only too few
to make any appreciable dent in a national election except in a situation where
every single vote counts (like the presidential election of 2000). Moreover, at
the national level, Muslims seem to be too unfocused. While nearly all African
American Muslims are traditionally Democrats, most immigrant Muslims
remain pragmatic and uncommitted. Even so, what emerged in the 2000 and
2004 national elections was the fact that immigrant Muslims tend to give a
block vote. This means that while the African American vote is a constant and
more or less predictable, the immigrant vote is a variable—a wild card that
cannot be taken for granted.

In the presidential election of 2000, immigrant Muslims overwhelmingly
voted Republican. The aides of the Democratic candidate Al Gore were too
slow in recognizing the very existence of the Muslim vote. On the other hand,
candidate George Bush recognized the importance of the Muslim vote and the
sensibilities of the Muslim population in the most closely fought presidential
election in American history. Soon after he criticized the policy of racial
profiling as selectively affecting the Muslim population, leaders of national
Muslim organizations, especially immigrants, made a collective recommendation to go Republican. Until today, American Muslims believe that but for the
Muslim vote, especially in Florida, candidate Bush could not have been elected
president of the United States in 2000.

However, few presidential elections in the future would be as closely contested as the election of 2000. For this reason, Muslim voters could be
expected to have limited clout in national elections for some time to come as
became evident in the 2000 election. There are two main sources of power that
American Muslims could harness. First, Muslims can play powerful political
role where their power is concentrated—at the community level. As the Muslim community is gaining in political clout, those running for positions of may-
ors, governors, congressmen, and senators would have to address themselves to
Muslim voters demands—be they local, regional, national, or international.

Secondly, American Muslims, unlike Muslims in Europe, are an economically successful and prosperous population. With their education and per capita
income being above the national average, they are capable of raising large
amounts of political dollars, which if used wisely, could affect state and even

national policies with respect to Muslim demands. Thus, although they may not have sufficient demographic strength at the national level, they may be in a position to exercise economic clout beyond their local communities, but only if they do not remain as unfocussed as they have remained so far.

A closer look at the programs of the national conferences and conventions of large Muslim organizations in the United States shows a great emphasis on children and the next generation. As the first generation of Muslim immigrants is aging, many believe that a new and a more focused generation is in the offing. Most Muslim leaders are now keeping their hopes in this new generation, which could soon be at the helm of Muslim affairs in the United States.

REFERENCES

Abugudeiri, alTijani. *A Survey of Mosques in America*. Indianapolis: American Trust Publications, 1980.

Mahmati, Hussein H. "Islamic Education in America: Problems and Prospects." Paper presented to the Southeastern Muslim Schools Symposium, Atlanta, Georgia, 1996.

Sakr, Ahmed H. *A Book of Juma' Khutub*. Lombard, IL : Society for Islamic Education, 1998.

Schumitz, Kali. "Children Inspire Her Activism." *Herndon Times*, July 15, 2003.

Shehan, Julie. "Performance and preferences of Muslim and Non-Muslim Students in Southern California." In *Muslim Education* 2002.

Shulman, Robin. "Rinker Drops Out of Race." *Washington Post*, July 31, 2003.

Zoll, Rachel. "Islam Today." *Austin-American Statesman*, July 28, 2003.

5

The Muslim Woman in the United States

There are approximately two million Muslim families in the United States alone. Additionally, there may be one hundred thousand household units in Canada.

The Muslim family in the United States comes in all shades and sizes, and from diverse origins. There are families rooted in immigration from Asia, the Middle East, Africa, Central Asia, Eastern Europe, and the Pacific Islands. Additionally, there are indigenous families, mostly of African American origin, with a sprinkling of people from European descent. Thus, indigenous Muslim families in North America are relatively more uniform in cultural background and ethnicity than immigrant families in general, who are more diverse in their national, linguistic, ethnic, historical, cultural, and other pertinent characteristics. Each Muslim group in the United States has, in its own way, tried to adjust and adapt to the dominant non-Muslim American culture. Whereas it has not been easy for the indigenous family to negotiate the transition toward Islam, it has often been traumatic for the immigrant family to articulate its Islamicity given the pressures inherent to assimilation in the United States. Their circumstances and practices force the first generation immigrant family to quickly adjust to new and often unforeseen situations.

A recent survey done for the Project MAPS (Muslims on American Public Square) at Georgetown University (see table 1 below), shows that the males and the females among Muslims in the United States are almost equal in numbers, with a rounded sex ratio (number of males per 100 females) at 100. However, a closer look shows that in absolute numbers, females outnumber males by a slight margin (2,565 females to 2,555 males). The survey also shows that the male children significantly outnumber the female children in the youngest

Table 1.
Gender Proportions by Age Group (American Muslim Population)

Age	M		F		Total		Sex Ratio
	N	%	N	%	N	%	
1–20	658	51	630	49	1,288	25	104
21–40	532	48	585	52	1,117	22	92
41–60	739	50	746	50	1,485	29	100
61–80	562	50	558	50	1,120	22	101
80+	64	58	46	42	110	2	152
Total	2,555	50	2,565	50	5,120	100	100

Percentages rounded to the nearest whole.
Source: Project MAPS, Georgetown University (2003).

age category (1–20). However, the same table also shows that in the two high-est age categories there is a preponderance of elderly males over elderly females, remarkably different from the general American demographic pattern.

Whatever the nature of the Muslim family in America, demands on Muslim women, especially immigrants, are greater than those on Muslim men. For instance, the demand for sexual modesty affects women more than men. Even if working, women bear a much greater responsibility for the children and others in the family. Although women play an important role in making decisions, husbands are still the patriarchs who have the last word. Women in the Muslim family are called on to play a more crucial role in shaping the family in the United States than women in the Muslim world are. In summary, in the Muslim household in the United States, the female family members play a central role.

Muslim girls in the United States are required to attend weekend religious instruction at the local mosque in addition to their full-time secular classes during the week. There, girls learn the Qur'an and the manners expected of a Muslim woman. Parents are protective of girls to the point of being paranoid lest they lose them to "male predators." They often do extremely well in school, ranking among the top ten or fifteen in a graduating class and often becoming valedictorian or salutatorian. Most female children, contrary to the general pattern in the Muslim world, look forward to college rather to becoming homemakers and mothers.

Whether in college or not, a Muslim woman is more responsive to the demands of her religion as conveyed by her family, the weekend school, and the Muslim community that she lives in. It is now common for indigenous Muslims and those of the immigrant stock to practice *hijab*, the covering of the head and torso with a scarf. Thus, while Muslim men remain indistinguishable from other men as far as their dress is concerned, Muslim women can be easily singled out as being Muslim at any public place. This results in unfortunate incidents of name-calling, use of insulting language, and outright obscene

Table 2.
Muslim Americans in Professions

Profession	M		F		Total	
	N	%	N	%	N	%
Engineering, Electronics	866	28	744	24	1,610	52
Computer Sc., Data Processing	435	14	371	12	806	26
Medicine, Doctors, and Others	122	4	126	4	248	8
Business and Finance	125	4	92	3	217	7
Self employed	94	3	60	2	154	5
Professor Teacher/Imam	19	.6	12	.4	31	1
Lawyer/Police Politics	13	.4	6	.2	19	.6
Other	9	.3	6	.2	15	.5
Total	1,683	54	1,417	46	3,100	100

Percentages are rounded to the nearest whole.
Source: Project MAPS, Georgetown University.

gestures toward these women (CAIR, 2003). A college campus is, perhaps, the safest place for them to be. This is where cultural diversity and "being different" are appreciated. In college, Muslim women often make the dean's list. They typically aspire to becoming professionals: doctors, lawyers, computer scientists, or engineers.

Secondly, few young Muslims, unlike their non-Muslim counterparts, engage in premarital sex or otherwise socialize with men in activities leading to intimate relations with them. There may always be a few exceptional cases, but in general having close and personal relations with an unrelated male is considered to be unbecoming and outright deviant (often with serious consequences) in the subculture of Muslim women.

Thirdly, in selecting a life partner, Muslim women (even indigenous) are expected to seek mediation on the part of their parents or some other elders of the family or the community, a practice imported from the Muslim world and implanted in the American practice. However, as specified in Islam, they retain the right to deny any young man as recommended by their parents if "he does not click."

The prime reproductive years for Muslim women coincide with the prime working age in the United States and most Muslim women pursue a career. This is not because an average Muslim family has to have two incomes in order to survive. In most cases, this is due to their education and their aspiration. Table 2 shows that 46 percent of all working American Muslims are females. The great majority of them are highly trained and in lucrative professions such as engineering, medicine, business, and finance. This helps to enhance their standard of living, makes wives less dependent upon their husbands, and helps women earn the respect of their husbands, enhancing their self respect. It is not easy to demean an educated woman who doubles the family income. This pattern seems to hold across ethnic lines in the Muslim population, whether immigrant or otherwise. In fact, young women in African

American Muslim families, because they are relatively more educated, show a sharp contrast with non-Muslim African American women in this respect.

Older women, who are past their reproductive age, or nearing that, are conspicuously less educated, especially among immigrant Muslims. African American Muslim women of this age, as a whole, are almost equal in education with men (14.5 versus 15 years for men) and immigrant Muslim women in this age category are, on average, 4.5 years behind their husbands in this regard. This results in the almost total dependence of immigrant Muslim women in their forties and above on their husbands. However, these women have typically raised 3.5 children. As their children become adults, Muslim women cast a much stronger influence on the family than their dependent status might imply.

In comparison to her counterpart in the Muslim world, a Muslim woman in the United States has a relatively greater degree of independence within her family. However, this may be a mixed blessing. We do not know whether there is a correlation between women's independence and marital instability, but Muslims in the United States, especially immigrants, have an unusually higher rate of divorce (Ba-Yunus, 2001, 2003). Hovering around 30 percent, which is not as high as that of the United States (almost 50 percent), it is, nonetheless, extremely high—much higher than that in the Muslim world in general.

Though we do not have comparable data for other new immigrant groups in the United States, it is nevertheless important to raise the following question: Are Muslim immigrants becoming Americanized faster than they think? Whereas Americanization may be a slow and a selective process, dissolution of marriage may be the least favored aspect of it among Muslims. What is surprising is that divorce among American Muslims (almost all of them from immigrant groups) seems to have a positive correlation with age. Married couples (in their twenties or early thirties), mostly born and raised in the United States, have the lowest incidence of divorce when compared with foreign-born married couples (in their late forties and early fifties), most of whom were married even before they migrated to the United States. Because those who are born and raised in the United States may be more American than their immigrant parents, who can only be "marginal men" (Park, 1901), the Americanization hypothesis does not appear to be quite plausible. Likewise, the relatively higher level of education among Muslim women and their relatively lower level of dependence on their husbands might not contribute to a higher divorce rate among American-born Muslims. This is so because in the age category with the higher divorce rate (immigrant Muslims), most women are relatively less educated. Most of them do not have any exposure to American schools or colleges, and most of them are homemakers without any outside jobs.

It is possible that the reason for such a high divorce rate among immigrant Muslims may be found in the dilemmas and the trauma of migration, which often entails long periods of separation between spouses before they finally get together and get settled in the United States. This conclusion is reinforced by

the observation that the divorce rate in the African American Muslim population is not even half that of the total Muslim immigrant population.

Perhaps because of their age, most divorced women, rather than remarry,
prefer to stay with their children, who are in most cases married and raising
their own families. This provides such women a secure living environment. It
also provides their children with responsible, experienced, and loving babysitters. Divorced women in younger age brackets, having just come out of dis-
tasteful experiences in marriage, generally do not seem to be in a hurry to
remarry either. Mostly educated and with some kind of employment, their transition from married life to being single all over again seems to be less traumatic. It may be more problematic if they have young children. In this case,
most would prefer to rejoin their parents, who may solve the problem of
babysitting.

A problem of far-reaching consequence facing Muslim women is that of
involuntary celibacy. Part of the problem stems from the fact that Islam allows
exogamy among Muslim men (they can marry women of Christian and Jewish
persuasion), but insists on endogamy among Muslim women. Consequently,
many eligible Muslim men in the United States do get married to non-Muslim
females. This practice leaves a sizeable number of Muslim females without
any matches. Another contributing factor seems to be that Muslim women,
especially those who are educated and have good jobs, like their non-Muslim
counterparts, are not in a big hurry to submit to the demands of their worrying
parents, who want them to get married as soon as possible. Their ability to say
"no" and their desire to wait for the one who "clicks" often reduces their
chances of finding a mate at all. This has been a rather persistent problem
among women of Muslim immigrant families in the United States. A sixty-
year-old woman born to Lebanese immigrant parents can always look back
and see where she missed the boat in her younger years.

Because Islamic injunction clearly poses a dilemma for them, Muslim
women of marriageable age often marry non-Muslim men, provided they first
accept Islam openly and publicly. This practice is quite visible among indigenous Muslim women, and is also, to a lesser extent, found among those of
immigrant stock. This practice has contributed to conversion to Islam on the
part of previously non-Muslim males at a higher rate than conversion of non-
Muslim women (non-Muslim wives of Muslim husbands do not have to convert to Islam).

An Islamic center or a mosque plays a significant role in the lives of a number of men and women. There are around twenty-five hundred such centers,
including those in large metropolitan areas as well as in smaller cities and
towns in the United States. These centers or mosques come to life on Fridays
(the congregation day) and the weekends with various educational and community activities. Because women in the Muslim world generally do not go to
mosques or attend any of their functions, Islamic centers or mosques in the
United States play a unique role, especially as far as Muslim women are concerned. Mosques in the United States are places where Muslim women do not

go for worship only. These are places where they serve on committees, teach if they are qualified, hold symposia and panel discussions, exchange information, and selectively cultivate relations with one another. Whether or not they have jobs or they are going to college, these activities help them in creating their own "primary groups," which provide them informal social circles, help resolve a great many problems in their lives, and provide desirable company for their children. This partly explains the active, although often unrecognized, contribution that Muslim women are making to the stability and growth of Islamic structure in the United States.

In short, Muslim women in the United States have made some gains while having to put up with some unforeseen and traumatic circumstances. In many cases, far from compromising their religious beliefs, they are making their religion into a social factor in their neighborhoods. They are making contributions to a non-Muslim society by playing traditional roles as homemakers, mothers, or babysitters as well as in their capacity as post-modern professionals.

While working on Project MAPS, we randomly chose two hundred Muslim women and requested them to briefly write about their life experiences. These women were chosen from five major cities and five smaller cities and towns. They were contacted through telephone directories, through their family members at different occasions, or through the snowball technique as often used in the social sciences. Out of these, we received life accounts from 113 women. Going through their accounts, we divided them roughly into five major categories. Subsequently, we randomly picked one autobiographical account from each category. Following McCloud (1991), we named these categories after the main character in each category—Aisha, Sara, Naima, Sahr, and Meryam. These categories do not exhaust all types among Muslim women in the United States. However, we believe they do give us a glimpse into the spectrum of important kinds in this population.

Aisha

In her late teens, Aisha graduated with honors from a suburban high school close to New York City. She was born in Queens, New York, where her father, an immigrant from Syria, ran a grocery store serving a growing Middle Eastern population. She has two elder brothers and a younger sister, who is in junior high. Her father now owns two more grocery stores. Her oldest brother is a medical doctor while the other one has an export-import business. Both are married and live close to where their father lives. Their mother, in her late forties, takes care of the family. Both their parents were going to college in Syria before her father came to the United States as a graduate student in 1965.

Aisha hopes to become a medical doctor following in her brother's footsteps. The Osman family has been quite active in Islamic activity in Queens. Her father, other than contributing generously to the establishment of a mosque and a weekend school, has also served as the *imam* of the mosque leading *Juma'* congregation on Fridays from time to time. From the moment of her birth,

Aisha has been breathing Islam. She started *hijab* (head cover) even before she was ten years old. She received her basic Islamic training from her mother, father, and older brothers, and from the weekend school in the mosque. In high school, she took part in the debating society. She read profusely, spoke with eloquence, and won awards. She had very close friends in school. She invited them to her place and often visited their families. They knew about her being a Muslim. This gave her a chance to speak to them about her background, her family, and her religion.

A junior in college, Aisha still loves to participate in the debating society. Early in college she was interested in American literature and political science, but biology and chemistry are her newfound interests that leave her with little time for other activities. Even so, she actively participates in student activities on her campus. She is a member of the student government and served as general secretary on its board. She is also very active in the Muslim Students Association (MSA) and attends *Juma'* congregation regularly. Her being a female does present a few problems in a male-dominated MSA, but she is a member of the executive committee of this organization. She arranges symposia and invites outside speakers as one of her responsibilities. The MSA, due to her role as the general secretary of the executive board of the student government, got a great deal of boost and prestige on the campus.

Aisha does not go out on dates but she does go to the dinner parties and other get-togethers among MSA members and others. "I may like some men better than others, but cultivating intimate relationships with them is against my religion. If someone really likes me and wants to marry me, he can tell me and I might consider him so he or his relatives could contact my parents with a proposal. This is the way it should be," she says. However, Aisha does not think that presently any young man is interested in marrying her. She is not overly concerned about it either.

For now, her vision about her future in the United States is that of becoming a doctor specializing in obstetrics and gynecology so she can serve women who do not want to frequent male doctors. She would like to have a husband working in the field of law or journalism. She would like him to be active in American politics. She hopes to have at least three or four children, educate them, and raise them as conscientious Muslims.

Sara

Presently in her late thirties, Sara is a teacher by profession. She teaches religion to sixth graders in a university town outside of Chicago. She has been a Muslim for more than ten years. She married an African American college graduate, who was attracted by the teachings of Imam Warith Deen Muhammad, head of the Muslim American Society.

Sara's father was a Baptist who wanted his children to become good Christians and respectable Americans. Her father worked for the Chicago Transit Authority. He could hardly afford to maintain a family of six children and an ailing wife. They lived in a rough neighborhood full of unemployed males in their twenties, unwed mothers collecting welfare checks, and street corner gangs on the brink of trouble with the law most of the time.

The community that Sara grew up in was, on all counts, a problematic one. There were churches, but only old people attended them. There were schools, where students learned violence, sex, drug use, and drug peddling. Men did not live very long. They used to disappear suddenly, having been murdered, taken away by the police, or they simply drifted away, never to come back. Women worked hard making money by any means they could—becoming prostitutes, having fatherless babies, or working long shifts as cooks, maids, or nurses' aides.

This community, however, remembered Elijah Muhammad and his Muslims, who lived a pure and religious life. They took care of their women who looked and behaved respectably. They did not drink, nor did they consume any drugs. They had their own small stores and independent businesses. But they practiced Islam, which did not teach Jesus Christ as being the savior. Their temples were neat and clean. In short, they provided their individual members with economic security and self respect that African Americans could not get from the Anglo-Saxon Christian establishment. Even while in school, Sara knew that there was no future for her or her brothers and sisters in the five-block area that they lived in. There certainly was no future for her or them in the city or the country beyond her community of residence. She was only sixteen when her mother died. They did not have enough money for the funeral. It was then that a Muslim woman with four others appeared. They washed the dead body of Sara's mother in their funeral home and buried her in their cemetery— without any charge.

Soon Sara started reading Muslim literature, particularly *Muhammad Speaks*, their newspaper. After Elijah Muhammad died in 1975, his movement went through internal convulsions for some time. One consequence of internal rivalry within the movement was active proselytization on the part of the rival groups. Exposed to their speeches, booklets, newspapers and other literature, Sara, now a high school dropout, found herself becoming inclined more toward the ideology of Imam Warith Deen Muhammad. Her meeting Jameel finally helped her in joining the *imam*'s group, which declared *Sunni* or mainstream Islam as their religion, and changing their temples into mosques. After she married Jameel in a short and simple ceremony, she started working as a receptionist in Imam Warith Deen's office, where Jameel also found work as a teacher in a school run by a neighborhood mosque. Her employers encouraged her to prepare for a high school equivalency examination, which she did in two years after her marriage to Jameel. She also had her first baby girl— Nafisa—at the same time. Soon after Nafisa's birth, Sara joined evening classes in a community college not far from their one-bedroom apartment.

Joining the movement of Imam Warith Deen, now known as the Muslim American Society (MAS), Sara and Jameel wanted to know more about Islam and Muslims in the world and especially in the United States. All of a sudden, her world expanded beyond her local community. She wanted to meet other Muslims in Chicago and beyond. In their quest they encountered several different Muslim groups among immigrants—*Sunni, Shia, Sufi*—Arabs, Pakistanis, Indians, Turks, Iranians, and others. For the first ten months after their marriage, they made it a practice to go to a different mosque in Chicago for the weekly *Juma'* prayers each Friday. This is how they were able to cultivate close contacts with other Muslims, especially among new immigrants. Jameel wanted to go to a Muslim country in order to learn Arabic, the main language of Islam. Soon he managed to get a scholarship for himself as well as Sara from a university in Saudi Arabia. They stayed in Saudi Arabia for one year and came back from there fluent in Arabic. This is how they both gained access to the sources of Islamic law and history.

After they came back from Saudi Arabia, Jameel remained unemployed for a while. Sara became a weekend school teacher in a mosque near Chicago. Soon Jameel got a position in a state prison as a Muslim chaplain, affording him economic security as well as an opportunity to do *dawa* in the prison population. He runs three-hour classes each day on Islam. His student inmates include a number of non-Muslims, all of whom are considered by the prison authorities to be model inmates.

They now have two more children. Both were adopted after their parents died in an accident. Sara and Jameel are raising their three children as Muslims, teaching them the Qur'an and Islamic manners and are hoping that their children will never have to experience what they did when they were growing up in Chicago's South Side.

What is characteristic of Sara and Jamil is that despite its notoriety as a den of crime, violence, and murder, the African American slum of Chicago provides its inhabitants with islands of opportunity for a cleaner and a more peaceful life. What their experience with Islam shows is that you could be saved even if you were destined to become an unwed mother or a drug peddler, and to disappear from life suddenly. More than that, their life shows that exposure to Islam can make you productive citizens raising healthy and respectable families.

Naima

Born in Pakistan, Naima migrated to the United States when she was only five years old. She was born in Karachi when her father was studying as a graduate student in a university in the United States. It was an especially trying time for her mother who became pregnant with Naima a few months before her husband left for the United States—for two years as he promised. It took him four years before he landed a respectable position as a chemical engineer in an oil refinery. It took him another year to receive a "green card," an immigrant visa, for himself and his family. Thus, Naima was almost five before she first set eyes on her father at the Los Angeles international airport. A year later she had a little brother named Rashid and then a sister, Salma, soon after.

Naima's father, Haseeb, was not a strict practicing Muslim, but her mother, Nazish, was. She prayed five times a day as prescribed in Islam. She fasted from dawn to dusk during the holy month of Ramadhan. She covered herself modestly in loose garb consisting of *kurta* (knee-length shirt), *shalwar* (baggy pants), and *dopatta* (long scarf covering her head and falling down to her shoulders and chest area). Naima, Rashid, and Salma used to receive presents of new sets of these traditional Pakistani suits, especially on the occasions of Islamic festivities. Soon, the whole family started going to the neighborhood mosque every Friday and over the weekend. While children joined the weekend Islamic school, their parents became active in other social activities initiated by the mosque. Thus, before Naima graduated from high school, her self perception as a Muslim woman was soundly established.

In college, Naima became active in the Muslim Students Association (MSA), reinforcing her identity through involvement in Islamic activities. As in high school, Naima made several friends in college. Because she prayed five times a day, dressed differently, and did not go out on dates, her friends talked to her about Islam and Muslims. She became a lay proselytizer of Islam within her small circle of friends. She invited them to different events of MSA, often getting them involved in sending invitations, cooking dinners, and occasionally participating in panel discussions on issues relevant to Islam and American society. She graduated from college with a very high grade point average, leaving an impact upon a number of her friends. Some of them accepted Islam. Others became Muslim sympathizers. Most importantly, her involvement in Islamic activities contributed greatly toward strengthening her own Islamic faith.

Having majored in accounting, Naima wanted to work soon after her graduation from college so that she could pay back her loans. However, as hard as she tried, she could not find a suitable position for some time. She attributed it to prejudice against her dress, which betrayed her religious affiliation. About six months after her graduation, she got a job as a clerk in a small bank not far from her home. Soon she found that they expected her to adopt American attire even if she was not directly involved in any public dealings. She was laid off because she refused to do so. For nearly two years she did odd jobs— as a telephone operator, as a substitute teacher, and lastly, as a clerk in an employment agency where she met her future husband—John, who was a Catholic. He wanted to take Naima out, but because of her refusal, he wanted to know about Islam. Before he met Naima, his knowledge about Islam was rudimentary and often biased. However, he remained interested in her and learned more about Islam until he came to know that the only way to take her out was to marry her, and that the only way to marry her was to become a Muslim himself. Soon Naima enrolled in graduate school and landed a position as a graduate teaching assistant in an MBA program. Even so John continued to see her. He took evening courses in Islam and eventually became a Muslim by taking *shehada* in the same mosque where Naima's father and mother had now become quite active. Having become a Muslim paved his way toward marrying Naima. He asked for her hand in marriage by proposing to her father. They got married the day she received her MBA degree in accounting.

John, now Yahya, and Naima have two children and a third baby is due in a few months. John is working as the manager of the same employment firm where he first met Naima, while Naima herself is teaching part-time in the evening in a nearby college.

Sahr

Born and raised in India, Sahr was married when she was not quite twenty years old. She was just beginning her third year in college when she was married to Najeeb, a civil engineer by profession. She never met him or even saw him before they got married. Their marriage was a typical arranged marriage. After her marriage she moved in with Najeeb's parents, who were living about a ten-hour train ride away in a town where there was no college. Najeeb was working on the construction of a dam about three hours away by bus. The construction site had no permanent dwellings. Because of this he could not take his bride to live there with him, but he would come home every weekend, and sometimes even more often. Two years later, when Sahr had a son and was expecting another child, she finally moved to live with her husband, who landed a well-paid job with an American firm in Bombay. Living in Bombay was very gratifying for Sahr and her family. They lived a comfortable life in a suburban development and observed Islamic beliefs and practices as much as they could. Her parents, as well as her in-laws, who were devout Muslims, used to visit them periodically. In sum, their fifteen years in Bombay were quite rewarding. Najeeb became a senior officer in the firm. Their children were doing quite well in school. Sahr was generally satisfied with her life.

However, Najeeb wanted to go to the United States for higher education, hoping to eventually settle there. At first, the very idea of her husband leaving the family behind at least for a while was a nightmare for Sahr. But as a good and a loving wife, Sahr finally reconciled herself with the notion of temporary separation from her husband. After Najeeb left his tearful family, Sahr went to live with her parents for a while, though they were quite old. Every few months she would also take her children to her in-laws. Najeeb took almost two years to finish his graduate studies in California. Soon he got a respectable position in the head office of the same firm that he was with in Bombay. The same firm sponsored him and his family for immigration to the United States. In all, it took him four years before he could go back to India and bring his family back to the United States with him.

By now his oldest son was almost eighteen. He was already in college. His older daughter, also in college, was seventeen. The other two were still in school. At first, for Sahr, as well as for the children, the United States was an exciting experience. They wrote beautiful letters home about friendly people, beautiful neighborhoods, their trips to Hollywood and Disneyland. Sahr was happy that her husband was happy there, although she wished they lived closer to the Islamic center or the mosque, which was about an hour's drive away. They bought another car. The older children took the train to college every day. She drove the younger children to their school every morning and picked them up in the afternoon. Like a typical middle-class wife, she then would go grocery shopping, prepare food, do the laundry, and keep the house clean. Soon she found herself waiting for her favorite soap operas every day and not wanting anything else to interfere with her television schedule.

Thus it seemed that all of them had adjusted themselves beautifully to their new life in the United States. Sahr was at first shocked but slowly reconciled with the discovery that Najeeb used to drink liquor once in a while, especially at office parties or occasional informal gatherings.

About ten months after their arrival in the United States, a telegram from home informed Sahr about the sudden death of her father, whom she loved very much. Evidently, she could not go back to India. According to the Muslim custom back home, she expected everyone to read passages from the Qur'an and pray for the salvation for her father. She also wanted to let the *imam* of the local mosque know about this so he could involve a larger number of people in praying for her father. But Najeeb was so busy. His daily schedule was to leave home early and to return quite late. Sometimes he used to work Saturdays also. This gave him less time to visit the local mosque with his family. He used to go to the downtown Los Angeles praying facility (*musalla*) every Friday for the *Juma'* congregation. Even so, it soon became apparent that the Najeeb family was becoming thoroughly Americanized with a secular character. In six months, the whole family quit using Urdu, their native tongue, and started conversing in English.

Only the older ones still conversed in Urdu. They also read the Qur'an every day. This is so because in college they met Muslim students who, at least among themselves, preferred to speak in Urdu. A strong chapter of the Muslim Students Association kept them involved in Islamic activities on the campus. Additionally, they both took Arabic as a second language in college. For a while it seemed that these college students in the family were the only ones who, while becoming Americans, could still maintain their Islamic faith. The younger children became almost full Americans—in accent, in dress, and in the choice of friends—quickly. Sahr met a few Indian families in a supermarket. She liked some of them and tried to cultivate close family relations with them. There were some Muslim families close by, but their women bored her a great deal. They could not speak English very well and generally covered themselves "unnecessarily from top to toe."

Sunday was almost the only day during the week when all family members could get together, even if only for breakfast. In two years time, it became evident that the older two had a much greater religious inclination than the rest of the family. They wanted to take the young ones to the mosque for the weekend school and tried to enroll them in other mosque activities. When the children went there, they did not like it at first. However, gradually they made good friends who invited them to their homes. One summer they also went to a

Muslim children's camp with their newfound friends. They liked it so much that they went to this camp for three consecutive summers before they graduated from high school. This is how the younger children were introduced to the world of Muslim children in the United States. This is how they started relearning about Islam, its basic beliefs, and practices. Sahr liked this new development among her children, but Najeeb remained indifferent and occasionally hostile.

In fact, as his children were inclining toward Islam, Najeeb was gradually moving away from it. Now in his forties, as his children grew up and were leaving home, his drinking had gradually become more frequent and more open. Sahr felt so lonely and often helpless. Three of her four children were living at least a hundred miles away. With few contacts in the Muslim community she hardly had any company beyond her family. In time Najeeb became louder and even abusive. He argued frequently until one evening he informed Sahr that he was divorcing her. Their youngest daughter, who was still living at home, took her mother's side, as did her brothers and sisters. Seemingly the whole household rebelling against him, Najeeb gave Sahr an Islamic divorce in front of his children as witnesses, and left home permanently.

Divorced Islamically but not legally, presently Sahr is living with her youngest daughter at home. Of her four children, her oldest son is the only one married—to a medical doctor from India. Now in her late forties, her divorce shocked Sahr tremendously, but she is more concerned about the marriage of her children, who are getting older and have no suitable prospects in sight.

Meryam

In her late thirties, Meryam used to be Marianne before she accepted Islam while still in college. Her forefathers migrated from Ireland during the great potato famine in the late nineteenth century. On her mother's side she is part German and part Dutch. Her father had a small printing business in a small town near Dallas. While a junior in college majoring in communications, she met Robert and started dating him. Soon they were engaged to be married. Marianne was always an outgoing person who could make friends easily. Among her other best friends were Naila and Masrour, two sisters from Jordan. These two Jordanian sisters were practicing Muslims, who observed *Hijab*, prayed five times daily, and fasted during the month of *Ramadhan*. It was mainly through her friendship with Naila and Masrour that Marianne became familiar with Islam. She also took two courses in religion, in which she wrote terms papers on Islamic topics. Soon she found herself reading more about Islam. She was still going to her church and often discussed her new interest with her priests, who told her to read about other religions also in her search of "the truth." However, in her quest for "the truth," she came closer to Islam. She attended a few Muslim conferences and conventions. The summer after her graduation from college, she also took a trip to Jordan with her two Muslim friends. As she came closer to Islam, she stopped having sex with

Robert, who although disturbed at first, found her insistence on premarital celibacy to be quite in line with his and her Catholic beliefs.

Soon after she came back from Jordan, she started working in the main library of the University of Texas. This gave her access to further her interest in Islamic literature. She remained in close contact with Muslim students on the campus and also became a regular visitor to the main mosque in the city, where she discussed Islamic issues with a number of people. She came to the conclusion that Islam gave her the most satisfactory answers to her questions. Thus, it did not come as a great shock to Robert when she informed him that she was going to convert to Islam. Though somewhat dismayed with her choice of her new religion, Robert still admired her being a seeker of "the truth." Marianne was invited to dinner by one of the Muslim students on campus. There she declared the *shehada* and took the name Meryam. Robert still loved Meryam and wanted to marry her. He remained intrigued with Islam as a religion. In a few months time he also converted to Islam and married Meryam in the city mosque.

Now proud parents of four children, Meryam and Robert are active participants in the activities of the mosque, as well as the MSA on the campus. Meryam, as outgoing as she always was, started contacts with non-Muslim students as well as their families. Her main goal is to create a balanced understanding about Islam and Muslims in the American population, which has historically as well as culturally had a number of misgivings about Islam. Especially after 9/11, her activities have intensified among non-Muslims. "Why do they hate us?" is the main question they ask about Muslims. Together with others, Meryam founded an organization of women named American Mothers for Peace (AMP), which is now drawing attention from the press and the media.

OVERVIEW

These five personalities mentioned above are not in every respect representative of the categories named after them. Understandably there are as many variations as there are people in each category. However each category has visible traits common to all or nearly all that are in it. For instance, Aisha represents her category in that most of the young women in this category were born and raised in Muslim families, which were immigrants from overseas. All of them were college students with rather high grade point averages. Most of them were practicing Muslims. Most of them were active in student activities, unmarried but without any intimate contacts with anybody and hoping to become respectable professionals. None of them was against marriage or eager to find a husband in the near future. Her character shows the ease with which relatively young Muslim women are able to relate with the larger non-Muslim society around them. Far from being hostile or prejudiced, these young Muslim women are American at the individual, familial, and the societal level.

Sara, on the other hand, represents those women who could have easily suffered or even been killed in the African slums of Chicago. Most women in this category belonged to large families. While growing up, they did not know what future they had other than attaching themselves with gangs, becoming prostitutes, or, if lucky, finishing high school and becoming nurse's aides. At the bottom of the socioeconomic ladder, they just did not have much control over their environment. They were lucky that they were living at a time when Islamic forces were competing to draw more adherents. Islam saved Sara and many others like her in that they have stable families, good education, and respectable sources of income. Not all women in this category have peaceful lives. Some had hard times due to divorce, lingering troubles with the law, and problems in raising children. However, Islam gave all of them a degree of self respect, social security, and status that they could not even dream of having before Islam entered their lives. It was not easy for them. They had to work hard for what they achieved.

Naima belongs to the group of Muslim female college graduates who struggled against the anti-Islamic prejudice and stereotyping that exists, especially in the job market in the United States. All employers naturally have to be careful in their dealings with their customers. One dimension of their timidity is their sensitivity to the customers' tastes, beliefs, and their cultural patterns of approval and rejection—of color, attire, and accent of the people they encounter in everyday life. In practice, only those that can attract rather than turn customers away are hired. Not all women in this category have insisted on wearing *hijab*. Not all of them resisted their employers' wishes to remove their *hijab*. Not all of them lost their jobs because of their insistence on wearing *hijab*, but nearly all of them encountered situations of prejudice of one kind or another when their religious affiliation became known. Evidently, these women were not qualified and experienced enough to be considered indispensable in the job market.

What is interesting to note is that quite a few Muslim women in this category were married to white American males who became Muslims; some of them becoming very active in local and national Islamic activities. Nobody can say if this is going to be a trend in the future because of the situations that eligible Muslim women find themselves in. However, this practice is very different and shows a much greater attachment to Islam on the part of those in our sample compared to the daughters of earlier immigrants (early or the middle twentieth century, for instance), who married non-Muslim men because they could not find Muslim husbands (Aswad, 1991).

Sahr is one of those women who saw happier days before. Very happy with a promising future in their early days of marriage back home, these Muslim women wished they had not migrated to the United States. All of them started with career-oriented husbands with promising job prospects. Not all of them were left behind when their husbands first embarked on their journey to the United States. Not all of them had become mothers before coming to the United States. Not all of them belonged to very religious families to begin with. However, what is common to all of these is their relatively low level of formal education. In any case, they were not educated enough to go on their own if something would happen to their marriage due to, say, death, divorce, or separation. In many cases, their families showed early signs of assimilation to American culture—giving up the native tongue, adopting American attire, drinking liquor even if occasionally, and having minimal contact with other Muslim families. In their late thirties or early forties, not all of the women in this category were divorced or facing divorce. But relations between husband and wife were strained in most cases. This created anxiety as to their future prospects because they were almost completely dependent on their husbands. "Where would I go, what would I do without him?"

Children were the most valuable assets they had. Not all of them married, which was another source of worry for their mothers. Children almost invariably supported their mothers against perceived highhanded dealings by their fathers. What is noteworthy is that of all Muslim women, this immigrant group is most susceptible to divorce or separation.

Lastly, Meryam belongs to the category of the Muslim women of European descent. As Meryam's account shows, not all white women become Muslim as a consequence of marrying Muslim men. Indeed, it seems that a growing number of them are becoming Muslims on their own because of what they call their search for the truth. However, there has to be some initial contact with the Muslims, not necessarily men, who leave an impact upon them and stimulate in them a desire and interest to study Islam with empathy. They may or may not end up having a Muslim husband. But what is important to them is that they remain active in creating an understanding of Islam among their colleagues, friends, children, and others. Like their black sisters, conversion to Islam to them means embarking on a mission.

It is clear from the above that for most Muslim women with an immigrant background, life in the United States revolves around their families. An exception to this rule has been relatively youthful college students or college graduates, who are hoping to pursue professional careers, or already working. Indigenous Muslim women, on the other hand, despite taking on the usual family obligations, are quite active in community activities, thus leaving an Islamic impact on their immediate social environment. Most of them who are going to college or have been to college seem to have been significantly affected by the activities of the MSA or similar organizations on most campuses in the United States. Although there is a national MSA, what has been important in the lives of most women of college age is the local MSA, which is primarily responsible for getting the flock involved in various Islamic activities on a campus-wide basis. It seems that locally MSAs draw their strength not merely from activating Muslim population, but also by relying on non-Muslim women. There is little doubt that the MSAs and individual Muslims have served as ambassadors of Islam in the United States for a long time.

Generally, one would expect an American Muslim woman to be apolitical. At best, she would be expected to follow her husband when it comes to politics. After all, the perception is that a woman observing *hijab* and married with children to care for would rather stay home most of the time. This scenario fits very well with the role a Muslim woman has been known for traditionally. At least, this is the impression that our subjects give in their accounts.

However, the traditional role of women has gone through some important changes in the Muslim world. Long before Golda Meir became prime minister of Israel and Margeret Thatcher that of the United Kingdom, Fatima Jinnah ran a very energetic campaign for the office of president of Pakistan against General Ayub Khan, the military ruler of Pakistan. Few people remember today that, in her bid, Jinnah was vigorously supported by *Jamaate Islami*, one of the most conservative Islamic parties of Pakistan.

It is a well-known fact by now that American Muslim women, especially those in college, have been quite active in politics. They have worked for the candidates of their choice in various capacities—locally as well as at the state level. The case of Afifa Saeed shows that, even if with *hijab* and married with a few children, Muslim women are now running for political offices themselves (CAIR, 2003). And there is no scarcity of Afeefa Sayeeds in the American Muslim community. This must not come as a big surprise. In fact, one may wonder why such an enterprising population took such a long time to register on the American political scene.

REFERENCES

Aswad, Barbara C. "Yemeni and Lebanese Muslim Immigrant Women in Southeast Dearborn, Michigan," in *Muslim Families in North America*, edited by Earl H. Waugh, Sharon McIrvin Abu-Laban and Regula Burckhardt Qureshi, eds. Alberta: The University of Alberta Press, 1991.

Ba-Yunus, Ilyas. 2003. "How do Muslims in North America Divorce?" In M. Akhtar (ed.) *Muslim Family in Dilemma: Quest for Western Identity*. Forthcoming.

Ba-Yunus, Ilyas. "How Do Muslims in America Divorce?" *Islamic Horizons*, Spring 2001.

Bukhari, Z., ed. *Muslims' Place in the American Public Square*. New York: Altamira Press, 2004.

CAIR (Council on American-Islamic Relations). "Muslim Women in Hijab," in Council on American-Islamic Relations. [http:www.cair@cairnet.org], November 30, 2003.

McCloud, Beverly Thomas. "African American Women." In *The Muslims of America*, edited by Yvonne Yazbeck Haddad. New York: Oxford University Press, 1991.

Park, Robert E. "Human Migration and the Marginal Man." *American Journal of Sociology* 33 (1901): 881–93.

6

Guilty until Proven Innocent: The Aftermath of 9/11

Paul Findley, an ex-congressman from Illinois once wrote (2001:61):

> Years of correspondence with Muslims and discussions in many parts of the Islamic world have not made me an authority on Islam, but I believe the experience has given me a realistic understanding of the religion's image problem in the United States.

Findley continues by cataloging incidents of what could be called "anti-Islamism" in the United States during the five-year period before the publication of his book. These incidents include, among others, the firing at the mosques full of worshippers in Memphis, Tennessee, the Muslim communities being denied the right to buy property in order to open a school in Chicago, Muslim women in *hijab* being publicly dishonored and ridiculed in Los Angeles, the Oklahoma City bombing being attributed to "jihad in America," and even a robber trying to rob a bank in New Jersey posing as a Muslim.

All these and many more regrettable incidents against Muslims took place before the terrorist attacks of 9/11. In fact, some believe that 9/11 brought to the surface sentiments that have only been dormant with respect to Islam and Muslims in American culture for a long time—from individual sensibilities and government actions to the proclamations of some very respectable religious leaders. The outrage of 9/11, it seems, liberated the prejudice against Islam and its adherents—a sentiment not to be expressed publicly without running the risk of being labeled as bigoted in this multiethnic and multireligious society loudly proclaiming pride in its secular values.

Americans are generally nice people. To say "thank you" or "sorry" to someone, to hold the door for someone, for instance, are American cultural traits. Americans in their individual capacity always seem to have pleasant surprises in reserve. Recently, one of the authors of this book, after finishing his burger in a mall, spilled the contents of his tray—dirty napkins, empty tomato ketchup packets, some mustard in a plastic cup—on the floor. Even before he was able to bend to pick the tray, a high-school-age youth suddenly left the line in front of the restaurant, and helped him gather all the contents and threw them in the garbage container. Why did he do this? Did he expect some favor in return? Did he expect some reward in heaven? Or, was he just being nice to a stranger? Examples of this kind of behavior abound in the United States. Most Americans, irrespective of race or religion, are neighborly, friendly, and charitable. Despite a great deal of opposition to immigration, most ordinary Americans go out of their way to accommodate new arrivals in their midst. Newcomers are often invited to churches, into homes, and are befriended. Even in states where race consciousness is high—southern California, Texas, and Florida among others—new arrivals, much to the dismay of Buchanan (2002), have outnumbered or are about to outnumber native-born Americans.

Is such a decent and polite nation like the United States really anti-Islamic at its core? We shall try to provide an answer to this question in this chapter.

THE ROOTS OF ANTI-ISLAMIC FEELINGS IN THE UNITED STATES

Many Muslims emphasize that anti-Islamic feelings in the United States are inherited from Europeans. What we know from history and pre-history is that the people clinging to the margins of the Mediterranean Sea have seldom remained friendly toward one another. Especially those on the northern shores—the Greeks, Romans, French, and even the British—have often collided with the Persians, Arabs, and the Turks living along the eastern and southern shores of this strategic sea. Throughout their long history, they have competed for each other's lands, tried to colonize one another, and even tried to ethnically cleanse the conquered territories. Thus, we see that the Romans once ruled nearly the whole coastal area of the Mediterranean. Greeks Hellenized nearly all of the eastern Mediterranean down to the Nile delta where Alexander the Great established a city, which, even centuries later, still carries his name. The conquerors looked at the conquered with contempt as being uncivilized savages worthy only of being sold as slaves and concubines. Then, united under Islam, came the Arabs and the Turks who turned the tables starting in the seventh century. They ruled Spain for six hundred years and were knocking at the doors of Vienna, which, more than once was forced to clamp behind the city walls trying desperately to stop the Turkish invaders. Christian Europe rallied temporarily under the banner of the Crusades, but only briefly (around one hundred years). It looked to many as if Islam could not be stopped and that the days of Christianity were numbered. The European Christian frustration is reflected in their anti-Islamist folklore and literature that was produced over the last few centuries.

However, starting in the sixteenth century, technological advances in Europe helped usher a new era, whereby the Arabs and the Turks were finally ejected. Europeans and the neo-Europeans—the Americans—again dominated the Middle East and, indeed, nearly the whole world.

This centuries-long history of mutual rivalry and warfare left little room for respect between the contenders living on different sides of the Mediterranean. One has to only turn pages of the post-Crusade literature to find out the negative stereotypes with which Europeans looked upon their adversaries to the south and east. The events of 9/11 may be a reminder that the one-hundred-year-long rule of the Crusaders in the Holy Land and the area around it must have created counter stereotypes of the *"Farangi"* (or the French the name the Europeans were known by in Palestine) in the minds of the people of the Middle East. It is, however, difficult to find anti-European references in Arabic or Persian writings of the period.

Most Americans, being descendants of European immigrants, grow up with a folklore in which negative images of the people, cultures, and religion of the Middle East persist. Now that Western colonialism is past history, it is replaced by a big-brother type attitude toward Muslims. According to Avineri, an Israeli scholar (1993:167):

> The underlying assumption has always been that Islam—as a culture and not merely a religious creed—was primitive, underdeveloped, retrograde, at best stuck in the memory hole of a medieval splendor out of which it could not disentangle itself without a radical transformation; and this could only be based on Western, "rational," "progressive" values. *Ex Occidente lux.*

In more recent history there have been three major events that have made Americans more apprehensive of Muslims in general. The first of these has been the nagging problem of Palestine, for which most Americans blame the Palestinians rather than the Israelis. The second event has been the oil embargo imposed by the oil-producing countries of the Middle East in 1973. This was not merely an act of defiance by a group of countries that were almost totally dependent on the United States for just about everything. The oil embargo hurt the feelings of the American public just as it hurt their pocketbook because of the sudden rise in the price of oil. Consequently, the American economy ran into a cycle of inflation and recession. The third major event in recent history was the Iranian Revolution of 1978, which came as an utter shock to both the American government and people. Initiated in the name of Islam, this revolution created exchanges of very negative pronouncements from either side. Naturally, the American public was affected by the events resulting in the creation of a negative image of Iran and of Islam in general. A new term "Islamic fundamentalism," conjuring up images of "Christian fundamentalism," was introduced into the American vocabulary.

This is how Islam became implicated in a long list of things that most Americans could do without. It seems America's first instinct is to look at the Arabs and the Muslims in general with some disdain. Just to illustrate the point, Saudi Arabia has consistently supported American policies ever since the administration of Franklin D. Roosevelt, who on his way back from Yalta, met King Ibn Saud on the U.S.S. *Quincy* in the Suez Canal in 1945. During the Cold War when the Soviets were arming Syria, Egypt, and Iraq, Saudi Arabia remained staunchly pro-American. In its efforts to drive the Soviet forces out of Afghanistan in 1980s, Saudi Arabia cooperated closely with the Reagan administration. In 1991, King Fahad hosted the Desert Storm troops in order to oust Saddam Hussein's armies from Kuwait. Few people are aware that in 2003 campaign against Iraq, Saudis secretly allowed coalition forces to use its three air bases, permitting special forces, having been provided with cheap oil, to stage attacks from its soil. Between 250 and 300 U.S. Air Force planes staged from Saudi Arabia, including AWACS, C-130s, refueling tankers, and F-16 fighters. In addition, Saudi Arabia also played a key role during the oil price explosion of 2004. At the personal request of President Bush, the Saudis cajoled its OPEC partners to control the price rise, thus mitigating the effects of the rising prices on the American economy. And, yet *National Review* calls Saudis "terror's bankers." Michael Ledeen includes Saudis on his target list of "terror masters." An article in *Commentary* magazine indicated that Saudi Arabia be "taken down" as part of a "World War IV" of hostile Arab regimes (Buchanan, 2004: 7). A Time/CNN poll shows that 72 percent of Americans are deeply distrustful of Saudi Arabia as an ally, 71 percent believe that Saudi Arabia is not cooperating with us in the war on terrorism, and 88 percent of Americans simply have an unfavorable impression of Saudi Arabia (Beyer & Macleod, 2003: 40). Understandably, the revelation that many of the hijackers of 9/11 were from Saudi Arabia did not help these perceptions.

On the other hand, the deeds and misdeeds of Europeans and neo-Europeans in the minds of the people of the Middle East are not merely a part of medieval history. For most of them, domination of Muslim lands, especially by Britain, France, and now the United States, is a matter of immediate past, even of the present. For most of them, the dismemberment of the Arab lands into feudal and semi-feudal principalities after World War I, the help extended to the local sultans and the military brass in order for them to remain in power, and the state of Israel, which could not be established and sustained without European and American help, are matters of the present and are a painful aspect of the ongoing Arab and Muslim experience. The American invasion of Iraq in spring 2003 is only the latest reason why "they hate us," Saddam Hussein notwithstanding. More recently, the sadistic treatment of Iraqi detainees at Abu Ghraib near Baghdad at the hands of their American captors provoked a flood of protests from all over the world and brought American prestige in the Arab world to its lowest point. Abu Ghraib should raise another question: "Why do we Americans seem to hate Muslims?"

Thus, it seems that history started on the wrong foot for the people living on opposite shores of the Mediterranean. Let us call it the Great Mediterranean Divide. Anti-Islamism is one aspect of this Great Divide. Over the years, Europeans and Americans have had serious misgivings about Islam and

Muslims just as the Muslims have harbored such sentiments about the West over the centuries. However, past history aside, contemporary Muslims have by and large come to admire Western economic and political values. The common man in the Arab street would like to have a taste of democracy, the rule of law, and a respectable quality of life for himself and his children in his lifetime.

It must not, therefore, come as a surprise to see how Muslim immigrants come to quickly settle and feel at home in American society despite innumerable setbacks. Unlike many Muslim immigrants in Europe, those who headed for the United States have prospered educationally, professionally, and economically. Having little prior experience with democracy, they seem to gain pleasure from seeing political candidates come regularly to their neighborhoods or even their homes. A few anti-Islamic gestures—some serious, some not so—would be a small price to pay. Some Muslims thought it might be that they had not done enough to educate their host society about themselves and the creed they belonged to. Then came 9/11.

THE AFTERMATH OF 9/11

What most Muslims would view as anti-Islamic attitudes flared up in the United States occasionally before 9/11 as evidenced by government proclamations, television debates, newspaper articles, and denial of opportunities to buy property, especially to establish mosques. Even occasional physical abuse had been reported. The anti-Islamic sentiment came to the surface each time an incident occurred in the Middle East, such as the Arab-Israeli wars or the oil embargo. Some even made a career of pointing their finger at American Muslims as potential terrorists. Findley (2001) lists some of these in his rather widely read book in the United States.

However, the story of anti-Islamic sentiment in the United States before 9/11, as un-American as it was, pales when compared with the way prominent Americans, some of them the gatekeepers of the law, treated their fellow citizens after 9/11. The way Muslim citizens and immigrants were treated has been painfully shocking. Muslim Americans, when approached, are often quite candid in expressing their anxieties and concerns. Responses of those in our sample are in general agreement with their responses, especially on the issues of their major concerns. For instance, to most of them, the government definitely looked more ugly, some Christian leaders suddenly became sinister, and the Zionist extremists had another chance to attack Muslim Americans as the American streets suddenly became dangerous. However, as the reaction of nongovernmental agencies and leaders seemed to be subsiding with time, the American government and its reactive agencies still seemed threatening in the Muslim perception.

The Perception of Muslims as Terrorists

The day of 9/11 was a numbing experience for most American citizens, as well as for the government. Everyone, including the Muslims, seemed to be in disbelief. At least for a few weeks it appeared that Muslim Americans were going to be spared (although television and especially radio broadcasts were already casting what looked like malicious and suggestive commentaries that were scary and suggested cause for concern). For a few days, at least, Muslims in the United States, citizens, resident or otherwise, were allowed to live their routine. There was no internment in the Japanese-American style. In this twenty-first century in the throes of globalization, in the United States there has to be a justifiable legal reason or at least some semblance of legality to warehouse even a fraction of any people. In addition, Muslims come in all colors and shades and the fact that they come from various cultural backgrounds makes it impossible to distinguish some Muslims from the non-Muslim American man or woman. Besides, it had been only ten years since the Japanese-American survivors of the World War II internment were asked to forgive the misdeeds of the government. The living memory of the Japanese internment probably prevented a similar project, but what was allowed was an unprecedented large-scale authority to arrest and detain people and transgress their civil rights

This time around, a whole new act—*Uniting and Strengthening America by Providing Appropriate Tools Required to Intercept and Obstruct Terrorism*, better known as the USA PATRIOT Act—was rushed to Congress and signed into law by the president on 26 October 2001. Critics have charged that the act gives the Executive branch the power to circumvent the requirement of the Fourth Amendment: probable cause when conducting wiretaps and searches. In his review of James Bouvard (2003), Raimondo (2003:27) writes:

> The sheer number—and absurdity—of the incidents described by Bouvard—in which innocent individuals have been charged, jailed and held incommunicado, their lives destroyed by callous, downright stupid government bureaucrats—is a phenomenon that would have conservatives up in arms if carried out by the Clinton administration, past or future. That people were being rounded up arbitrarily to jack up the numbers of "apprehended terrorists" recalls the Soviet style of rule, where "it did not matter how many bushels of potatoes were rotten" as long as the five year plan was fulfilled. In the same way ... the success of the investigation after 9/11 was gauged largely by the number of people rounded up, regardless of their guilt or innocence.

Although neither Bouvard nor Raimondo mention that Muslims were the main sufferers under the impact of the USA PATRIOT Act, others have pointed out the extent to which Muslims have suffered from the government's action. In fact, the USA PATRIOT Act seems to have come into effect a few days before it was signed into law. According to Arshad, our main informant in Chicago, less than a week after 9/11, the bustling Devon Avenue in Chicago became a ghost town. Agents of the Immigration and Naturalization Service and those of Alcohol, Tobacco, and Firearms apprehended people almost at will. It was like a "bum rap." Those who were not rounded up by the police did not dare to come out on the street. Arshad was slow to realize what was happening. He had to pay for his folly by spending one harrowing night behind bars during which he was fingerprinted and photographed. They did not let him sleep. They subjected him to a barrage of questions, some embarrassing and demeaning. He was lucky. The following morning, they grudgingly came to accept his claim that he was a bona fide student and let him go, hungry, suffering from lack of sleep, and under severe psychological trauma.

Even out-of-town visitors, some from as far as California invited to dine with their hosts in Chicago, had to face the same ordeal. It almost looked as if the USA PATRIOT Act was introduced *ex post facto* in order to justify what government agents were doing to begin with. One anonymous Iranian remarked, "It was like my country under the Shah—a knock at the door after midnight was the most feared sound." Tim Thomas from Haiti noted that "it was like the regime of Baby Doc all over again." In short, in the wake of 9/11, the spirit of vengeance against Muslims by the authorities brought the United States down to the level of some of the worst Third World states.

According to Mujahid (2003), writing two years after 9/11, according to government admission, 27,000 Muslims were interviewed, interrogated, investigated, or had their homes raided. Of these, 6,483 were detained or arrested, 3,208 were deported, and 13,434 were in the process of being deported. Additionally, 144,513 Muslims were specially registered, interviewed, fingerprinted, and photographed under NSEERS (National Security Entry Exist Registration System) as introduced by the Justice Department. The FBI, the INS (Immigration and Naturalization Service), the U.S. Customs Service, and the agents of the Department of Alcohol, Tobacco, and Firearms raided Muslim homes and businesses. Often the victims and their families were raided twice, some even three times, because of a lack of coordination among the agents of these departments. Often, the victims were some of the most respectable members of their respective communities.

Just to illustrate the point, on 20 March 2002, federal agents raided a number of offices of the International Institute of Islamic Thought (IIIT) and the Graduate School of Islamic and Social Sciences in Virginia. The homes of the workers in these offices were also raided the same day. Safa, the daughter of one of those workers, was at home with her mother that morning. She was getting ready to go to college when, just outside the living room window, she saw a few suspicious-looking, heavily-armed characters proceeding toward the front door. They broke into the house and put Safa and her mother down, handcuffed them, and dragged both women by their hands into the living room sofa. They did not identify themselves, nor did they explain the purpose of their visit. They ransacked the whole house. They took away with them practically everything in the house, even children's toys. Both women requested the raiders to let them cover their hair as is customary for Muslim women, but to no avail. "It would have been much worse if you were in your country," said one of the federal agents to Safa. 'What are you talking about?' she asked. "This is my country. I am an American. I was born and raised here."

In yet another case that day, Aisha was still asleep in bed when the agents raided her home. Pulled out of her bed, she found herself staring into the barrel of a machine gun. They threw her on the living room sofa and ransacked the whole place. The irony is that her husband was out of town—on a federal government assignment in the Caribbean.

According to a report by CAIR (2003:4), affidavits that led to these raids were sealed and thus the targeted individuals and organizations were not informed about what the government suspected and why these measures were taken in these cases. No criminal charges were filed. The government did not produce any evidence of suspicion either. These are not isolated cases. As mentioned above, federal agents engaged in 27,000 such cases of search, interviews, and raids in the aftermath of 9/11. How many more American citizens like Safa and Aisha had and would have to go through such physical, psychologically shocking, and demeaning ordeals is anybody's guess.

The government did not merely introduce the USA PATRIOT Act. It openly encouraged people to report if they saw any suspicious characters without realizing that but for a fundamental trusting character of most Americans, this could have easily created a nationwide environment of mutual suspicion and vendetta reminiscent of Nazi Germany during World War II. Even so, as reported by CAIR (2003), the FBI received, in less than a year, a few hundred thousand calls by private citizens regarding "suspicious characters." Naturally, the FBI could follow through only a few thousand of these leads, nearly all of which were found to be false, with near tragic consequences for these American citizens.

One such case, which immediately received wide, minute-by-minute coverage from the media, involved three Muslim medical graduates traveling in August 2002 from Chicago to Miami to resume their internships in a hospital. After driving for more than twelve hours, they took a break in order to freshen up and eat breakfast in a restaurant in a small town in Georgia. As they ate, chatting and laughing, they hardly knew that they were under surveillance by a woman who suspected them of plotting an attack in Miami similar to that of 9/11. She wrote down their license plate number and called the police. This triggered an incident that proved to be a hoax, but resulted in disastrous consequences for the three interns, an embarrassment for the federal and state of Florida authorities, as well as for the media due to the false accusations against the interns.

A statewide advisory in Florida was issued against these students traveling in two cars. A trap was laid for them at a tollbooth on the Alligator Alley part of I-75 in south Florida. The occupants of both cars soon found themselves surrounded by the agents yelling, shouting orders, and dragging them out of their cars without identifying themselves. They were strip-searched and their baggage was torn open and thrown on the roadside. Then their cars were stripped with the help of robots and sniffing dogs. Panic-stricken and bewildered, the interns were grilled over and over again individually for nearly twelve hours. The national media had a field day telecasting live coverage of the capture of "possible Islamic terrorists," focusing on their belongings, their wrecked cars, and even their home-cooked food. Their bewildered relatives in

Chicago were not spared either; their homes were searched and they were also subjected to hours of questioning. The twelve-hour search of these medical graduates did not yield anything for which to arrest them. To cap the whole episode, they were falsely accused of driving through the toll booth without paying the toll, which later proved to be an outright lie. The Miami hospital wasted little time in canceling their internships.

Finally, they were released in their battered cars. The caller, who initiated the whole incident, entered a local hospital complaining of chest pains. To be fair to the media, Larry King invited these interns for a live interview on CNN, in which it came to the fore that even the accusation that they did not pay the toll at the booth on I-75 was false. The Miami hospital, under pressure from the local Muslim community, gave them back their internships. Subsequently, they finished their internships in due course.

Although after 9/11 nearly all American Muslims became suspect overnight, Americans of Afghani, Egyptian, Pakistani, and Saudi origin had to worry the most. In less than a year after that fateful day in September 2001, more than thirty-five hundred Pakistani residents of only one state, New York, were forced to leave the United States According to a report in the *Washington Post*, this resulted in a nine billion dollar net gain in the foreign reserves of Pakistan (Powell, 2003). Naturally, in this case what was a gain for Pakistan was a loss for New York, which could hardly afford it in those dire economic times. As the neoconservatives increased their pressure on the Bush administration to attack Iraq toward the end of 2002 and the beginning of 2003, more and more Iraqi Americans also came under surveillance. Immigrants or citizens of Iraqi background, who were sending the usual money to poor relatives back home, were suddenly under suspicion regardless of their feelings for Saddam Hussein and his Bathist gang, how long they had lived in the United States, or what they contributed to their community. Iraqis could be deported, detained indefinitely without charge, or indicted on numerous charges with the amount of bail set way beyond their ability to pay.

An illustration of the above is the case of Dr. Rafil Dhafir and his Texan wife who came to Syracuse, New York, in 1978. Dr. Rafil, as he is generally known, was born and raised in Iraq. He escaped from the oppressive rule of Saddam Hussein in the early 1970s and came to Texas where he finished his internship and residency in oncology. In the quarter of a century that he had been in the Syracuse area, he established a respectable practice. He became an active and an honorable member of the Islamic Society of Central New York centered at the mosque across the street from Syracuse University. He became known for his own very generous donations to the mosque and especially the help that he gave to the African American families in need. He became known among senior citizens of Oneida, New York, for the great care and concern with which he treated them. Sally Perkins, an eighty-year-old of Camden "knew" that, with Dr. Rafil around, she was not going to die of breast cancer although her mother and two of her aunts had died of this disease. Approaching eighty-five, she visited Dr. Rafil numerous times for matters that turned out to be false alarms in the course of years. Robert Dovailes of Oneida, New York, remembers how his wife, dying of cancer at age sixty-seven, thought so highly of Dr. Rafil.

Among others, Dr. Rafil did two things that he thought were extremely important contributions he could make as a Muslim American, but which came to haunt him later. First, he actively participated in the Islamic Assembly of North America (IANA), an organization dedicated to creating a good understanding of the Qur'an and the *Sunnah* and cultivating Islamic personal character.

Secondly, after sending money to the poor relatives back home for some time, he laid the foundation of Feed the Needy, as a charitable organization, supposedly a part of IANA, dedicated to providing food to the starving children of Iraq under Saddam Hussein's dictatorial rule. On the occasion of *Eid al Adha* (the Feast of Sacrifice commemorating the divine saving of Ishmael from being sacrificed), Muslims all over the world sacrifice animals (a goat, a sheep, or a cow) and distribute meat among the poor. American Muslims also do this, but many of them send money overseas to their relatives or to different organizations so they can perform this act of sacrifice on their behalf and give the meat to the poor and the needy. Feed the Needy was aimed at tapping, although not exclusively, this very resource. Many Muslims, not necessarily Iraqi Americans, out of a feeling for the Iraqis under Saddam's rule, contributed to the efforts of this charitable organization. By writing a check or giving one's credit card number to Feed the Needy, one would have fulfilled one's religious obligation.

Over the years, Feed the Needy expanded and was doing quite well until one cold snowy day in March 2003 when the axe fell. As usual, Dr. Rafil got up at five in the morning, washed for the *fajr* (early morning prayers) and drove in his car toward the mosque, about twenty miles away in Syracuse. He was hardly a few minutes on road when the federal agents stopped him and took him away. That very day three other employees of Feed the Needy were also apprehended.

The apprehension of Dr. Rafil resulted in serious economic shockwaves in the Syracuse area. Three of his employees at Feed the Needy lost their jobs. Three of his employees at his Oneida clinic and four of them at his Camden clinic lost their jobs. In addition, scores of poor families, mainly African American, who received regular weekly or monthly stipends from him, were all of a sudden left out in the cold. All those who were put behind bars could hardly afford to bail themselves out. One of his employees at Feed the Needy was a part-time worker. He also worked as a part-time Muslim chaplain in a nearby New York state correctional facility. He was fired from the facility the day after he was apprehended. He was also teaching as a part-time instructor of mathematics at the State University of New York campus at Oswego. Three days after his arrest, the president of the university went to his class. She announced to the students that he was no longer their teacher, period.

Dr. Rafil was charged on eleven counts. Considered to be a flight risk, his bail was fixed at an impossible fourteen million dollars. Generally sleepy and somewhat boring, the upstate New York newspapers suddenly had something exciting to report. The day after the arrest of Dr. Rafil and his two employees in Feed the Needy, a full two-page story sketching their histories and the reasons for their arrest was published. Many wasted little time in convicting him before the court. "I did not know that terrorists were living in our midst," wrote one reader. However, most other readers, including the area clergies, wrote lengthy letters in support of these men.

The federal agents interviewed and searched three hundred additional Muslim individuals in Syracuse, some of them more than once. Individuals were commonly asked about their county of birth and their date of entry into the United States. They could hardly believe when one Muslim woman replied that her ancestors came to the United States from Ireland soon after the Civil War. "Then how come you are a Muslim?" one interrogator asked.

For the Syracuse Muslim community, the incident was like a collective punishment; they felt like second-class citizens. Six months after their arrest, three of Dr. Rafil's companions were freed on bail. None of the charges against Dr. Rafil himself were dropped. The worst charge against him was that of money laundering. He was using IANA's tax exemption for Feed the Needy operations, and for Feed the Needy's sending of money rather than food to Iraq as required by the law. Evidently, even these charges have nothing whatsoever to do with terrorism, money laundering, or breaking the rules of charity. Being the only Iraqi American among those arrested in the Syracuse area, it is apparent that he would be the last to go free. Even that may take some time as long as hostilities continue in Iraq. However, he is quickly becoming a test of the American criminal justice. How long can he be kept behind bars without a day in court? After all, he was not arrested under the USA PATRIOT Act. Dr. Rafil's case was finally brought to court more than a year and half after his arrest on October 19, 2004. At the time of this writing, his case is still pending in the Federal Court in Syracuse.[1]

These are only some of the multitudes of cases that involve American citizens. The government seems to have gone on a wild goose chase. The case of the three medical students in Florida was particularly embarrassing because the media covered it live. But raids on family homes in Virginia and Dr. Rafil's arrest in Syracuse are no less embarrassing because the government agents could not find a shred of evidence linking them with terrorism. In nearly five hundred similar cases in the two years after 9/11, the government was partly successful only in three cases, ending in plea-bargaining for lesser charges, and those on technical grounds. What the government action did succeed in doing was to harm innocent American citizens and to put them under conditions of extreme physical as well as psychological trauma and hardship.

According to some of our informants in New Jersey, in the early days after 9/11, arrests were made so indiscriminately that on the New Jersey turnpike,

---

[1]Since that writing Dr. Rafil has been convicted and sentenced to fifteen years' time in the Jamesville penitentiary outside of Syracuse.

traffic would be stopped and people with brown skin would be randomly detained. This trapping of brown-skinned citizens and immigrants resulted in the detention of thousands of people who were later released without being charged.

To some, the pursuit of the terrorists in the United States became an obsession on the part of the federal authorities seemingly incensed with anger and feelings of revenge. The Department of Justice particularly went on a relentless hunt for Muslims. While few blame them for their seeming lack of restraint during a time of high anxiety, many of their critics blame them for their prejudice and the methods they adopted in doing this. First, they assumed that no American is exempt from engaging in terrorist acts. Secondly, they adopted, among others, a "hold-until-cleared" policy.

This "guilty until proven innocent" mindset (Mujahid, 2003) resulted in the arrest of close to a thousand Muslims, who voluntarily participated in the INS's Special Registration call in California in December 2002. Since the immigration officers could not possibly handle such a heavy workload, instead of sending them back and letting them come the next day, they detained these people and put them behind bars for days—even those who had applied for extension and were waiting to hear from the INS. This California event had a ripple effect among Muslim immigrants, as well as visitors nearly all over the country. Thousands of those who had overstayed their visas, even those who had applied for an extension and were waiting to hear from the INS, decided to leave the United States (435 in November 2002, 871 in January 2003, and 952 in February 2003) and cross the border into Canada rather than be forced into American detention indefinitely (Hukill, 2003).

This deluge of would-be asylum seekers took Canadian immigration authorities at the border by utter surprise. This was especially true in Detroit and Buffalo, where swelling crowds, including families with children and women, old and young, left their homes, jobs, businesses, and schools behind, disenchanted and eager to leave the United States in disbelief. The weather did not cooperate either. The 2002–2003 winter was more severe than usual in the northern tier states. Were it not for the timely help from local Muslim communities, a number of churches and Vive La Casa (a local shelter in Buffalo, New York), which came forward with food, medicine, and blankets, a catastrophe of massive proportion was in the offing well within American borders. Most major newspapers, especially those on the eastern seaboard, did manage to find some space in their columns to cover the event briefly. However, the television media, for the most part, remained quiet. Curiously, few of them could afford to spare time for this unique migratory episode, whereby the migrants were leaving the United States in droves, perhaps for the first time in modern American history. How many Muslims emigrated from the United States at this time? Nobody knows. According to the Canadian immigration authorities, the total number of those who entered Canada from United States at this time was at least ten times higher than usual for this period (December to January). The *Herald* estimated that 50,000 would return to Pakistan before it is all over (Hukill, 2003).

Why these Bangladeshis, Egyptians, Indonesians, Jordanians, Pakistanis, and many others from Muslim countries decided to run from the United States is exemplified by the case of Ejaz Haider, a visiting scholar from Pakistan at the Brookings Institute in Washington, D.C. On January 28, 2002, two agents from the INS arrested him outside his office. "In a matter of moments I was transformed from research scholar in a venerable Washington think tank to a suspect, from a person with a name and a face to a body, a non-person. I was put in a car, taken to a detention center, locked in a cell, and stripped not just of my belt and shoelaces but of my pride and dignity—all because of my nationality" (Haider, 2003).

Now, Haider was not an ordinary Pakistani residing in the United States on a temporary visa. Other than being a scholar engaged in research at a reputable institution in Washington, he was personally known by many among Washington's elite. He was nabbed, presumably for missing a deadline for registration with the INS, which changed its registration requirement for Pakistanis three times. Consequently he stated, "I did not know I was in violation of the INS policy. Brookings did not know I was in violation. My friends in the State Department did not know I was in violation."

Fortunately for Haider, Khurshid Ahmed Kusuri, the Pakistani foreign minister and a good friend of Haider, was in town to discuss Pakistan's inclusion in the NSEERS program. The day after Haider's unceremonious arrest, Kusuri raised the matter with Attorney General John Ashcroft. "Everybody was embarrassed," Kusuri told a *Washington Post* reporter. "If this is the sort of person that can be nabbed, then no one is safe." The fact remains, as Haider (2003) writes, "For more than a century, people from all over the world came to the United States to escape repression and enjoy its freedoms. Perhaps for the first time in American history, we are witnessing the spectacle of families migrating from the United States in search of safety."

The Perception of Muslims as Anti-Semitic

There are around five or six million of those who identify themselves as Jews in the United States today. Not all of them are necessarily practicing or even believing Jews. Their main identity stems from the fact that they consider themselves to be the direct descendants of the prophet Abraham (Ibrahim in Islam). In this sense they are a clan or a tribe spread rather thinly around the world. Because the Arabs, especially those of the peninsula, also trace their descent from Abraham, they consider themselves to be closely related cousins of the Jews. However, not all-modern day Arabs are from the peninsula. Many of those who became Muslims, especially in the Middle East, also became thoroughly Arabized over time. Unlike a Jew, then, an Arab generally means a person who speaks Arabic as mother tongue. However, because in the United States Arab is often mistaken for a race, a person whose parents or ancestors were Arabic speakers is also looked at as being an Arab.

Jews are found in many parts of the world. Hence, they may be culturally and linguistically diversified. On the other hand, most Arabs live in a large but a more or less contiguous territory and speak one language—Arabic—as their mother tongue.

As divided as Jews may be among different nationalities, languages, and cultural backgrounds, what unites most of them in the United States and makes them a pressure group *par excellence* is, by far, their seemingly passionate support for the state of Israel. For many, the establishment of the state of Israel is like a response to years of prayers. As a result, many Jews strive to defend Israel and the hostile environment it finds itself in.

Whereas the Zionists have a theological claim over *Erd Israel*, Palestinians have a purely historical claim over the same parcel of land. Whereas most Jews left for better pastures somewhere else and their population in Palestine shrank during the Diaspora, Palestinians remained behind as the natives of their land for the past at least a few thousand years. When before he became a prophet, Muhammad visited Palestine as a trader, most Palestinians were Christians, probably of Orthodox faith for at least five centuries. Even after most of them accepted Islam under the reign of the second pious Caliph Omar, Christianity remained the second most important religion among the Palestinians, which still is the case. Because of common nativity and heritage, Muslim and Christian Palestinians seldom had religious prejudices dividing them.

The persecution of the Jews in Christian Europe is quite old. However, ever since the failed Nazi efforts to exterminate Jews from Europe, anti-Semitism has become something like a swear word in the Western world. In a multiethnic America, it has the same connotation as "the N word." Americans in general and American political hopefuls in particular have, therefore, come to learn how to evade this label and do not criticize Israel publicly. However, lately the term *anti-Semite* is being used so frequently by the self-styled caretakers of the state of Israel that it is becoming stale. For instance, in his critique of neoconservatives, Pat Buchanan (2004:12) writes:

> The neoconservatives have also begun to injure their reputations and isolate themselves with the nastiness and irrationality of their attacks. French cannon once bore the inscription *ultima ratio regun*, the last argument of kings. The toxic charge of "Anti-Semite!" has become the last charge of neoconservatives. But they have wheeled out the cannon too many times. People are less intimidated now. They have seen people look into the muzzle and walk away.

The confusion is partially due to the way this terminology has been used. Does anti-Semitism mean hating Jews for being Jews? Or is criticizing a Jewish institution or even the state of Israel also anti-Semitism? In our opinion, most Muslims do not seem to hate Jews. They rather agree with Avneri (2004), and Finkelstein (2000), namely that the term anti-Semitism must not be extended to criticizing Israel and any other Jewish institution or partisan groups. Ruder (2004) stated, "It is not anti-Semite to oppose Israel."

Moreover, with the quickly changing ethnic and religious composition of the United States, many Americans, including the Hispanics, the Sikhs, the Hindus, the Asians, and the African Americans and Muslims of all colors, do not care for or even understand the true meaning of anti-Semitism. This is partly because they did not cause or contribute to the Holocaust. They do not harbor any guilt with respect to Jews. On the contrary, Muslims always valued Jews highly as "People of the Book" who often took refuge in Muslim lands during attempts to escape Christian pogroms in Europe. Moreover, many Muslims, especially Arabs also consider themselves to be the Semites. "How could we ever be anti-Semitic?" they ask.

Nonetheless, one of the main targets of this labeling in the United States especially during the past few decades has been American Islam, whose expansion pro-Zionists elements (quite a few non-Jews among them) have always been looked at with great apprehension due to their concern for Israel. As Findley (2001) pointed out, American Zionists have not been the least active in cultivating this psyche in the United States. The difference 9/11 brought about is the change of the label. Muslim Americans are now being touted as terrorists, implying that Muslims are not merely anti-Semite, they are anti-West, and especially anti-American. Furthermore, some feel that Muslim Americans hate Western values of equality, the emancipation of woman, secularism, freedom of expression, and democracy.

From the Muslim point of view, because God calls the Jews and the Christians the "People of the Book," Muslims are not supposed to hate Jews or, for that matter, the Christians for being what they are. Even the Nation of Islam under the leadership of Louis Farrakhan quit calling Jews names since he embraced Sunni Islam. For centuries, when Jews were subjected to pogroms in Europe, many of them took refuge in Muslim lands where they became renowned scholars, successful businessmen, and trusted diplomats. According to Ahmed (1973), in Arab countries, Jewish ghettos never existed. Muslims, Jews, and Christians lived next door to one another as good neighbors. Our thesis is that much of what is becoming known these days as "Islamophobia" is produced in a conflict of interest that involves, among other factors, American support for the state of Israel, especially among some American Jews and Evangelical Christians. Our experience shows that at the individual level, Muslims and Jews interact freely and make friends as fellow students, as neighbors, or as colleagues in colleges, business, industry, and so on. In fact, the contemporary enmity between Muslims and Jews arose with the establishment of Israel in 1948.

Even if they are not anti-Semitic, Arabs, whether Muslims or Christians, differentiate between liberal pro-Muslim Zionists and extremist anti-Muslim Zionists. Many liberal Zionists belong to the Israeli Peace Now movement, which, according to Nader (2004) is very substantial. These peace-loving Israelis recognize the right of the Palestinians as a people who are demanding their own sovereign country in their own homeland or whatever is left of it after the establishment of Israel in 1948 and its subsequent expansion in Palestinian territories. These are the Jews (in Israel, as well as in the United States) who have been in the forefront of the Oslo and the proposed Geneva accords, and are actively encouraging Israel and the Palestinians to reach a negotiated settlement.

Then there are other Zionists who, from the Muslim point of view, support Israel even to the point of being ruthless. They support extreme anti-Arab and anti-Palestinian policies that the Likud and other right-wing parties have been trying to impose. Other than destroying and demoralizing Palestinians and their homes, such policies are aimed at the creation of another Bantustan in Palestine. Palestine is at present and continues to be further divided into smaller parcels of districts separated by Israeli highways, which Palestinians cannot cross in case they want to go from one district to another district of their newly achieved independent state.

There are three distinct extremist Zionist strains of labeling Muslims as terrorists in the United States today. One of them is openly opportunistic, the other distinctly anti-intellectual, and yet another is trying to occupy most powerful positions in American politics and government.

During the past fifteen years, Hollywood released two movies on the linkage between Islam and terrorism. Few in the United States today remember the names and plots of these movies. They certainly do not belong among the Hollywood classics. As mediocre as these two have been, their basic theme is being revived by a few enthusiastic American Zionists who got a foothold in the media by using a new battle cry, "Jihad in the United States," filled with the same old contraption—anti-Islamism. Sometimes they make serious mistakes, which, however, are soon forgotten by an oft-forgiving media. For instance, Tim McVeigh was still racing north on I-35 when the Oklahoma City bombing was quickly attributed to "Islamic terrorism." In a rare coincidence, quick FBI work came to the rescue of Muslim Americans when Tim McVeigh was apprehended minutes before he was to be released by the Oklahoma Highway patrol. However, a linkage between Islam and terrorism is the old pastime in the United States and it often pays good dividends to those who cry wolf. As the late Edward Said once noted:

> What matters to "experts" like Judith Miller, Samuel Huntington, and Martin Kramer, Bernard Lewis, Daniel Pipes, Steve Emerson and Barry Rubin, plus a whole battery of Israeli academics, is that the "threat" (of Islam) is kept before our eyes, the better to excoriate Islam for terror, despotism and violence while assuring themselves profitable consultancies, frequent T.V. appearances and book contracts. The Islamic threat is made to seem disproportionately fearsome lending support to the thesis [which is an interesting parallel to anti-Semitic paranoia] that there is a worldwide conspiracy behind every explosion. (Findley, 2001:66)

Evidently, these "terrorism experts" are selling their wares because in the post-9/11 climate, there exists an elevated Islamophobia. Besides, this has generated in the United States an aroused curiosity about Islam, which they capitalize on. These self-styled experts proclaim at the outset that Muslims in general are not that bad, thus trying to evade any label of anti-Islamism. On the other hand, there is always an underlying theme in their proclamations, namely, that these innocent-looking Muslims must be kept under close watch and need to be shaken up frequently, for they harbor and hide terrorists—sleeper cells—in their communities, mosques, colleges, and businesses. It is therefore emphasized that all registered and unregistered mosques (no one knows their exact number or their locations), organizations, associations, institutions, and businesses must be subjected to close police scrutiny. The cases of IIIT in Northern Virginia, Professor Sami Al-Arian in Miami, Dr. Rafil in Syracuse, and many others speak loudly of a government establishment eager to listen to the recommendations of such Zionist "experts" on terrorism.

Few mosques have been violated so far. However, when federal agents surprised a few Muslim businesses and colleges and ransacked the homes of their employees at the advice of such "experts," they came out empty-handed. Even CBS's *60 Minutes* made a fool of itself when, at the behest of an undercover Zionist woman posing as a Muslim, they surprised a chicken farm in Gainesville, Georgia, and a Muslim publishing house in northern Virginia and were, slapped with a multimillion dollar civil suit (Sugg, 2003; Bray, 2003).

Another vintage of anti-Islamism in the United States is what was sometimes touted as "campus watch." It is anti-intellectual not in a traditional but a real sense of the word. At the very outset, proponents of this movement deny that they are anti-Islamic, but that the supporters of Islam, especially those on the campuses, better keep their mouth shut. Within this overall American culture with traditions of misgivings about Islam, American universities and colleges represent, perhaps, the only subculture that has raised questions rather than blindly follow the Zionist demands supporting the government of Israel and concocting hitherto unknown and misleading anecdotes in Islamic history in order to prove that the Muslims could be very unreliable at times. Here lies the double-talk in their claim. On one hand, we are told that in general Muslims are really good folks. On the other hand, we are told that they must not be trusted. If some professors or college students do not agree with this stereotyping of the Muslims, it is a good idea to keep an eye on these professors—intimidate them with respect to their promotions, their careers, even their lives. Reminiscent of the Nazis, students were encouraged to inform on professors that express the wrong views. A rather long list including names of such scholars was prepared. This list generated a few threats against these intellectuals. According to Strindberg (2004: 20):

> First it was necessary to popularize the view of universities across the country as an unmitigated breeding ground for "terrorist thought." This was accompanied by the monitoring of scholars and institutions that expressed criticism of Israel and of U.S. foreign policy (i.e. "anti-Semitic" and anti-American views), "naming and shaming them" on the Internet and in columns and editorials. While thus "raising public awareness," Congress was being lobbied for legislation to confront the threat from this enemy within: the fifth column in the ivory tower.

How closely "campus watch" has come to committing a criminal act (intimidating, blackmailing), only a lawyer could tell, but so far it has failed to stifle the voices of these intellectuals. Moreover, American academia prides itself on perpetuating diversity and difference of opinion that enriches academic inquiry and improves the knowledge base. Among other things, this is what has made the United States home to some of the very best and most sought-after seats of learning in the world. Once you start stifling this practice of freedom of inquiry and expression on the campus, it is the beginning of the demise of the quality of American higher education that the world has come to admire.

Yet another example of extremist Zionist elements in the United States is the so-called neoconservatives, Jews as well as non-Jews. Having lived as an ethnic minority under persecution for centuries in Christian-dominated Europe and the United States, Jews have mastered the art of living as a minority. Of the five major contributors to the Western civilization—Newton, Darwin, Marx, Freud, and Einstein, the latter three were Jews. While they excelled in education and the professions, by adopting the host culture, many nonetheless retained their fundamental Jewish traits and identity. Superficially, at least, the Jewish subculture became indistinguishable from the larger cultures of host societies. They have been in the forefront of atheistic socialism as well as secular democracy, both of which distance themselves from religion. Politically active, they raise large amounts of funds. Jewish donors make up an estimated 50–70 percent of the Democratic Party's large contributors (*The American Conservative*, June 21, 2004, p. 4) and use this fund wisely to support a political candidate, intimidate a candidate, or defeat a candidate. Cynthia McKinney of Georgia knows through personal experience in 2002 that even being an African American as well as a woman does not automatically make you an "untouchable" or put you out of the extremist Zionist reach. J. William Fulbright of Arkansas and Charles Percy of Illinois, both chairmen of the Senate Foreign Relations Committee in their own times, as well as Paul Findley of Illinois and many others, would tell you the same thing.

Moreover, what worries Muslim Americans most is that Zionist extremists—Jews as well as non-Jews—have, during the past few decades, established themselves in crucial decision-making positions at the highest level. Sitting in the Pentagon, the White House, or on Capitol Hill, they are able to gradually extend their reach almost worldwide. The so-called neoconservatives are a case in point: they constitute a sort of a small club of those who passionately defend and support Israeli extremist Likud policy. The neoconservatives as gathered in the Pentagon and in the office of the vice president are generally recognized as being responsible for pushing the United States into invading Iraq in order to topple Saddam Hussein. They initiated and pushed the Bush administration in a policy which defied and angered nearly all the major allies of the United States who had serious reservations about President Bush's war on Iraq. These neoconservatives are the ones who have been directly or indirectly responsible for putting in President Bush's State of the Union address a lie about Saddam having acquired uranium from "an African country." They are the ones who have made the president vocalize the by-now infamous expression "Axis of Evil, that is, Iraq, Iran, and North Korea." More seriously, the neoconservatives are pushing the United States toward reversing its established policy of not being the first to strike. Instead, preemption is being forged as a policy for self-defense against the adversaries of Israel and seems to be the answer on the part of many critics of this policy. The Soviet Union does not exist any more. China seems to have developed a taste for diplomacy. On the other hand, despite massive doses of continued American help, which have made it the superpower of the region, Israel continues to harbor an elevated and almost a paranoid sense of insecurity. So do the neoconservatives and, as they see it, so should the United States! This explains what one may call "jumping justifications" to invade Iraq in 2003—Saddam is a bloody tyrant; he has links to al-Qaeda; he has weapons of mass destruction; he could attack the United Kingdom in a matter of minutes; he is an imminent danger. As it turned out, these proved to be blatant excuses, which made many, including Bob Schieffer of CBS wonder if maybe Saddam Hussein, as bad as he was, was really not that bad.

The Perception of Muslims as Anti-American

The fourth most troublesome dimension of anti-Islamism that emerged in America in the wake of 9/11 has been a widespread belief, especially among laymen, that Muslims are America's enemies. Actions of government agents, pronouncements of Southern Baptist ministers, and the efforts of pro-Zionist elements appear to have helped to inflame this belief. In the wake of 9/11, many asked the question: What do they have against us, or why do they hate us? There seems to be a presumption of innocence in raising this question— we are a humanitarian, helpful, and nice people—implying that there must be something terribly wrong with those who hate us or do not agree with us. What is wrong with them, we are often told, is that they hate the American values of freedom and progress. Many in the Bush administration, especially the so-called neoconservatives, loudly espouse this explanation. We have explained in the preceding pages how this view of Muslims is overly simplistic. The same question, "why do they hate us?" was raised just before and during the second war on Iraq in 2003. Only this time, the presumed America haters also included such traditional European allies as Germany, France, Belgium, and Holland, all of which champion values of democracy, freedom, and progress no less than the United States. Understandably, Muslims in general would disagree with this line of reasoning. They came to settle in the United States looking for freedom, equality before the law, and quality of life for themselves and their children. As one American Muslim scholar writes:

> Nothing can be further from the truth. Indeed most Muslims are great admirers of democracy and freedom and insist that these values are not only consistent with Islam but were the bedrock of glorious Islamic civilization. They point to the diversity, tolerance and harmony at the peak of Islamic civilization to substantiate their claim. As Islamic awareness increases in postcolonial Muslim societies and Islamic activists try to rebuild their civilization they find that the

economically motivated alliance between secular authoritarian regimes in the Muslim world and the West, in particular the U.S., is the biggest barrier to freedom, democracy and self determination. Turkey, Algeria, Saudi Arabia, Bahrain, Kuwait are just a few examples of states where non-democratic regimes thrive and repress popular movements with U.S./Western support. (Khan, 2002: 125–26)

In short, the claim that Muslims hate the United States because of its emphasis on freedom and democracy is too flimsy to be taken seriously. But more seriously, what Khan is trying to tell us is that America, the champion of freedom and democracy, is in cahoots with and supports some of the worst enemies of freedom and democracy in the Muslim world from Uzbekistan to Saudi Arabia and Egypt. Even this is only a part of the explanation. What enrages the ordinary man in the Arab street is that the United States does not act evenhandedly in the problem of Palestine. On the contrary, today the United States is only one of the few unconditional supporters of the state of Israel despite all the atrocities that it continues to commit against rock-throwing Palestinians who are now forced to become suicide bombers—terrorists in the jargon of the American government and the media. Theodoracopules (2004) put this more succinctly:

> The pro-war lobby in the United States as well as Europe has it that radical Islam wishes to destroy the whole basis of Western society—secular democracy, individual liberty, equality before the law, toleration and pluralism are all anathema. Of course they would say that, but it is nonsense. I have lived in Arab countries and traveled extensively throughout the Arab world. Most Arabs that I've met simply want to live in peace. ... I have said it before and I will say it until the day the Israelis pull out. As long as the Palestinians live under Israeli control and are humiliated daily—not to mention the killing of innocent civilians by Israeli soldiers—America will be hated by all Arabs, not just radical Islamists.

Whatever the reason for Arab or Muslim anger about American foreign policy in the Middle East, for an American layman, perhaps, it was maddening to see a bunch of suicidal maniacs attack America's centers of economic and military power. Palestinian terrorists were bad enough. The 9/11 hijackers proved to be something else. Evidently, you cannot do anything about those suicidal fanatics after the fact. Consequently, it seems to us that many are trying to get even with their kind—the Muslims, if you can reach them, especially the ones who are living in the United States. In short, 9/11 gave rise to a widespread feeling of anti-Islamism among laymen who, like their preachers and a number of other elites, wanted to take revenge against those who subscribed to Islam.

There is a long list of such attacks by lay individuals since 9/11, and it is becoming longer still. Muslim women in *hijab* have been particularly easy targets because of their visibility. They have been accosted, verbally attacked with profanity, and profiled racially in stores, at jobs, in trains, and at airports. In Santa Clara, California, a Muslim woman was assaulted in the laundry room of her apartment building on February 28, 2003, more than two years after 9/11. She was punched in the face and suffered a split lip and several bruises. Every item in her laundry was later found torn having been stabbed with a sharp object (CAIR, 2003).

Zulfiqar Ahmed, age thirty-three, came to Irvington, New Jersey, in 1993 on an immigrant visa. His wife and their six children joined him five years later. He established a telephone card business and was living comfortably when in the night of February 21, 2003, two white males attacked him in a parking lot of a supermarket. They kicked him in the head, in the stomach, and the groin and said, "You are killing our people in America. You have to go back to your country"(Roberts, 2003).

According to a report by CAIR (March 2003) a Muslim teenager was severely beaten on 22 February 2003 in Yorba Linda, California, by a group of some twenty attackers using baseball bats and golf clubs. The assailants, at least two of whom were reported to be white supremacists, shouted racial slurs such as "F... the Arabs," "You Arab pieces of s...", and "camel jockeys." The eighteen-year-old victim sustained multiple head injuries and stab wounds. He underwent reconstructive surgery during which metal plates were used to repair his facial bones.

The mildest anti-Islamic reaction recorded so far was from Williams (2003). It reads:

> Why don't you lead a "Million Muslim march" on Washington, D.C. against terrorism? It would probably result in the end of terrorism. Until you do I can only assume you, and all Muslims, support terrorism.

Even non-Muslims confused with being Muslims were called names, threatened, and even killed. Of these "Muslim-looking" men, Sikhs have been the most unfortunate. According to the *Observer-Tribune* (September 29, 2003), there are about five hundred thousand Sikhs in the United States out of a total estimated at one million in North America. Sikhs are a religious group from India. Because they must not cut their hair nor shave, they generally have long hair, thick moustaches, and bushy beards. Additionally, they cover their head with a *Pagree or* a turban. In fact, the *Pagree* and thick beard are the insignia of one being a Sikh. Evidently, some Americans have come to take these as the characteristic features of Muslims with tragic consequences for the Sikhs, who do not have anything to do with Bin Laden and his religion.

Balbir Singh Sodhi, a forty-nine-year-old Sikh immigrant from India, wore a *Pagree* and beard all his adult life in accordance with his religious teachings. Sodhi was a hard-working man. After years of thrift and working long hours, he was able to save enough money to buy a business of his own—a gas station where he was working the day he was assassinated in cold blood (Ghouse, 2003).

On September 15, four days after 9/11, Frank Roque, a resident of Mesa, Arizona, went on a rampage, which included shooting at those who were or appeared to be Middle Eastern. On that day, Balbir Singh Sodhi was working outside of his gas station when a bullet from Roque's gun, in a drive-by shooting, hit him in the chest and killed him instantly.

Sikhs are a rather small but well-organized religious community in the United States. Although Frank Roque was convicted for first-degree murder, according to Manjit Singh, president of the Sikh Mediawatch and Resource Task Force (SMART), with their main breadwinner gone, the Sodhi family has suffered a great deal since his death. According to Manjit Singh:

> This honest and hard-working man was killed simply because of the way he looked. We hope this conviction would shed light on the persisting problem of hate crimes, which are rooted in sheer ignorance and intimidate entire communities.

SMART has noticed an increase in hate crimes with tragic consequences since the war in Iraq. A Sikh college student and his Caucasian girlfriend were pelted with rocks while returning from an evening class in Jersey City. A Sikh woman traveling in a subway in New York was shouted at, "You Moslem bitch. Didn't your man...?" According to a report by the Sikh Coalition (www.sikhcoalition.org), two Sikh teenagers were attacked in the evening of March 3, 2004 in Lodi, New Jersey. Their turbans were removed and their hair was cut with a pair of scissors. A Sikh gentleman was shouted at and publicly insulted by a flight attendant while flying on a commercial flight. According to a story in the *Observer-Tribune* (September 29, 2003), Handsdip Bindar, an executive vice president of Innov8 Computer Solutions, a software firm in Newark, planned to visit family in Ohio over Thanksgiving. He took a Delta flight from Newark and changed to an Atlantic Coast Airlines flight in Cincinnati. He was reading a magazine in the plane when the flight attendant, Janet Thomas, suspicious of him because of his looks (full beard and a large turban), came to him and literally shouted at him. One witness, Wayne Hill of Springboro, Ohio, said he overheard the attendant telling passengers that as long as she was in control of the passenger cabin, she had no intention of whatever happened in the past happening all over again. She indicated that there might be a problem and "she might need their help," and said, "If I give a signal I might need help subduing the guy." Mathew Gordon, a professor of Middle Eastern Studies at Miami University of Ohio, was sitting in a seat just behind Bindar. According to him the whole scene "was horrifying. He was just a normal Joe going about his business." In taking the airlines, Delta and Atlantic Coast, to court, Bindar said that the incident on the Atlantic Coast plane was due to ignorance and lack of training. In a statement he observed:

> I, however, have not been the only Sikh, Muslim, Arab or other individual perceived to be from the Middle East who has experienced the trauma and humiliation that results from racial profiling after September 11. Just as thousands of African Americans and Hispanics were victimized by racial profiling on the highways of New Jersey and across the country, today, Sikhs, Muslims, Arabs and others perceived to be from the Middle East are being illegally harassed and racially profiled by persons like this attendant.

Of course, Sodhi's assassination was a sad incident, especially for the Sikhs who have been victimized by ignorant men. Being beaten severely in the face and stomach, females being attacked in the laundry room of their own apartment building, being pelted with rocks and being called names, or shouted at for no apparent reason are no less intimidating and demeaning for the Sikhs or others being victimized by men who are acting out of sheer ignorance as to who their victims really are or what they really believe.

In these post-9/11 days, anti-Islamism may not merely be related to ignorance about Islam and Muslims, it may also be seemingly self-motivated for personal gains. Far from being an uncivilized act, anti-Islamism these days could be used to further personal interests. Peter King is a Republican congressman from Long Island, New York. While being interviewed by WNBC-TV's *News Forum* on February 9, 2004, he declared that 85 percent of the nation's mosques are involved in terrorist activities. The occasion was a discussion of his recently published novel, *Veil of Tears* about the World Trade Center attacks. King is not an expert on Muslim demographics. Before putting the figure at 85 percent, he ought to know how many mosques there are in the United States. In fact, the number of mosques in the United States has eluded even expert researchers in the field. Furthermore, to say that people like Steve Emerson or Daniel Pipes know this figure quite well is to elevate these men to an expertise that they do not possess. Had these remarks come from a layman in the street, they could be overlooked. However, an author and congressman uttering these words do not merely show his ignorance about what he is asserting. He is being blatantly insensitive to Muslim Americans in general and especially to those in his constituency in Nassau County for the sake of selling his book.

There are many other lawmakers who do not mince their words when it comes to making anti-Islamic pronouncements. They do not even care as to how ridiculous their anti-Islamist pronouncement may be. For instance, Guy W. Goldis, a member of Massachusetts's senate, sent a flier to his fellow senators that says terrorist attacks could be deterred if convicted Muslim extremists were buried with pig entrails (Abraham, 2003).

Why should an American with the rank of a state senator make a statement like the following, according to Abraham:

The flier, which Goldis's 39 colleagues received ... said an execution of Muslim extremists in the Philippines was ordered by General John Joseph "Black Jack" Pershing before World War I, in which the terrorists were shot with bullets dipped in pig's blood entrails, etc. According to the flier, contact with the blood and entrails of pigs "instantly" barred Muslims from paradise, dooming them to hell. It said news of the burial deterred other terrorist attacks for the "next forty-two years."

An additional, and outrageous, claim was made by Congressman Cass Ballenger, a Republican from North Carolina, who said that the stress of living near a Muslim civil rights group in Washington "bugged the hell" out of his wife and caused the breakup of his fifty-year marriage (CAIR, October 4, 2003).

These are only a few examples randomly drawn from hundreds of such cases that have been recorded over the last two-year period. As is evident, such cases are not limited in time and place. Anti-Islamism in the United States does not have any season and such cases are happening all over—Arizona, California, Florida, Illinois, New York, New Jersey, and Texas.

These are difficult times for American Muslim citizens and residents. Even if you are not at fault, you may still suffer from government action motivated by faulty information. Even if you are not a practicing Muslim, your religion and your community are under attack by "reputable" Christian fundamentalists, who demonstrate a high level of ignorance about Islam and Muslims. Then, not surprisingly, pro-Zionist extremists have a field day of anti-Islamic actions, projecting Muslim citizens as being the fifth column. With all this going on it is not surprising if laymen also take the law into their hands. Police and other local law enforcement agencies are particularly concerned about this rush of violent anti-Islamism in American streets. As usual, there is a wide gap between cases "reported" and cases "cleared" by the police. As long as this gap exists, no police action can stop these hate crimes against Muslim citizens of the United States. What is urgently needed is a change of social environment starting from the highest reaches of law enforcement, the religious discourse, and of course the media, which has often shown a tendency for thrill seeking and overenthusiasm, thus implicating itself in anti-Islamism.

SUPPORT FOR ISLAM IN THE UNITED STATES

Can the United States really be that bad for Muslims? President George Bush would, most probably, say no. After all he is the only American president who visited some important places of Islamic worship in the Washington area. He is the one who has repeatedly praised Islam as the religion of peace and, more recently, declared that Islam is compatible with democracy. That some in his administration, especially the Department of Justice, reacted to 9/11 with unusual security measures lurking at the brink of vengeance must not have come as a big surprise either. The attorney general had to take steps to prevent any further attacks on the United States. Accuse him as you may of trying to overstep the constitutional limits or of anti-Islamist bigotry, how else could any other attorney general react to 9/11? Although none of the 9/11 suicide attackers was an American, all of them were Muslims of Arab decent. There are a few million Muslims of Arab background residing in the United States lawfully: how could one be certain that these 9/11 attackers were not in agreement with at least some Muslim Americans, many of them first-generation immigrants? Though none of those hijackers, not even the twentieth one, was found to have any contacts with Muslim American communities or individuals, still the suspicion and bias naturally remain and linger. In the first attack on the World Trade Center in 1993, all convicted conspirators, except for the main character who got away, were lawful American residents. Although there are some serious unanswered questions about the conviction of the blind Sheik Abdul Rahman, could the highest-ranking officer of the law responsible for preventing such attacks in the future afford not to put Muslim Americans under close watch? At this time the warnings to the State Department in 1990 by Ahmed Kabbani, supreme leader of the American Sufi movement (all Muslim students are trying to find out how to make the atomic bomb; all Muslim women in *hijab* during the day are prostituting in the night in order to find official secrets; and nearly all the mosques in the United States are dominated by the Saudi agents) must have been like bells ringing in the ears of the officials, especially those of the Department of Justice. Although there is evidence of widespread abuse of Muslim detainees on the part of the rank-and-file government agents approaching religious prejudice and racial profiling (some of which was reported by the inspector general of the Department of Justice), it seems that far from being anti-Islamic, the Bush administration has been, at worst, acting upon a "good cop, bad cop" policy. While President Bush continued to soothe Muslim emotions, his attorney general was seemingly out on a witch hunt.

What is particularly disappointing, although not altogether unexpected, has been the reaction to 9/11 on the part of some of the leaders of the evangelical fundamentalists. Although anti-Islamism was the pasttime of many of them even before 9/11, Islam has seldom been the exclusive target of these evangelicals, who are dogmatic rejectionists. From its very inception in the latter part of the nineteenth century, fundamentalism condemned even other Christian churches as being heretical.

It seems that prejudice, which has been the hallmark of the culture of the American south, has not been limited to race only. About the same time as slavery was being abolished, it developed a religious dimension as an additional outlet for their tradition of rejecting others. Anti-Semitism has been as rampant in the American South, as has been racial prejudice against former African slaves. It seems it is the turn of the Muslims this time around.

Prejudice against others, whether racial, religious, or otherwise is one of the ways of telling the "other" that they are not merely different, but inferior. This sense of inherent superiority characterizes the Hindu caste system of India, although there is little evidence that it is borrowed from the Hindu fundamentalists. It is home grown and some of the prominent practitioners of this prejudice achieved prominence by virtue of practicing it. Attacking others from the pulpit is a cheaper way to gain notoriety, especially in front of the spellbound crowd eager to achieve nirvana.

However, what is refreshing from the Muslim point of view is that these anti-Islamic pronouncements on the part of some Southern Baptist leaders quickly became a source of great embarrassment for other Christians in the United States. For instance, the day after the First Conservative Baptist Church in Jacksonville, Florida, erected the sign stating "Jesus Forbade Murder.

Mathew 26–52. Muhammad Approved Murder. Surah 8:65," Reverend Fred
Morris, the executive director of the Florida Council of Churches, which represents 3,500 congregations with 1.5 million worshippers, strongly denounced
this attempt to attack the founder of Islam:

> As a Christian, I am disappointed at this unchristian effort to disparage Islam.
> Jesus never attacked other faiths... I am proud to regard Islam as our sister
> among the Abramic religions. (Associated Press, January 22, 2003)

The Reverend Richard Cizik, vice president for governmental affairs of the
National Association of Evangelicals, has been quite vocal in trying to stop
demonization of Islam. "We do not worship the same God," he says, "but I
also of do not believe in Islam as the new 'evil empire'" (Lattin, 2004).

Interestingly, Christians of nonfundamentalist persuasions, who read the
same religious book as the fundamentalists do, have adopted a more concilia-
tory approach toward Islam and Muslims. Some have even tried to defend the
Prophet Muhammad. Alex Kronemer, a graduate of Harvard Divinity School,
is a coproducer of the PBS documentary *Muhammad: Legacy of a Prophet*. In
his article "Understanding Muhammad" (Kronemer, 2002), he rejects the
notion that Islam is fundamentally warlike, that Muslims are dangerous, and
that the Prophet Muhammad was primarily a military leader:

> Historical context must likewise be remembered when judging Muhammad. The
> notion that Muhammad was a man of war as contrasted Jesus and Moses, as
> Jerry Falwell recently asserted, ignores the fact that Muhammad fought only a
> handful of battles in his lifetime, resulting in barely one thousand casualties on
> all sides.
> This might be compared to such Biblical figures as David, who is praised in I
> Samuel 18 for killing his "tens of thousands," famously earning the murderous
> jealousy of Saul who only killed his "thousands"; or to Moses who, in the book
> of Numbers 31, chastises his army for sparing the women and children of the
> vanquished Midianites.

In his article, Kronemer does not imply that Southern Baptist preachers do
not know their Bible. His objection seems to be that they are guilty of serious
anti-Islamic bias in that they conveniently ignore the fact that passages of the
Bible condone and encourage bloodshed, not sparing even noncombatant innocent women and children.

According to an Associated Press report of December 6, 2003, a leading
evangelical Christian organization, Fuller Theological Seminary, is using federal funds to launch a one-million dollar program to ease strained relations
with Muslims through an interfaith code of ethics. The initiative, funded by a
grant from the Justice Department, includes teaching the code to Muslims and
Christian community leaders in the Los Angeles area and publishing a book on
this topic. According to Sherwood Lingenfelter, Fuller's provost and senior
vice president, "We hope to lead a large portion of evangelical Christians into
a better understanding of Islam. After 9/11 there was a great deal of hostility
in the Christian community toward Muslims."

However, those who objected to portions of the code belong to the Southern Baptist church. For instance, John Revel, a spokesman for the Southern Baptist's executive committee observed, "For Fuller to declare that Christians and Muslims worship the same God would be a radical departure, not only from the evangelical tradition but also the tenets of orthodox Christianity."

Likewise, as the war began in Iraq in March 2003, the Miami-based John S. and James L. Knight Foundation of Miami in a press release on 19 March 2003 announced three grants totaling $2.9 million aimed at helping Americans and Arabs better understand each other by promoting the free flow of news and information and training Middle Eastern journalists. According to Hodding Carter III, president and CEO of the Knight Foundation, "This effort to expand understanding of and an appreciation for Arab culture and the Muslim faith in the United States is important. At the same time, we act in the interest of ensuring that the same principles are finding their way to the Middle East so that people in these historical lands have access to facts and opinions relevant to understanding American culture and values."

Evidently, not all Christians, not even all evangelicals, are anti-Islamists. Presently some Southern Baptist leaders could be the only ones who, over the past few years, have adopted a vocal, hard-line anti-Islamic bias. On the other hand, large numbers of American Christian leaders, including the Methodists, Catholics, and even some evangelicals have given their support to Muslims and Islam quite openly. There is no doubt that readership about Islam and Muslims has increased tremendously in the aftermath of 9/11. More Muslims than before are being invited by the churches and the schools to give talks on Islam and Muslims. In a Unitarian church in Cortland, New York, in a Sunday class on Islam, children are taught to say "peace be on him" each time the name of the Prophet Muhammad is mentioned. College professors and students have in general kept an open mind about Islam and Muslims. New chairs for Islamic studies are being established in universities where there were none before. Still there are scores of campus churches that let their premises be used by Muslim students for their weekly congregational (*Juma'*) prayers and other functions.

There are more rabbis and other Jewish individuals attending large Islamic conferences and conventions in increasing numbers each year. In fact, for the past few years, Jewish rabbis are conspicuously present in and have made significant contributions to interreligious dialogue in the annual convention of the Islamic Society of North America (ISNA), the largest organization of Muslims in the United States. None of these Jewish activists is anti-Israel, but they do not condone injustices being done to the Palestinians in territories occupied by Israel since 1967. Here we reproduce a letter by Deaton (2004) to illustrate the internal anguish that many Jews in North America are experiencing due to Israel's merciless overkilling of the Palestinian people.

As a Jew I am disgusted by Israel's Law breaking
Re: At least 10 killed as Israelis fire on Gaza protesters, May 20 and
Israel threatens to raze hundreds more homes in Gaza, May 17.

I am ashamed to be Jewish, because Israel has become a pariah among nations
by continually ignoring and violating international law. Isn't time that Israel was
condemned for its hypocrisy and double standards?

Israel's ongoing policy, approved by its Supreme Court, of destroying
the homes of Palestinian families who fight against the Israeli occupation in
Gaza and the West Bank is a clear violation of the Geneva Accords regarding
the treatment of the civilians and their property.

Israel has continuously refused to implement the many United Nations resolutions with respect to withdrawing from the Gaza and the West Bank. No sanc-
tions have been taken against it. Why?

Israel is a nuclear power and now has a first-strike capacity from submarines, but
has steadfastly refused to become a signatory to the Nuclear Non-Proliferation
Treaty. Israel has more weapons of mass destruction than ever existed in Iraq.

Building the so-called security fence through Palestinian territory is nothing but
a land grab in contravention of international law. The Israelis, however, should
ask whether they are keeping the Palestinians out, or locking themselves in.

Israel targets and assassinates anyone it wants. Israel seems to feel that it is
above the international law. In recent years, the U.S. State Department has cited,
and Amnesty international has condemned, the human rights violations and abuse
of Palestinians in Israeli prisons.

The Israelis make a mockery of international law and besmirch the name of Judaism. Isn't it time for the international community to demand that Israel adhere
to the rule of law like everyone else?

Some major Jewish community organizations are becoming increasingly
respectful of the sensibilities of their Muslim neighbors. For instance, the Jewish Federation of Volusia and Flagler counties (Daytona Beach) had invited an
Israeli speaker, Avi Lipkin, to speak at a community Holocaust Memorial Observance on April 25, 2004. Mr. Lipkin is known for his extreme views on
Islam, which he equates with Nazism and calls it a psychosis (Callea, 2004). A
press release was sent out of his appearance at the Temple Israel, which, however, withdrew its invitation as soon as the community became aware of his
extreme views on Islam. "He was yanked for the simple reason that we want
good relations with other faiths. ... We are not down on Islam," said Rabbi
Gary Perras of Temple Israel.

The emergence of American Jews with more liberal attitudes toward Palestinians is paralleled by a similar development in Israel. There is little doubt that
liberal American Jews and those in Israel are in close contact with and coordi-
nate their activities with the fast emerging pro-Palestinian Israeli Peace Now
movement, which was instrumental in presenting the Oslo and now the Geneva
accord. In this respect, the observations of Uri Avnery, an Israeli journalist and
peace activist, are attracting wide readership in Israel as well as in the United
States.

As most Muslims see it, anti-Islamism has increased in American society
ever since 9/11. For that matter, each time American policy comes under
attack in the Middle East or in some Muslim country, many American laymen
are provoked into showing their anger or dismay in various ways, some of

them not altogether very candid. However, American foreign policy with respect to the Arab and the Muslim world in general has been attacked by some of the prominent American talk show hosts, media personalities, and journalists such as Chris Matthews, Phil Donahue, Robert Novak, and Patrick Buchanan, just to name a few. Such support of the Muslim cause, especially from the American media, was almost unthinkable only a few years ago.

As for the seemingly pro-Israeli policy of the Bush administration, no one can deny that this administration, like so many administrations before, and perhaps after, cannot whisk the Zionist pressure away even if it wants to. The pro-Zionist elements in the United States as a pressure group are too strong to be shaken off. They are becoming even more so with unexpected help coming from the Southern Baptist leadership and their millions of followers. In part, this allows Israel to continue to behave like a naughty boy, and the best an American president can do is slap it on the wrist. Saddam Hussein was a bad man, we were told, because, among other things, he broke at least a dozen U.N. resolutions. How many U.N. resolutions did Israel choose to ignore during the same period that the media did not care to discuss?

In short, from the Muslim point of view, the American president and, for that matter any political hopeful in the United States, is a hostage to Zionist extremist elements. It does not make a difference who the president is, a Republican or a Democrat, the American Muslim dream of American policy in Palestine becoming even-handed may not be realized until Muslim Americans themselves quickly learn the rules by which the American Zionists play their hand. Even if there exists an inherent anti-Islamism fueling American policy toward Palestine or the Middle East, at its core it is pure pragmatism—fat political contributions—leading the way. We maintain that if the growing Muslim American population is able to generate greater monetary resources and play the political game skillfully, American democracy would shed the remaining vestiges of anti-Islamism. Muslim Americans do not need any fanatics. They need an ability to get together and in a calm, cool, businesslike manner, be able to find friends and strengthen the hands of those who are ready to extend help.

CONCLUSION

Are Americans hopelessly anti-Islamists? Evidence so far suggests that this is not really the case. America is a complex pluralistic society. American culture is a mosaic composed of several different subcultures based on class, religion, race, education, profession, income, and national origin, among others. Americans, therefore, are not of one kind. They cannot be expected to be. Because American law permits freedom of expression, there is a free flow of opinion in the nation. In this climate, it must not be unexpected that if anti-Islamic feelings exist and are expressed in the words and actions of multitudes of people who were raised in subcultures used to anti-Islamic symbols, upbringing, and experiences. Frequently, the publicity from incidents in the Muslim world not compatible with American foreign policy (e.g., the Iranian

Revolution, the oil embargo) only reinforces and provokes anti-Islamic feel-ings among the uneducated, ignorant, insecure, and highly biased persons within such subcultures. In this sense, 9/11 was a highly provocative incident. It did not only hurt the American sense of security, it hurt American pride.

While it is expected that many Americans would express anti-Islamism in their words and deeds occasionally and especially so in the wake of 9/11, it is also expected and comforting to find many others who are embarrassed at such anti-Islamic outbursts. Many proceed to mend the situation with their words, their pens, and their actions in private as well as in public. Far from living in an anti-Islamic America, it seems that Muslim Americans are living in a nation divided among anti-Islamic, anti-anti-Islamic, and pro-Islamic. Far from being hateful toward Islam, many Americans might even be respectful of Islam.

Evidently, the roots of anti-Islamic forces in the United States lie in a highly ethnocentric view of Islam. This resulted in widespread ignorance about Islam and yielded a distorted picture and ridiculous pronouncements. With the excep-tion of a few highly biased clergy or the Zionist pro-Likud zealots, most anti-Islamists are the uneducated people who could not distinguish between a Muslim and a Sikh living among them. Most probably, they do not know any Muslims closely—as colleagues, classmates, as neighbors, or as friends. For that matter, they might not even like to know or befriend new immigrants, African Americans, or Hispanics. They seem to harbor a skewed sense of nationalism. In the past, their kind used to be anti-Black, anti-Japanese, anti-Chinese, and anti-Russian. Now that the specter of socialism is gone, Islam is being put in its place as an emerging enemy in the world.

However, there is another kind of ignorance about Islam. This is spread by the educated fundamentalist clergy, many of them from some of the very best schools in the nation. But, their ignorance of Islam is unenviable. They create ig-norance of Islam by trying to falsify it. For instance, Jimmy Swaggart's Bible College taught that Muslims worshipped the black stone tucked in the side of the *Kaaba* in Mecca. While every scholar of religion recognizes Islam as one of the three major monotheistic religions, the Yale law graduate, Pat Robertson, still goes on harping on the tune of the "moon God" of Islam (Nelson, 2003). Some-how it is difficult to understand why Christian fundamentalists are obsessed with trying to prove that Muslims worship a god different from their own. Jerry Falwell is of the opinion that this is so because his God has a son while the Muslim God does not. Does this mean that the Muslim God is the same as the Jewish God, "the one and the only," is different from the God that Jerry Falwell worships? Evidently, his anti-Islamic logic makes him anti-Semitic too.

Why is it that these educated clergy are so ethnocentrically ignorant of Islam and Muslims that they are fond of speaking about so frequently these days? The answer is that these clergy are not students of religion. They could, at best, be students of Christianity, looking at it mainly from their specific point of view. However, when this point of view becomes a lens through which to look at other Christian denominations as well as other religions, indeed the whole universe, then it promotes ignorance because it necessarily means selective reading of others, resulting in highly biased interpretations.

Above all, these Southern Baptist clergy have increasingly become businessmen selling their religion. This business provides them their primary means of living lavishly. In this sense, their anti-Islamism may only be a dimension of their general pattern of rejectionism as a marketing technique in a rather crowded bazaar of competing denominations.

However, in response to massive criticism, evangelical anti-Islamism is showing clear signs of waning or readjusting itself. Lately, there is a feeling among important Southern Baptist leaders, namely, that the Muslims should be saved rather than attacked. There are numerous evangelical preachers trying to spread the word of gospel in Muslim countries, increasingly so in Iraq lately (Avneri, 2003). There is a fear that attacking Islam and Muslims would create a negative reaction against these evangelical efforts. A new strategy includes distributing copies of the Bible in native Muslim tongues and preaching while helping poor Muslims with food and medicine. Muslim Americans hope that these efforts would create a greater understanding between these two monotheistic communities in the United States.

American Zionist extremists, on the other hand, do not speak of Islam so much as they talk about Muslims—fundamentalists, extremists, unreliable characters, terrorists, anti-Semites, and so on. Their anti-Muslim diatribe is understandable. From a Muslim point of view, they are not merely Zionists; they are the main apologists for the extreme right-wing policies in Israel. However, while these extremists do not have a monopoly over Israel, their philosophy itself is under increasing attack in Israel as well as in the United States lately. Anti-Likud elements in Israel made significant contributions to the Oslo as well as the Geneva accords. These Jewish pro-Palestinian elements in Israel as well as in the United States still have a long way to go, yet their influence is certainly on the rise in both the United States and Israel, and as their influence is rising, Likud influence is bound to decline. With increase in cooperation and understanding between the Israelis and the Palestinians resulting in the creation of the Palestinian State, one may foresee a change for the better between these two communities in the Middle East and, for that matter, in the United States.

Meanwhile, as Muslim participation and influence in American politics increases, especially during election times, American government policies toward Muslim citizens and residents need to mellow. With a total strength of around nine million Muslim Americans and non-Muslim Arab Americans, there may be around three million very resourceful and highly sensitized voters. Generally called Arab Americans, this voter population is further augmented by other Muslims, such as African Americans, South Asians, Southeast Asians, and African Muslims. In short, the voting power of American Muslims seems to be on the rise. American Muslims are convinced that heir block vote (especially close to sixty thousand in Florida) was the deciding factor, which gave victory to George Bush in the 2000 national election. Although their candidate in the 2004 election did not win, the "Muslim Block Vote" remains a hotly debated topic these days.

In the wake of 9/11, it is the first time Muslim Americans are now being targeted from an unexpected direction. They are now getting welcome attention from American businesses. According to a report (Potrikus, 2003), in 2003 for the first time ever, Hallmark introduced greeting cards for *Eid al Fitr*, the Muslim feast rejoicing the first revelation of the Qur'an to the Prophet Muhammad. The Eid immediately follows the fasting month of holy Ramadhan. In 2002, the American postal service printed thirty-five million Eid stamps of its holiday celebration series. In 2003 they sold forty-four million stamps that featured *"Eid Mubara'"* in Arabic (blessed be your holiday).

Everything from *burqas* or the hiding gowns for Muslim women to pop religious music that celebrates pious living are hot sellers. One reason for the interest is the market's growing size and the growing visibility of the Muslims since 9/11. It is not lost on the American market that more than seven million Muslims could be targeted for their own special ethnic needs.

James Zogby, the president of the Arab American Institute in Washington, D.C. says," It is the good old logic of the free marketplace. If you got a market, products will find their way into it."

REFERENCES

Abraham, Evan. "Flier from Senator Angers Muslims." *Boston Globe*, June 26, 2003.

Ahmed, Niaz Sharif. "Muslims Yahud aur Moujuda Tarikh" [Muslims and Jews in Contemporary History]. *Akhbar Jahan Weekly* 5, no. 4 (1973): 15–18.

Avineri, Sholomo. "The Return to Islam." In *Global Studies: The Middle East*, 167–170. Guilford, CT: Dushkin Group, Inc., 1993.

Avneri, Uri. *The Great Game* 2002. joverman@stny.rr.com.

———. "To Drink From the Sea of Gaza." *The Mirror*, June 9, 2003.

———. "Questions on Anti-Semitism." *International News*, May 24, 2003.

Beyer, Lisa, and Scott Macleod. "Saudi Arabia: Inside the Kingdom," *Time*, Sept. 15, 2003, 40.

Bray, Mahdi. "MAS Freedom Supports Lawsuit Against CBS 60 Minutes Terrorist Hunter," communications@masnet.org, June 5, 2003.

Buchanan, Patrick J. *Death of the West: How Dying Populations and Immigrant Invasions Imperil Our Country and Civilization*. New York: Thomas Dune Books, 2002.

Buchanan, Patrick J. "Fatal Friendship," *The American Conservative*, May 24, 2004, 7.

CAIR (Council on American-Islamic Relations). *American Muslims One Year After 9/11*. Washington, D.C.: Council on American-Islamic Relations, 2002.

CAIR (Council on American-Islamic Relations). "Beating of California Muslim Prompts call for FBI Probe." Council on American-Islamic Relations, www.cair@cair-net.org. March 3, 2003.

CAIR (Council on American-Islamic Relations). "Congressman Blames a Muslim Advocacy Group to Break His Marriage." Council on American-Islamic Relations, www.cair@cair-net.org. October 4, 2003.

CAIR (Council on American-Islamic Relations). *The Status of Muslim Civil Rights in the United States: 2003*. Washington, D.C.: Council on American-Islamic Relations, 2004.

Callea, Donna, personal communication from *News Journal* online, May 4, 2004.

Chadwick, John. "The Rev. Dr. Norman L. Geisler Doesn't Like Islam." (July 13, 2002).

Deaton, Richard. "As a Jew I Am Disgusted by Israel's Law Breaking." *The Ottawa Citizen*, May 24, 2004.

Findley, Paul. Sil*ent No More*. Beltsville, MD: Amana Publications, 2001.

Finkelstein, Norman G. *The Holocaust Industry: Reflections on the Exploitation of the Jewish Suffering*, 2000.

Ghouse, Mike, personal communication to author, October 1, 2003.

Goldstein, Laurie. "Seeing Islam as 'Evil' Faith, Evangelicals Seek Converts." *The New York Times*, May 27, 2003.

Haider, Ejaz. "Wrong Message to the Muslim World." *Washington Post*, February 5, 2003, A23.

Hukill, Traci. "A Safe Heaven Turns Hostile." www.alternet.org (March 27, 2003).

Khan, Muqtader. *American Muslims: Bridging Faith and Freedom*. Beltsville, MD: Amana Publications, 2002.

Kronemer, Alex. "Understanding Muhammad," *Christian Science Monitor* 95, no. 10 (2002).

Lattin, Don. "Trying to Avert a Clash of Biblical Proportion. Evangelical Works to Cool Christian Rhetoric on Islam." *San Francisco Chronicle*, June 11, 2004.

Mujahid, Abdul Malik. "In a Virtual Internment Camp: Muslim Americans since 9/11." Chicago: Sound Vision, 2003.

Nader, Ralph. "An Interview with Ralph Nader," *The American Conservative*, June 21, 2004, 6.

Nelson, Craig. "Fundamentalist Christian Receives Standing Ovation in Israel." *The Atlanta Journal-Constitution*, December 25, 2003.

Potrikus, Alaina Sue. "America's Muslims are Hot New Market." *Ridder Newspapers*, November 23, 2003.

Powell, Michael. "An Exodus Grows in Brooklyn: 9/11 Still Rippling Through Pakistani Neighborhood." *The Washington Post*, May 29, 2003, A01.

Raimondo, Justin. "The Last Word on America First." *The American Conservative*, May 19, 2003, 40.

Roberts, Reginald. "Attack on Muslim Probed as Bias Crime." *The Star-Ledger*, March 2, 2003.

Ruder, Eric. "Is it Anti-Semitic to Oppose Israel?" July 26, 2004.

Strindberg, Anders."The New Commissars," *The American Conservative*, February 2, 2004, 20.

Sugg, John. "Was CBS Suckered by 'Anonymous'?" *Creative Loafing*, June 12, 2003.

Theodoracopules, Taki. "The Pain in Spain." *The American Conservative*, April 12, 2004, 39.

Thomas, Tim. Personal Communication. 2001.

Williams, Steve. Personal Communication, December 17, 2003.

7

Major Internal Concerns

HIJAB, HALAL, HILAL

Our treatment of the Muslim American population so far may mislead the reader into believing that it is more or less unified in its basic day-to-day practice of Islam. This, however, is far from the truth. The very fact that Muslim Americans originated in vastly different cultures makes them differ in their emphases with respect to several different daily practices of interaction within the Muslim community. Of these, three differences stand out among them. These are *hijab* among the females, the *halal* or properly slaughtered meat, and the *hilal* or the new crescent, which marks the beginning of the new lunar month.

Hijab

Literally, *hijab* means modesty as it is applied to women as much as to men. First and foremost, it means controlling your words and actions in everyday life. For instance, it has come to mean not to gaze at a member of the opposite sex, not to engage in lewd acts, and not to exhibit parts of your body in a suggestive manner. It means a controlled manner of speech, including one's choice of words (i.e., no double meaning and no small or leading talk). Thirdly, and quite commonly, it means the way you cover up as a man and as a woman.

Both men and women are supposed to wear loose-fitting attire that covers them from the neck down to the ankles. Women, especially when in public, are also supposed to cover up their head with a piece of cloth, which may also come down to cover their shoulders and the chest area. Thus, while dress requirements for Muslim men as well as women are roughly the same, women are supposed to remain a bit more covered than men. In fact, but for the head-gear for women, Muslim dress code is fairly unisex. Among Arabs, this means a long, loose shirt (*thop*) that comes down up to the ankles with a loose pajama, and among non-Arabs (from Turkey to Pakistan and Central Asia) a pair of baggy pants (*shalwar*) worn over with a loose shirt (*qamis*) coming down somewhat below the knees. In West Africa, Muslims wear the grand *boubou* (loose big gowns), while North Africans wear the *jelabiya* (oversized, loose shirt).

Over the years, in local cultures in the Muslim world, *hijab* has come to mean the sign of feminine modesty. In Malaysia, for instance, highly educated professional women, such as doctors and bankers, come to work in *hijab*. In yet other Muslim cultures, like in Saudi Arabia and Afghanistan, *hijab* refers to the seclusion of women. They are not supposed to come out of their homes. In smaller towns in the Middle East and South Asia, for instance, this is a distinguishing factor between Muslim and non-Muslim women. In case they have to come out, they must be clad in an additional covering, a burqa or a chador, which Hanna Papaneck (1971) calls "portable seclusion." Whether or not one covers her face, her burqa allows a Muslim woman to venture out of her home for the sake of, say, visiting, shopping, working in offices, or even going to college.

On the other hand, many other cultures in the Muslim world allow their women to relax rules of *hijab*. Especially in large cities such as Cairo, Karachi, or Beirut, Muslim women do not always follow the rules of *hijab* and often venture outside of their homes without their heads covered and often even wearing tight-fitting attire. At an extreme, it is quite common to see Turkish women in Istanbul and Ankara clad in the Western attire.

The Muslim female population in the United States more or less reflects the way women in the Muslim world, especially in urban areas, choose their attire. There are some among them who observe *hijab* meticulously. There are others who do not wear *hijab* or do so only when they are praying or are in a mosque. There are still others who feel comfortable in unisex American attire. Indigenous American Muslim women seem to be about the only ones who consistently abide by the rules of *hijab*, even while at work.

Hijab is so completely foreign to American culture, and indeed the West, that a woman in *hijab* stands out, although this must not necessarily be so. After all, not too many years ago, Catholic nuns clad in black, loosely-fitted clothes with tightly wrapped headgear were a common sight in public places. Lately, American Muslim women have taken full advantage of contemporary American unisex dress code. However, they have generally preferred to use somewhat longer shirts, which allow them to leave their belly buttons hidden from the eyes of the gazers.

Broadly speaking, there are three categories of American Muslim women as far as dress preferences are concerned. First, there are women who do not prefer to use *hijab* at all, although their unisex attire may not be too far from the

Islamic code. This probably is the largest category of American Muslim women. With mostly second-generation immigrant women, there may be little, if any, tradition of *hijab* in their families to begin with. Job considerations may further help promote this practice among them. They might even detest *hijab* as being too archaic and unfitting for modern society. Most Muslim women, especially those who belong to recent migrant groups, belong in this category.

Then there are women whose family or cultural traditions make them use *hijab* each time they are in public or in the presence of unrelated men. Women whose families originated in the Middle East have been used to and insist on this practice. They continue to practice *hijab* as they practiced it in their home countries. Indigenous American women who accepted Islam lately are very prominent newcomers in this category.

Lastly, there are Muslim women who have lately adopted *hijab* voluntarily, although in many such cases their mothers, aunts, or other female relatives did not call for such practice. This last category must be of great interest, especially to the student of religion, which seems under pressure to make uneasy adjustments in the face of individual modernity. The question as to how many Muslim women in the United States (or elsewhere) fall in this category is not easy to answer. However, these days it is not difficult to find American-born young Muslim women who wear *hijab* as they are going to college or are working as engineers, doctors, lawyers, teachers, college professors, cash clerks, or office secretaries. If they are adopting this Islamic practice that did not exist in their family before, such *hijab* observing Muslim women are conveying the message that they are proud to be Muslims and that one does not have to be coerced into going back to this practice.

This voluntary observance of *hijab* is not limited to the United States only. It has become almost a universal phenomenon, especially in the Western world. It is almost an act of defiance—you have every right to practice Islam even if you are living in a secular society. One has to only recall the struggle between the French government, which insists that you may not be allowed in a government school if you are in *hijab*, and the *hijab*-observing young Muslim women who insist on receiving modern education as their birthright even if they want to cover themselves in *hijab*.

While there is no such controversy in the United States, it is safe to assume that the practice of *hijab* raises a few eyebrows. Some may display quiet curiosity. Others might not be so tolerant. Dena Kassim (Boettcher, 2004) found that the reaction of others may be as mild as them considering you to be a foreigner or an immigrant who is a newcomer to the United States. Or, it may be as serious as some driver of a car yelling, shouting at you, and trying to force your car in another lane with his vehicle. Boettcher's experience (2004) of wearing *hijab* for a day shows that she was more self-conscious than arousing the consciousness of others except for the older people:

In fact, no one under about age forty-five anywhere in the city gave us much of a look. Older people, however, were a different matter. Within the first ten minutes of walking through the grocery store, we were stared at by at least six grey-haired couples in the store. Elderly Caucasian women were the worst in this regard.

Evidently, *hijab* as a social phenomenon is presently on the increase. It deserves serious empirical research to show how a minority as different as Muslim women is coping with the daily problems associated with adjusting to American culture.

Halal

Because contemporary American culture is so rich in its variety of subcultures, *haram* (that which is prohibited by Islam) exists just around the corner. Muslim Americans, a subculture in themselves, have to be careful as to what they are doing, drinking, eating, wearing, and even uttering. For instance, Muslims must not have sex outside of marriage. They must not drink alcohol. They must not eat pork. They must not take or give interest. They must not use obscene language or rob or kill unjustifiably. These are only a few examples of what is *haram* (prohibited), and, broadly speaking, what is not *haram* is *halal* or permissible in Islam. However, not all Muslims necessarily abide by all the rules of *halal* and *haram*. Neither is there a complete agreement among them as to exactly what constitutes *haram*. The controversy about this seemingly very obvious situation, is, in fact, so serious that Yusuf alQardawi, a contemporary Muslim scholar, became famous for devoting a whole book (1990) on this topic.

Of all the issues of *halal* and *haram*, Muslim Americans seem to be visibly concerned with what they eat. For instance, nearly all of them avoid eating pork as if it is not merely prohibited, but it is rotten. Furthermore, some Muslims will drink, but usually not in public. The meat of most other animals such as goat, sheep, cow, and most other animals and birds of prey is permissible under specified conditions. According to the Qur'an (5:3):

> Prohibited is for you dead animal
> and blood
> and the meat of swine
> and the one that is slaughtered in the name of other than God
> and the animal, which died (or was killed) of suffocation
> and that died of being hit
> and that died of falling
> and that died of being gored
> and also the animal, which was torn apart
> except that you cleaned it before it died
> and that, which was sacrificed on an altar...

Following these verses and the practice of the Prophet Mohammed, Muslims derived a norm, which is followed all over in the community of Islam, namely that the animal must be slaughtered. It must be slaughtered only in the name of God for it to be permissible or *halal* for consumption. In practice, the animal is slaughtered as quickly as possible while the one who is doing the slaughtering repeatedly utters something like, "I slaughter you in the name of Allah," or simply "in the name of Allah."

This is the general rule of slaughtering animals for consumption among Muslims all over the world. It is almost taken for granted that this is the only way that meat could become *halal*. Any deviation from this practice would render meat *haram* and therefore unfit for consumption. Because this practice is so pervasive among Muslims, few are hardly aware of any other alternative. For instance, according to the Qur'an (5:3), a camel could be sacrificed by piercing its jugular vein. Also, it is reported that often hunters invoke the name of Allah before shooting a bird or animal of prey lest it dies before they are able to properly slaughter it.

Evidently, this norm poses a dilemma for Muslim Americans. It means that all the meat and meat products that are being sold in the supermarkets are not available for consumption. It means that as a Muslim you could only become a vegetarian or survive on eggs and fish (and other seafood), which is *halal* without any slaughtering.

Because a large but unspecified number of Muslim Americans insist on this norm, limited alternative arrangements are gradually appearing in the United States. Some individuals, for instance, go to the shops run by the Jews and buy kosher meat from there (kosher is deemed *halal* for Muslims). Some Muslim businesses have bought slaughterhouses. Some slaughterhouses (owned by the non-Muslims) have hired Muslims who could slaughter animals or the fowl. Some Muslim businesses or individuals have made special arrangements with slaughterhouses allowing them to perform the act of slaughtering and leave the processing to the slaughterhouse. In short, in about half a century of their explosion in the United States, Muslim Americans have learned how to use American resources serving their norm of *halal* meat.

However, there are equally large numbers of Muslim Americans (presumably also Muslim Europeans) who do not insist on *halal* meat. They buy their beef, lamb, or chicken from any grocery store. Besides, they may also not hesitate in eating in any restaurant, including those serving fast food. Evidently, this practice makes their life much more convenient and in tune with the American pattern of consumption (except for pork, of course).

However, not insisting on *halal* meat is not merely a matter of convenience. A number of highly reputable Muslim scholars have argued to the effect that the animal not slaughtered in the traditional manner may still be *halal* or permissible. For instance, none other than Yusuf alQardawi (1990) writes about an occasion when the Prophet Mohammed was invited by a Christian family. Knowing that the Christians do not slaughter animals according to the Islamic prescription, his companions asked the Prophet what to do about the meat as served by their hosts. The Prophet replied to the effect that it did not matter as long as they ate it by reciting the name of Allah or God on it before they ate it, and this is what they did. From this alQardawi concludes that although slaughtering the animal in the name of Allah is and has been a universal norm among Muslims, not doing so does not make the meat *haram* or not permissible for consumption as long as you recite the name of Allah on it at the time of eating. This legal ruling justifies what millions of Muslim Americans have been doing on their own ever since they came to the United States.

American Muslims are clearly divided regarding their daily food consumption. This division creates some awkward situations. Because most Muslim Americans most often socialize within the larger Muslim community, the question of *halal* meat becomes a difficult one, especially for those who still insist on *halal* or the meat of properly slaughtered animal. For instance, they will decline an invitation from a family which is known for not insisting on *halal* meat. When you are invited to a large reception, there is always a lingering question as to whether or not the caterer could be trusted with respect to the *halal* meat. *Halal* meat looms significantly in marriage considerations. Those insisting on consuming *halal* meat look down upon others as committing *haram* knowingly, while others may look at them as being irrational conservatives who reduce Islam to consuming *halal* meat. However, as widespread as not insisting on *halal* meat is among Muslim Americans, insistence on *halal* meat by some has promoted *halal* meat business in an unforeseen manner. Nearly all eateries run by the Muslims (as well as some non-Muslims) now advertise prominently that they serve *halal* meat exclusively. In conventions and conferences of large Muslim organizations, nearby hotels and restaurants, owned mostly by the non-Muslims, prominently claim serving *halal* meat. *Halal* meat may never replace kosher in American food industry. However, that it is appearing as yet another element in religious economics of the United States, there is no doubt in it.

Hilal

The new crescent, or the *hilal*, has almost become synonymous with Islam these days. It appears on the flags of numerous Muslim countries. Red Crescent is an alternative to the Red Cross in many Muslim countries. A number of mosques in the United States and Europe display a crescent on top of their domes or the minarets.

However, there is no religious significance to the crescent in Islam except that the Islamic calendar is a lunar calendar. The day following the new crescent or the *hilal* is the first day of the new month and the evening when the *hilal* appears on the horizon constitutes the culminating point of the month gone by. Thus, determination of the appearance of *hilal* is of utmost importance in Islam for the simple reason of the determination of the calendar and not because, as Reverend Pat Robertson erroneously claimed, that Muslims worship the new moon.

Other than determining the calendar, the significance of *hilal* for the Muslims is the determination of the beginning and the end of Ramadhan, the holy month of fasting. Likewise, the determination of *hilal* is important for the determination of *hajj* or the annual Islamic pilgrimage, which falls on the tenth day of the twelfth and last month of the Islamic calendar. Thus, *hilal* is intimately connected with the two most important occasions of Islam. For *shia* Muslims, *hilal* has an additional significance—determining the beginning of the first month in the Islamic calendar, *Muharram*, during which Imam Hussein, the grandson of the Prophet, was martyred.

Ever since the days of the Prophet Muhammad, the sighting of *hilal* is performed with a great deal of care and enthusiasm in the Muslim world. Especially at the beginning and the end of Ramadhan, small crowds of people are seen at several nooks and corners trying to locate the new moon. Because no artificial means of sighting, such as the telescope, were invented until relatively lately, experienced "sharp sighters" were used to watch for the new moon. Concerns about sighting the new moon with the naked eye, because it varies with the weather, season, width of the sun's rays on the moon, and the brightness of the sun itself, gave rise in later centuries to Islamic astronomy based on observations of the solar system and the constellations, as well as highly sophisticated mathematical calculations. In Islamic astronomy, following the Prophet, the new moon is defined as a crescent (or *hilal*) visible on the western horizon soon after the sunset. This is different from the practice in modern astronomy, which defines the new moon as the completely dark moon preceding the *hilal*.

The new moon, as defined by modern astronomy, is observable through sophisticated telescopes, regardless of the time of the day or night. As well, it is mathematically predictable. *Hilal*, on the other hand, is the Islamic new moon on the western horizon with a line of sun rays illuminating a small part of it, is following the setting sun by a short margin of time. Islamic tradition, as well as modern astronomy, are quite capable of predicting the occurrence of the *hilal*. Is it visible by the human eye is the question. For some, *hilal* must be visible by the human eye (may be with the help of a simple telescope). The traditionalist may also concede a witness or witnesses of the moon from a neighboring district in case you are not able to see the moon yourself. For others, astronomical computations are preferable provided they inform us that the *hilal* is following the setting sun by a margin only of a few minutes, regardless of whether it is visible with the human eye.

Because most parts of the North American sky often remain partly or fully cloudy, most Muslim Americans cannot do the moon sighting, except those living in the southwest. For most Muslim Americans the controversy lies in whether to rely on traditional moon sighting with the naked eye or to go by modern astronomical techniques. Because astronomically visible *hilal* might still not be visible to the naked eye (because of the factors mentioned above), most traditionalists rely on the news of moon sighting, say, in New Mexico or Southern California, or even places east of North America.

Most important in this respect has been Saudi Arabia, which would announce moon sighting and the traditionalists (mostly Arab American Muslims) would accept this announcement as a "witness" account. However, from the beginning, non-Arabs remained uneasy about the authenticity of the Saudi sighting of the *hilal*, mainly because the Saudi sighting often did not coincide with astronomical observations. "Could we accept Saudi *hilal* sighting on the fifteenth of Ramadhan?" retorted a Muslim living in Chicago.

The controversy about *hilal* did not seem to abate with time. Indeed, it was becoming more serious as new batches of Muslim immigrants poured into the United States, especially before 9/11. Mosque leadership was split in the middle at several places. For some, fasting and Ramadhan started on one day. Others waited for a day before their Ramadhan started. Likewise, confusion prevailed among Muslim Americans regarding *eid alFitr* and *eid alAdha*. Muslim Americans just could not pray on and celebrate these occasions on the same day.

In order to resolve the controversy, a meeting of heads of large national organizations was called in Orange County, California, in 1993. The meeting resulted in the formation of the North American *Majlis al Shura* (consultative assembly), comprising five major organizations of national stature and a number of large mosques. Although according to the announcement, the *Majlis* would like to address itself to all major *Sharia* or legal problems besetting the Muslim community in North America, the one major issue that the *Majlis* has been partly successful in satisfying most Muslim Americans is the issue of the *hilal*. Especially for the *hilal* of the beginning and end of Ramadhan (which also signifies the celebration of *eid alFitr* the day after Ramadhan), the *Majlis* recommended that it will abide by the news of sighting of the crescent in North America provided it does not contradict astronomical determination. This is how the *Majlis* was able to combine the traditional with the modern and this seems to be acceptable by most mosques save a few in the United States. For *eid alAdha*, falling on the next day of the *hajj* or the annual pilgrimage to Mecca, the question of the moon was completely bypassed, insisting that moon sighting for *hajj* is up to the governor of Mecca. If he errs, we err too, but we are not responsible for this mistake.

This ruling regarding *eid alAdha* on the part of the *Majlis* has relatively less unanimous response on the part a number of some large mosques in the United States. For them, *eid alAdha*, contrary to what the members of the *Majlis* say, is directly determined by the moon (falling on the tenth day of *ZulHijjah*) and not connected with *Hajj* as most Arab Americans would insist.

It seems that these controversies under the surface in the Muslim American community at large would continue as long as immigration from Muslim countries would go on, for these are the new immigrants who bring with them practices and traditions, which do not always overlap. It seems that until the native American-born Muslim generation takes over the leadership, these controversies will continue to haunt the Muslim American community trying to redefine its identity in a modern but a predominantly non-Muslim society.

THE SAUDI CONNECTION

Starting in 2003, some of the prominent Muslim organizations of national stature, which remained hitherto untouched by the federal authorities, came under scrutiny. Congress asked the Internal Revenue Service (IRS) to present financial records of these Muslim organizations and disclose names and addresses of their donors. In fact, federal agents raided the offices of the College of Islamic and Arabic Sciences in Northern Virginia on July 1, 2004 and confiscated their computers and official records, although they did not take any official of the college under their custody. In itself this looks like a relatively mild action taken by the American establishment, but many suspect that this congressional action is aimed at deliberately finding faults with large nonprofit and tax-exempt Muslim organizations. Even before brought to court, they stand a chance of their funds being frozen and their tax-exempt status being cancelled. Although no legal action has yet been taken against them, they may have to hire expensive legal services. Should this happen, the number of existing donors might drop. There is no doubt that to make the donors withdraw is a legal and an effective way to destroy a nonprofit, tax-exempt organization, no matter how broad its donor base.

This action on the part of Congress and the IRS might also have a negative impact on local mosques and their associated schools and programs, which cannot sustain themselves without generous donations from their respective constituencies. Any shrinkage in the donor population would, no doubt, have a negative impact of serious proportion, at least in the short run, on Muslim organizations in the United States and Canada, which have no one else to turn to except their own. All this talk of Saudi Arabia spending millions of dollars on American mosques and other organizations trying to sell its Wahabi ideology sounds extremely unrealistic and ludicrous. Claims that 10 percent to 20 percent of Canada's 580,000 Muslims adhere to Wahabism ("After 9/11: The Saudis" *Time*, 2003:50) seems to be an idle remark without any empirical basis and needs serious revisiting. To date we do not know any such scientific work done in Canada. Likewise, we believe that *Time*'s claim (2003) that "virtually every Muslim child in the U.S. is receiving religious instruction in Arabic using Saudi textbooks" is an overgeneralization. How many Muslim children are in the United States, one might ask. Of course, every Muslim child has to start with some Arabic when he or she starts taking lessons in Islam. As to the books used by these children, *Time* reporters are not aware that in the United States there exists a lucrative free market of Islamic books, in which Saudi books (if there exist any) have to compete with numerous titles from Pakistan, Turkey, Malaysia, and other Arab countries, including Egypt. According to *Time* (2003), an American official says that Saudi gifts to American mosques and community centers are "...conditioned on the preaching of Wahabism." This implies that most, if not all, mosques in the United States are practicing and preaching Wahabism. More than a thousand large and small mosques that were the backbone of our Muslim demography project (chapter 2) do not testify to this proposition. Moreover, how could the Saudi elites, having rightly or wrongly gained a reputation to flout Islam, be expected to ask others to follow their forefathers' religion of yesteryear? In fact, the claim of the authors of the bestseller *9/11 Commission Report* seems to be more plausible when they point out that, for a few years, Saudi Arabia tried to counter the impact of the Iranian revolution by influencing the Muslim world with its petrodollars.

During roughly fifteen years from the mid-1970s through the 1980s, Muslims, indigenous as well as immigrants, were still struggling to find their place in the United States. Muslim community leaders, in order to finance their mosque and school projects, used to send fundraisers all over the Muslim world, especially to the Middle Eastern countries such as Kuwait, Bahrain, Qattar, the United Arab Emirates, and Saudi Arabia. These American fundraisers, as well as others, remained especially interested in collecting donations from the *Awqaf* (official religious charities) and, quite significantly, from the yearly *Zakah* (the Islamic poor tax) from other private sources, such as newly expanding business community in the newly oil-rich states. Many of these fundraisers did a good job at least for some time. The decade of the 1980s remains unmatched as far as this fundraising was concerned.

Although representatives from a few American Muslim institutions still tend not to waste a chance of collecting donations from a rich and generous party overseas, the situation of collecting charity has since its heyday changed drastically. Most of the then-young Muslim Americans—indigenous as well as immigrant—are, in their preretirement or early retirement age now, monetarily secure seniors with few dependents still living at home. Their children, having become educated and successful professionals, have left home. Consequently, like many other denominations in the United States, the Muslim community has already become self-sufficient for quite some time (although fundraising in the Muslim community, like in others, does not come easy.)

In the meanwhile, the Gulf States, including the mighty Saudi Arabia, went through serious financial convulsions, mostly of their own making. What most OPEC countries failed to foresee at the time of their oil revolution in the early 1970s was that with a steep hike in the price of oil, the price of everything else in the mainly oil-based world economy would shoot up too. This is how almost in no time, the massive showpiece development programs of these oil-producing countries—ornate palaces, beautiful mosques, as well as spacious university campuses, oversupplied hospital complexes, multilane highways, modern air and seaports, water and sewage systems, water desalination plants—became unbearably expensive, chewing up their newly earned wealth. This is what happened to Mexico and to Venezuela. This is what happened to the Gulf sheikdoms. They had to seriously curtail their development programs, which resulted in massive shrinkage in employment and sky-high inflation. Some of these states made quick adjustments. Others did not or could not. One has to only look at Qatar, Bahrain, and tiny Dubai to see how they diversified their development in order to maintain the standard of living bestowed on them by oil profits.

However, Saudi Arabia is a somewhat different case. Its economy is still too problematic to spend any riyals on *Awqaf* as generously as it used to thirty years ago. In fact, for all practical purposes, Saudi money is just not available for any mosques or any public works anywhere in the world. This is so because Saudi Arabia became a total welfare state from the beginning of the oil revolution of the early 1970s, underwriting even the most basic expenses of its citizens. Moreover, long-time Saudi princes, Prince Abdallah notwithstanding, were used to looking at the oil money as their inherited dynastic property and preferred to spend it mostly in keeping a flotilla of expensive cars, building and condemning palaces, and visiting the casinos of Europe. Now many of them, along with their cronies, are racing over the newly constructed bridge to neighboring Bahrain where fair-skinned prostitutes and other "female companions" recruited from all over the world tango with their half-drunk customers clad in full compliment of their traditional *jullabiah* and *ghutra*. Or they help them lose their money lavishly on gambling. Saudi Arabia—the birthplace of Islam, the center of the annual *Hajj* or the Muslim pilgrimage, the home of the two holiest sites of Islam—cannot afford to make fast buck the way neighboring Gulf emirates have ventured. Gambling, prostitution, and liquor have to remain legally, and therefore publicly, prohibited within Saudi borders. Otherwise, Saudi Arabia is blessed with very long, sun-drenched, lonely beaches, which could be a haven for tan-loving Westerners and now the Japanese in growing numbers. Moreover, as its population has more than doubled in three decades, bad economic planning or no planning over the years, never let Saudi Arabia develop beyond its status as a primitive raw material (oil) exporting country. A nation where only two decades ago almost every mildly educated citizen was aspiring to become a pompous bureaucrat surrounded by a number of telephones, the jobless rate is quite high (about 15 percent by some estimates). In the meanwhile, there are cropping up some other, completely unforeseen problems, of which to politely reject foreign donation seekers has been the easiest to resolve. Their real problem is twofold: first how to pacify the *baddu* who, having left his traditional oasis, invokes Wahabism each time he needs funds to boot in the *souq* of Jeddah or Riyadh; and secondly, how to control the children of those who became too rich too fast.

To be fair to the Saudi elites in the government as well those in business, at first they did donate lavishly and sincerely to almost all those who came asking for money for mosques, for schools, and for other Islamic causes. A few hundred million dollars a year given in religious charity would not hurt a gigantic system generating almost fifty billion dollars yearly. If some of them, as unapproachable as they are becoming lately, are approached anyway, they still pay large amounts of money by our standards, Prince Bundar bin Sultan, the Saudi ambassador in Washington, being one of them. He is known for giving from his own personal *Zakah* and what he collects from his near relatives. Several members of the Saudi household as well as old, established businesspeople gave lavishly to help the needy Muslims in Palestine, Bosnia, Kosovo, Kashmir, and especially Afghanistan during the Soviet occupation of the early 1980s. However, not even a decade of this generosity had gone by before Saudi Arabia had to all but close its *Awqaf* purse in a hurry as much as the *Zakah* started dwindling at the same time. Those who maintain that Saudi money is flowing to American and European mosques, seem to be doing their homework using some very dated texts. Empirical research on mosques and the mosque builders in the Chicago area, or in Houston, New Jersey, Boston, Pittsburgh, or Whapinger Falls, New York, may reveal how proud and independent these Islamic centers have become over time. In fact, they are generally much too independent of one another, even if they have a token although legal affiliation with some national organizations. Furthermore, they are much too independent of one another in their school curricula, in observing the beginning and the end of holy Ramadhan, the fasting month, and in fixing the timings of the two holiest celebrations of *eid al Fitr* and *eid al Adha*. Likewise, they hire their own *imams* according to their needs, with an American degree increasingly becoming an extra qualification (e.g., Imam Shafiq of Rochester, New York, originally from Pakistan with a Ph.D. from Temple University; Imam Ahmed Nazar of Syracuse, New York, originally from Egypt with a Ph.D. in counseling from Syracuse; Imam Mukhtar alMaghravi at Albany, New York with a Ph.D. from Syracuse; Imam Muzammil Siddiqui of Orange County, California, from India with a Ph.D. from Harvard, and Imam Qasim at Binghamton, New York, originally from Turkey and a doctoral candidate at SUNY, Binghamton). Obviously, *imams* in the United States, from as diverse Muslim background as Pakistan, Turkey, Egypt, Algeria, and India, with their modern American education, can hardly be expected to tow the Wahabi line. If you look closely, they generally agree about the basic universal practices of Islam. What they have often fought among themselves is about the authenticity of sighting of the new crescent in Saudi Arabia.

Likewise, in claiming that "Wahabi control over mosques means control of property, buildings, appointments of imams, content of preaching—including faxing of Friday sermons from Riyadh, Saudi Arabia—and of literature distributed in mosques and mosque bookstores, notices on bulletin boards, and organizational solicitations" (Schwartz, 2003) it seems that the authors of this claim have never visited any mosques, what to speak of studying them carefully, save a very few of them in the United States. As deplorable as it is, this almost total ignorance about Islam in the United States is widespread, from government functionaries to religious leaders and pop experts in the media and in society at large. It is widespread mostly because, in the absence of objective research, highly biased information about Islam in the United States is being concocted on a large scale.

Selective observations like the one above ignores the fact that during the past two decades or so numerous neighborhood mosques, especially in larger inner cities, are coming into existence (see chapter 2). Who is supporting them? How do they get their *imams*? Who pays their salaries? Who runs these mosques? What books are they using and who pays for them? What are the educational and professional qualifications of people run these mosques? How do these neighborhood mosques relate with larger Islamic center nearby? Our data from Chicago shows that, as quickly as they are proliferating, they do not need any help from Saudi Arabia or any other outside agency. Their members raise more than enough for these neighborhood mosques and schools associated with them. We do not have any reason to believe that the same pattern does not exist in other cities of high Muslim concentration.

Moreover, even if for a short time some thirty years ago, Muslim mosque makers looked to Saudi Arabia for help, Saudi kings, Saudi princes, and even most Saudi individuals, save a few, who visited Europe and the United States were hardly admired by other Muslims. This is so because, seemingly, most Saudis remained most of the time more interested in doing something more amusing and far less serious than spreading their Wahabi ideology.

Who is practicing Wahabi ideology these days anyway? Perhaps a handful of princes with a love for horses, the desert, and the oases, a few powerless descendants of late Imam Abdul Wahab (the founder of the Wahabi school in Arabia), and previously small-time businessmen, who became multimillionaires during the "oil revolution" of the early 1970s, are just about all who remember God for his favors upon them. These are not the rest of the Saudi elites whose forefathers fought to establish Wahabism with their swords. The only place where the Wahabi sword roosts these days is the Saudi flag, which speaks loudly of a gnawing generation gap. Even if you have a fear of flying, craving to have a shot of whisky as soon as your plane takes off from Jeddah does not qualify you as a fanatic Wahabi by a long shot. Likewise, Saudi women would hardly wait for the plane to taxi before they peel off their black chador and appear in their most fashionable Western colors. In its heyday, the Wahabis looked at other Muslims as being heretics, and the "heretics" looked at them with contempt as being narrow-minded desert Bedouins. Yet, for a long time, a number of Muslim countries sent donations to the cash-strapped Saudi government for the upkeep of the *Kabah or* grand mosque in Mecca and the mosque of the Prophet in Medina.

However, since the flood of oil money drenched Saudi Arabia in the early 1970s, things changed quickly. Outsiders flocked around Saudi elites for donations, but the façade of Wahabism came crashing down. Those who are still afraid that there are ongoing efforts at spreading Wahabi ideology in the world, including Europe and the United States, are overrating Saudi religiosity and underrating the impact of material prosperity on demanding ideologies. It may not be too surprising to see that far from trying to spread a Wahabi version of Islam in the world during the past thirty years, the Saudi dynasty is fighting its own Wahabier-than-thou rebels.

For a while, it looked as if there was a resurgence of Wahabism in Saudi Arabia after all. Juheman's surprise takeover of the *Haram* or the grand mosque in Mecca in December 1979 and the emergence of Osama Bin Laden and his entourage in the late 1980s looked to some like a revival of Wahabi Arabia. Far from it, in reality these characters are products of breathtaking socioeconomic change, which, as mentioned above, made some Saudis mind-boggling millionaires, while leaving others frustrated with nothing to show but their abandoned date palms in the desert valleys. Both have their own axes to grind. The poor, with no prospects in sight, want their share in the national wealth.

Many of the newly rich, having gained economic power, want to have a taste of political power. As different as they may be on the economic and consumption ladder, they have one thing in common: both evoke Islam in order to seek justifications for their demands. Naturally, there does not seem to exist any love lost between the ruling Saudi dynasty and these seemingly Wahabi insurgents. Far from embracing them, at first the ruling elite tried to root the rebels out of their domain. If Saudi Arabia is exporting its Wahabism at all, it is mainly through its rebellious dissidents who are forced to take refuge in other countries, including European countries where exposure to modern education and overall democratic culture further fanned their antimonarchial sentiments. However, as Iraqi insurgency looked like it was spreading within their borders, the wily Saudis, much to the dismay of their American allies, announced a policy of pardon if the insurgents would voluntarily submit themselves to the authorities. To "embrace your deviant 'brother'" and let him live him under your watch rather than killing him and making a martyr out of him, is a long-held tradition of the Arabian peninsula. It has often paid off in the past. It is worth trying again.

In fact all this talk about Saudis trying to buy the fidelity of Muslim masses to their ideology smacks of something more sinister for American interests in the Middle East. A number of neoconservatives are portraying Saudi Arabia in a counter-American posture. For instance, according to Buchanan (2004):

> Here is *National Review* on the Saudis; "Potentially the most dangerous foreign-policy issue confronting the Bush Administration, and its greatest dereliction in the War on Terror, is its See-no-evil approach to terror's bankers, the Saudis."

Michael Ledeen includes the Saudis on his largest list of "terror masters," though Riyadh, given recent attacks, seems at the top of Bin Laden's list of enemies. *Commentary* magazine wants the Saudis "taken down" as part of a "World War IV" on hostile regimes.

How many of these people asked themselves who would take power in Saudi Arabia should the monarchy fall? Do they care? Do they want instability, chaos, and revolution to throw up an Islamic republic in Saudi Arabia and similar regimes across the Persian Gulf so that the United States will have no choice but to fight a thirty-year war?

The talk of the town inside the Washington beltway is that the neoconservatives who got us belly-deep in the Iraqi morass had their eyes on Saudi Arabia and other Middle Eastern states in order to secure the Israelis' hinterland (Klein, 2004; Hollings, 2004)). Moreover, until lately, the Saudis openly declared that the Palestinians were freedom fighters and not terrorists as defined by the Israelis. This is something that would enrage any blue-blood Zionist extremist. Consequently, we see that the American strategy that unravels in the wake of 9/11 has to serve Israel first. Richard Pearl, the guru of the neoconservatives at the Pentagon, provided the rationale for forcing American presence in Israel's vicinity with the pretext of establishing freedom and democracy in that volatile region.

It is in light of this neoconservative approach that one may understand efforts at implicating Muslim American communities with Saudi Arabia—kill two birds with one stone. Abolish Saudi Arabia, which is perceived as being the financial supporter of the Palestinian cause, and destroy American Muslim communities, which are emerging as a new challenge to the Zionists strangle-hold in American politics. However, the claim that Saudi Arabia is using its oil money to spread its Wahabi ideology in the United States and elsewhere in the world is to make fanatic missionaries of Saudi elites, a highly questionable proposition, to put it mildly. In fact, Wahabi ideology was seriously compro-mised the day the Saudi warrior, Abdul Aziz Ibn Saud, the father of the pres-ent King Fahad, negotiated the frontiers of modern Saudi Arabia with the British in the 1930s. When a faction of his army of the *Ikhwan* (brothers in faith) rebelled against this decision, he crushed the rebellion using British-made armored cars. That Wahabism was a thing of the past as a political force and could not provide any security to the ruling Saudis came to the fore when, in 1944, the aging king personally met Roosevelt, the president of a newly emerging world power and offered him a perpetual supply of oil in exchange for American protection of his dynastic rule. Nobody in the world since then ever heard of Wahabism as a force to reckon with, until the American neocon-servatives started demonizing the dynasty lately. Indeed, to suspect the sons of the late Ibn Saud to embark on a mission to conquer the whole world for Wahabism is like seeing Saddam Hussein getting ready to attack the United States with his so-called WMDs. This scary story could have been more believable in the early twentieth century. Our storytellers seem to be almost one hundred years too late.

"SLEEPERS" AND AMERICAN DEMOCRACY

For better or worse, Muslim American communities have, for a long time, become used to raising their funds locally. This is not an easy task, as men-tioned earlier, but this makes each Muslim community independent of any other community or organization. This independence, as we shall see later, is its strength as well as weakness.

Sometimes it looks as if with the passage of time the situation is improving a bit. The Justice Department seems to have slowed down a little because thousands of Muslims have been deported or have left in search of security elsewhere; it seems there are few Muslims left to be caught and thrown out with impunity. To their utter embarrassment, a few surprise raids against some reputable Muslim institutions conducted under the direction of self-styled "ter-rorism experts" backfired. Moreover, a number of senators and congressmen are wondering how to reverse the USA PATRIOT Act, which was forced upon them in the wake of 9/11.

Also, some of the more anti-Islamic clergy seem to have been quiet about Islam, at least, for now. Likewise, since the beginning of 2004, the Southern Baptist pundits have not made any arousing anti-Islamic pronouncements. In fact, lately there have been explicit efforts toward reconciliation with Islam. Even the Zionist extremists seem to be pondering the limits of neoconservatism. Should Iraqi insurgency continue longer, there is always a chance that the United States would pay heed to what some conservatives (Buchanan, 2004) are wondering in anger: why should American young men and women shed their blood serving the cause of Likud? There is no doubt that as the similarity between Vietnam and Iraq is being invoked even in the halls of American Congress lately, identifying with Likud ambitions at the cost of the lives of young Americans may prove to be counterproductive.

The only instances of anti-Islamism we notice these days are the continuing attacks on Muslim Americans and their institutions by "more American than thou" individuals who become incensed at wartime incidents occurring in the Middle East as portrayed by the media. The best and worst that may be happening to Muslim Americans at the time of this writing, however, is American democracy. Starting in the latter half of the twentieth century, national elections in the United States are becoming close and, therefore unpredictable (Truman in 1948, Kennedy in 1960, Nixon in 1968, and Bush in 2000). This benefits minority communities disproportionately, including the Muslims. Whether or not the next president keeps his promises is beside the point. What is important is that a closely contested election keeps political candidates on their toes. They have to remain open to the demands of the minorities no matter how small they are. A closely contested election disproportionately favors small minorities. History has a tendency to forget about a candidate who does not understand this principle. Ask Al Gore.

This is the best aspect of American democracy that makes Muslim Americans feel that they could make the difference. With enthusiasm, they are registering in large numbers. There are animated discussions in the conferences and conventions. However, the worst part of American democracy that Muslim Americans are beginning to see is that it promotes opportunism, false promises, double-talk, and outright lies on the part of power-hungry, selfish, and pandering politicians. They are learning that American democracy is for sale. Irrespective of what is good for the nation as a whole, a political candidate may be primarily motivated to support the interest of the group or groups, which contribute most dollars to his or her campaign. Despite their growing numbers, enthusiasm for American political processes, and growing prosperity, Muslim Americans are still baffled by their naivet

However, in our opinion, the greatest weakness of Muslim Americans is their impotence regarding any future 9/11-like attacks on the United States. If another conspiracy on the part of bin Laden or his followers is hatching, Muslim Americans are in no position to stop it. The best they can do is pray that it would not materialize as another 9/11, in which case the civil rights of Muslim Americans may be threatened, even if it is election time.

Considering Muslim Americans and their social investment, the next attack on American soil would almost necessarily incubate beyond American borders in utter secrecy beyond the reach of American intelligence. There is no proof that any Americans—Muslims or non-Muslims—were involved in the conspiracy that led to the attacks on 9/11. This is, in all probability, going to be the case in the next attack, if it is going to happen at all. We believe that the ongoing talk about "sleepers," in all probability, is nothing but a heightened degree of paranoid Islamic-phobia that overtook the nation in the wake of 9/11. It may be an attempt to make people feel that their government is not sitting idle and that they too should keep their eyes open—a strategy that has failed time and time again with serious consequences to Muslim citizens, their families, and their institutions, as we noted above. Or it could be a deliberate rumor to make Muslim Americans look suspect.

But who is a "sleeper"? Let us look into the concept more closely. We are simply told that a sleeper is a conspirator who is ordered to lie low for a period of months or even years, provide vital information as needed, and then remain available to participate in the strike when the time comes—a very mysterious figure indeed. Did any sleepers help the 9/11 terrorists? Those nineteen hijackers, even the so-called twentieth one, do not fit this description unless one insists that the flight schedules of the hijacked planes could not be obtained without the help of the sleepers. Moreover, one who has been sleeping for several months or years cannot remain anonymous in the "gemeinschaft" Muslim community where he, his wife, and children must necessarily be cultivating contacts in the mosque, in the neighborhood, and in schools. Is he working or is he not? If not, what is his source of income? If he is working, where is he working? Which neighborhood does he live in? Finally, children being born to him and as they are growing in age and going to schools and colleges—all of these are confounding factors, which militate against one being a sleeper for years.

For all practical purposes a sleeper has to be a deliberate loner without any family of his own and without any other larger family contacts, a personality seen rather rarely in the Muslim community in the United States. He is a big city dweller living farther away from where most other Muslims live or congregate. He may be working for a living. If not, he may be receiving stipends from some unknown source. He must be residing in the United States legally, which entails having lived here for a protracted period of time, say, five to ten years. Can any one live a cultivated loner's life for so many years in an alien society and survive with his sanity remaining intact? As Tom Ridge, the former secretary of the Homeland Security department, pointed out (Fox News, May 18, 2004), not a single sleeper has been apprehended so far (although the FBI must have been watching several Muslim suspects for years). One may conclude that a sleeper is only a fictitious being, whose pursuit will only lead to a dead end and, therefore, a waste of taxpayer's money. It is unnecessarily making the lives of several Muslim citizens miserable and running psychological havoc in the Muslim community.

As in the past, most Muslim Americans are not going to play any role in future attacks on the United States because their being Americans involves a heavy social investment in society. It is not only that Muslim Americans are getting rewards for being Americans; they have been busy, despite some serious setbacks of late, seeking power and influence in the United States, following the legal-political route that is a proven path to success in American democracy. This appears to be preferable to hurling yourself in suicidal attacks against skyscrapers or other monuments, something that enrages Americans more than it hurts its power. In short, American Muslims are Americans who have plenty of opportunities available to them and in which they have invested readily. Unlike Europeans, first-generation Muslim immigrants and their children who are desperately trying to get out of the ghettos, most American Muslims, immigrant as well as indigenous, are already in suburbs, which, unlike European ghettos, are not fertile grounds for hatching revolutions or violent action. They provide fertile grounds for political participation.

Barring any mishap, Muslim Americans have the ability to use the opportunities available to those who are living in the United States legally or even illegally. Despite mass arrests in the wake of 9/11, Devon Avenue is back in business. The ISNA attracted almost fifty thousand participants in its annual convention held in Chicago over the 2004 Labor Day weekend, promising to field at least one million new voters in national election. Three major Muslim groups, that is, African Americans, Arab Americans, and South Asians, along with their vote-eligible children, have already made their presence felt due mainly to block votes the second time around. It seems that 9/11 did put American Muslims and Arab Americans at a disadvantage. It demoralized them momentarily. It did not break them.

ISLAM IN THE AMERICAN MOSAIC

Islam is now rooted in American soil. American Muslims now outnumber Jews, Episcopalians, and Methodists. Anti-Islamists in the United States must be sensitive to this new American reality, namely, that Islam is the second largest American religion and it is gaining strength by each passing day. Anti-Islamism, therefore, is anti-Americanism and it would not pay in the long run even if Muslim Americans have had a temporary setback. Any witch hunt, any anti-Islamic diatribe, any attempt at painting Muslims as terrorists, any prejudicial act or attack against Muslim individuals or institutions does not make Muslim citizens less concerned about their priorities. If at all, their self-perception as being victims of racial and ethnic prejudice has made their resolve even stronger.

Far from being a melting pot, the United States remains, by and large, a mosaic with different ethnic communities living next to one another in a moral symbiotic balance. This symbiotic interaction is what made the United States a culturally rich society that harnesses innovative abilities of people of different traditions, faiths, and ideologies from all over the world. Anti-Islamism tends to seriously disturb this balance, and therefore, must be put under serious checks.

With the passage of time, Islamic roots are getting deeper in American soils. Before 9/11, Islam was generally described as being the fastest growing religion in the United States. Even if its growth is slowed due to immigration restrictions from the Muslim countries lately, its growth is not owed to immigration only. As we have seen in the preceding pages, reproduction and conversion have been two other contributing factors. Not only Muslims as a whole have a much higher birth rate than the national average, Islam has had a traditional appeal for many, especially the African Americans in the United States. Thus even if one attempts to restrict Muslim immigration from overseas, no one can stop runaway reproduction and conversion to Islam. There are findings that reproduction and conversion combined amount to more than one third of the growth of the Muslim population in the United States. This fact alone is notable on two important counts. First, it means that Islam has the potential to outnumber many other religious and ethnic groups, which have been showing declining growth rates for quite some time. Secondly, Muslims in the United States are a very knowledgeable and resourceful people who have of late become acutely sensitized politically, thanks to the perception of widespread anti-Islamism in the wake of 9/11.

As we know, American Muslims are racially and ethnically a highly diverse people with highly varied national and linguistic background. This ethnic variation is reflected even in their mosques, which, otherwise, have almost identical mode of prayers couched in the Qur'an and the *Sunnah* of the Prophet. In ordinary circumstances, before 9/11, these mosques were enhancing rather than minimizing these ethnic divisions in the Muslim community at large. As if this was not enough, Muslim organizations of national stature were also increasingly following ethnic divisions. A function of 9/11—and the resulting sudden rise of anti-Islamism in its aftermath—was to bring these ethnic divisions under control. Many Muslims who were not too enthusiastic about their Muslim identity before 9/11 became self-conscious of being Muslims. Acts of selective apprehension on the part of the government, anti-Islamic proclamations by the Christian fundamentalist leadership, perceived machinations of the Zionists, and blind Muslim-bashing and prejudice by individuals in the street—all contributed to Muslim Americans crossing ethnic lines and trying to come together as Muslims. Efforts are underway to bring major Muslim organizations such as ISNA, ICNA, and MAS closer together at least in their annual conventions, which bring together Muslims literally in the thousands on an annual basis. Civil rights have become the common slogan. Active political activity in the Muslim community became a priority overnight. National organizations with a focus on civil rights such as CAIR and those with political agendas such as AMC gained stature. In the national election of 2000, Muslims became known as block voters. In the last election, the Muslim block vote was even larger. It may be larger for a number of reasons: first, because there were more Muslim voters in 2004 than in 2000 as a result of more Muslim voters becoming age-eligible; secondly, voter registration has almost become a movement in the Muslim community; thirdly, because most immigrant Muslims show a preference to reject President Bush's policies. They, along with African American Muslims who traditionally prefer to vote for the

Democratic Party candidate, might follow the same political direction, thus swelling the size of the block vote in favor of the democratic candidate.

However, most immigrant Muslims are more pragmatic than indigenous Muslims in this respect. They are more inclined to support a party or a candidate who supports their cause as Muslims. Rejecting Mr. Bush, therefore, did not automatically mean support for Mr. Kerry, the Democratic candidate who did not support the most important Muslim demand, namely, that the United States should be even-handed trying to resolve the Palestinian conflict. If not, the Muslim block vote might even be in support of Mr. Ralph Nader, the Green party candidate in the election. The Muslim vote in closely contested elections in the future might always play a critical role. Muslim Americans constitute a resourceful and an expanding population. This speaks for their potential, which a political hopeful could ignore only at a great cost to his or her political hopes.

THE FUTURE OF ISLAM IN THE UNITED STATES

The United States is not going to have a Muslim president anytime soon. Although some members of the second generation of Christian Arabs, such as Ralph Nader, John Sununu, Spencer Abraham, and the Zogby brothers, have made their name in politics and public opinion, Muslims have some catching up to do.

In fact, as things stand at the time of this writing (summer 2004), Muslims, whether citizens or not, are, by and large, a demoralized community struggling against a tide of prejudice, injustices, and even physical attacks forcing them to look above their shoulder. It seems that the days of "bum rap" from the street are over. However, the so-called USA PATRIOT Act is still in force. According to the latest report as complied by CAIR (2004), the year 2003 was so far the worst for American Muslims. Anti-Islamic incidents, according to this report, jumped 70 percent, from a high of 602 in 2002 to a total of 1,019 in 2003.

Although this sudden rise in the rate of anti-Islamism in 2003 may partly be due to increase in the number of reporting chapters, several other contributing factors must also be considered, according to CAIR. These factors include a lingering atmosphere of post-9/11 fear of further attacks on the United States; the pro-war rhetoric before and after the invasion of Iraq in March 2003 must have played a significant role; and abuses associated with the implementation of the USA PATRIOT Act continued from the previous years. We may add extreme anti-Islamic diatribes on the part of major evangelical leaders, and radio commentators must have played their share in the attacks on Muslim Americans.

Presently, as a Muslim, you do not know if you are under surveillance or even those who call you or write e-mails to you are not being investigated. In short, the politics of the "big brother watching you," which characterizes the culture of totalitarian societies of the Third World in general and the Muslim World in particular, has been imported lock, stock, and barrel to the United States. As strange as it may sound, the tyrants of the world still have a few tricks up their sleeves that we like to borrow in the name of national security. This is ironic because many of the Muslims who came to the United States in search of economic and political security and became citizens or legal immigrants have nowhere else to go. For better or worse, they are stuck in their newly adopted homeland where they have already raised at least two generations of American-born citizens. African American Muslims are facing a double jeopardy—for being African American and for being Muslims. Color, which was shoved under the rug for a few years as a basis for explicit prejudice, all of a sudden comes to life, often quite unexpectedly. Ask an African or African American woman who ventures in the street in *hijab*.

Sami alAriyan, Rafil Dhafir, Abdul Rahman alAmoudi, and Jose Padilla, just to name a few, have become household names in the Muslim community because of their being imprisoned on what many believe are trumped-up charges. Government prosecutors seem to be in no hurry to bring their cases to the court. Judges continue to deny them bail, and the defense lawyers consistently complain about hindrances put in their way by highly biased and often under-educated detention officers. A few, who have been convicted, were convicted on plea bargaining and were found to have nothing to do with Osama Bin Laden and his terrorist activities.

A number of active Muslim charities were shut down, mostly due to technical violations. For instance, Benevolence International was shut down because after it ran out of clothing and food, it transferred a few thousand dollars to the needy Bosnian families at a time when American forces were fighting against the marauding Serbs. The Holy Land Foundation was brought to court in July 2004 after being locked up for two years accused of having transferred funds to Hamas, a Palestinian organization that has nothing to do with Osama Bin Laden. It is never known to have hurt any Americans and is never known to have engaged in any anti-American policies. In fact, Hamas is an organization of Palestinians who, tired of Israeli atrocities and the PLO corruption, started a poor man's war—a pro-active campaign of *intifada* against Israel. It relies on multitudes of young children throwing rocks at Israeli soldiers and uprooted and distraught young men and women becoming suicide bombers in Israel. In short, they are fighting illegal Israeli occupation of their land with whatever limited means that are available to them. They are fighting a poor man's war against one of the best-equipped armies. Moreover, Hamas also runs a health care system, a family care system, and school systems that have to be maintained if they have to survive as a society. It is beyond most Arab and Muslim Americans as to what is wrong in helping a people who never tried to harm the United States.

None of the mosques or major Islamic centers had been invaded by the police or federal agents in almost three years after 9/11 until 6:30 in the morning on August 5, 2004. That day, in a sting operation, the local police as well as federal agents surrounded *Masjid al Salaam* situated near downtown in Albany, New York. Its founder, a former Bangladeshi gentleman with graying temples and its *imam*, a former Syrian, were paraded in handcuffs in front of the television cameras and taken away. We were informed by CNN that these men were apprehended on a charge of money laundering in connection with *Ansarul Islam*, one of the groups fighting against the American occupation of Iraq. Later, as the day progressed, we were told again by CNN that the charge was about an effort on their part to buy a handheld missile in order to destroy the Pakistani embassy in Washington. A clearly agitated Governor Pataki of New York, finding yet another chance for a television appearance, all but convicted them even before their appearance before a court. What is interesting is that by the evening news time none of the other major news corporations devoted more than a fraction of a minute to this incidence. BBC from Washington did not even mention it.

Regular worshippers in *Masjid al Salaam* were so scared that its attendance fell and the donations almost evaporated. However, in about three weeks time, a magistrate in Albany freed the accused on bail on their own recognizance, confining them to their own homes, places of work, and their mosque. What is interesting from the point of view of sympathizers of the accused was the rebuke that the magistrate gave to the FBI for doing an extremely sloppy job of the sting operation, which almost amounted to a harassment of innocent citizens.

In short, by now for more than two years after 9/11, Muslim Americans, individuals as well as organizations, are continuously faced with the worst of times in the United States to say the least. Or, as Vickers (2002) writes:

> Ironically, it is this crucible experience that now places the American Muslim in the position of being the conscience of America. The government's treatment of Muslim Americans during this period of near hysteria about homeland security is the new barometer of justice in the United States. Simply put, the yardstick today for measuring whether this country lives up to all the egalitarian ideas and principles embedded in the constitution and espoused to the world is its relationship with the over seven million Muslims who call the United States home.

How long is this going to continue? Are Muslim Americans going to get their civil rights back anytime soon? Whereas you cannot be too cautious, we do not foresee any repetition of 9/11, at least, not in the near future. Our terror alert system has become much too strong for Osama Bin Laden and his followers to take a shot at the United States with impunity again any time soon. Of all people, ask Senator Ted Kennedy who was denied a boarding card (five times) on a flight to Washington, D.C. that he has been taking for the past almost half a century. However, Bin Laden's *al Qaeda* provides juicy fodder for American politics, because its ghost will not die any time soon. And as long as the specter of terrorism on American soil remains alive, American Muslims will remain a suspect minority.

REFERENCES

alQardawi, Yusuf. *Halal and Haram in Islam*. Indianapolis, IN: American Trust, 1990.
Boettcher, Shelly. "Walk a Mile in My Hijab." *Calgary Herald*, July 30, 2004.

Buchanan, Patrick J. "Our Ill-Conceived Vendetta against Saudis," *The American Conservative*, May 24, 2004, 7.

Buchanan, Patrick J. "No End to War," *The American Conservative*, March 1, 2004, 6–14).

CAIR. *American Muslims One Year after 9–11*. Washington, DC: The Council on American-Islamic Relations, 2003.

CAIR. *The Status of the Muslim Civil Rights in the United States*. Washington, DC: The Council on American-Islamic Relations, 2004.

Hollings, Earnest F. "Bush's Failed Mideast Policy is Creating More Terrorism." *Charleston Post and Courier*, May 6, 2004.

Klein, Joe. "The Perils of a Righteous President," *Time*, May 17, 2004, 25.

Papaneck, Hanna. "Purdah in Pakistan: Seclusion and Modern Occupations for Women," *Journal of Marriage and the Family* 33, no.3 (August 1971): 517–530.

Schwartz, Stephen. "Wahabism and Islam in the U.S.: Two Faced Policy Fosters Danger." Text of testimony before the Senate Subcommittee on Terrorism, Technology, and Homeland Security, June 26, 2003.

Vickers, Erik A. "American Muslims: The New Conscience of America." Washington, D.C.: American Muslim Council, AMC@amconline.org: October 7, 2002.

Glossary

Abu Bakr: First Khalifah, or the pious Caliph elected to head the Muslim community after the death of the Prophet.

Adhan (Azzan): call for the prayers.

Aghakhanis: the followers of Aghakhan.

Ahmedies: those who consider Gulam Ahmed of Qadian a prophet.

al-Ameen: (literally, reliable) the Meccans called the Prophet by this title because of his character.

alAqsa: the great mosque in Jerusalem.

al-Hajj or Hajji (Hajja): one who has performed the Hajj.

al-Khobar: oil rich eastern coastal province of Saudi Arabia.

al-Qaeda: (literally, the base) name of an international movement initiated by Osama bin Laden.

al Madinat al Nabi: (literally, the city of the Prophet). It is only called Medina, a city in Arabia with the Prophet's tomb in it.

Ameen: same as Amen (may God accept).

Ameer: head of the community or the nation.

Amileen: those who collect Zakat.

Asabiya: ethnic or tribal prejudice.

Asr: later part of the afternoon.

Asslamo alaikum: "Peace be on You," usual Islamic greeting.

Baddu: desert dweller.

Banu Hashim: "children of Hashim," great-grandfather of the Prophet.

Bilal: An African companion of the Prophet who was the first caller of the prayers.

Burqa: (Pakistan and India) a covering that women hide under while in public.

Dawah: (literally, invitation) has come to mean inviting others to Islam.

Deen: Islam as a total way of life.

Dopatta: (Pakistan and India) a piece of cloth that women use in order to cover their head and shoulder.

Eid al Fitr: first great celebration in Islam marking the end of Ramadhan, the fasting month.

Eid al Adha: second great celebration in Islam commemorating Ismail's escape from being slaughtered.

Eisa: Prophet Jesus.

Fajr: early dawn, time for the very first prayers of the day.

Fiqh: Islamic jurisprudence.

Fuqra: plural of faqeer, meaning a beggar.

Hadith: saying of the Prophet.

Haj: annual pilgrimage to Mecca and the surrounding area.

Halal: permissible.

Hanafi: followers of Imam Abu Hanifah.

Haram: prohibited.

Hijab: modesty and distance between members of the two sexes.

Hijrah: (literally, migration) the migration of the Prophet from Mecca to Medina.

Hira: the cave where the Qura'an was first revealed to the Prophet on top of the hill Jabl al Noor.

Ibraheem: Prophet Ibrahim.

Imam: leader of a community, also one who leads the prayers.

Injeel: the Evangel.

Insha Allah: If God so wishes.

Isha: later part of the evening (time of retirement).

Jabl alNoor: the hill where the Qura'an was first revealed to the Prophet.

Jamaate Islami: Islamic Party, an Islamic political party in Pakistan.

Jelabiya: long loose shirt which covers from neck to the ankles.

Juma: Friday.

Ka'bah: focus of Islamic worship, the grand mosque in Mecca.

Khutba (Khutub): sermon in Juma' or Eid prayers.

Kurta: shirt.

Madrasa: school.

Maghrib: west and/or sunset.

Majlis al Shura: consultative assembly.

Masakeen: (plural of miskeen) poor and needy.

Masjid (Masajid): mosque.

Milad al Nabi: birth of the Prophet.

Musa: Prophet Moses.

Musalla: a small mosque, or a place where you pray regularly.

Nihari: hot breakfast curry (Pakistan and India).

Pagri: turban.

Paye: shank bones.

Qamis: shirt.

Quari: one who recites the Qur'ran.

Qureish: the Meccan tribe to which the Prophet belonged.

Ramadhan: fasting month, ninth month in the Islamic calendar.

Riba: interest which is prohibited.

Salat: regular prayer.

Shahadah: witness.

Shalwar: baggy pants.

Sharia: law.

Shia: supporter (of Ali).

Shura: consultation.

Siyam: fast.

Subhan Allah: praise be to God.

Sufi: a sect in Islam.

Sunnah: practical tradition of the Prophet.

Surah: chapter from the Qura'an.

Tafseer: explanation of the Qura'an.

Taqwa: piety.

Thop: long, loose shirt from neck to the ankles.

Torait (Taurat): torah.

Ummah: Islamic nation as a whole.

Ummi: an illiterate person.

Wahabi: follower of Imam Abdel Wahab.

Wakeel: one who represents or stands for something.

Waqf (awqaf): property that is given to a religious cause.

Wiratha: property left by a deceased.

Yatama: plural of yateem (orphans).

Yathrib: name of Madinah before the Prophet moved in.

Zakat: to be given to the poor, 2.5 percent of the property not in use for one whole year.

Zohr: early afternoon.

ZulHijjah: last month of the Islamic calendar.

Index

About the Authors

ILYAS BA-YUNUS is professor emeritus of sociology and associate professor of anthropology at the State University of New York, Cortland.

KASSIM KONE is associate professor of anthropology at the State University of New York, Cortland.